TEACHINGS
from the
WORLDLY
PHILOSOPHY

TEACHINGS
from the
WORLDLY
PHILOSOPHY

Robert Heilbroner

W. W. NORTON & COMPANY

NEW YORK · LONDON

Copyright © 1996 by Robert Heilbroner
All rights reserved
Printed in the United States of America

First Edition

The text of this book is composed in Palatino
with the display set in Centaur
Composition and manufacturing by the Maple-Vail Book Manufacturing Group.
Book design by JAM Design

Library of Congress Cataloging-in-Publication Data
Heilbroner, Robert L.
Teachings from the worldly philosophy / Robert Heilbroner.
p.   cm.
Includes bibliographical references and index.
ISBN 0-393-03919-6
1. Economics—History.   I. Title.

HB75.H375   1996   95-37470
330—dc20   CIP

W. W. Norton & Company, Inc., 500 Fifth Avenue, New York, N.Y. 10110

http://web.wwnorton.com

W.W. Norton & Company Ltd., 10 Coptic Street, London WC1A 1PU

1 2 3 4 5 6 7 8 9 0

This book of teachings
is dedicated with gratitude to Stanley Burnshaw,
scholar, poet, critic, and very good friend.

CONTENTS

PREFACE

⸺

Forty-odd years ago, in what I once described as the combination of confidence and ignorance that only a graduate student could have possessed, I undertook to write a history of the evolution of economic thought, under what I hoped would be the catchy title of *The Worldly Philosophers*. I did not know at the time that Edward Gibbon, in his classic *Decline and Fall of the Roman Empire*, had used those very words to describe, not economists— there were none in those days—but the counselors to the Roman imperium who sought to counter the other-worldly recommendations of the early Christian church fathers.[1] Whether on account of the title, or because it filled a niche, my book did indeed find a market, and continues to be used to this very day, knock wood.

Over the four decades of its publication I have fleshed out the text in several editions, but one major emendation has always remained beyond reach. It was to find a way of introducing readers who were interested in the rise and permutations of eco-

---

[1] Edward Gibbon, *The Decline and Fall of the Roman Empire*, Modern Library, n.d., Vol. I, p. 412.

nomic thought to the actual texts of the great economists themselves. That is the aim I hope to fulfill in this new book which, although obviously connected with its middle-aged parent, stands on its own feet as a different way of presenting the ideas of its progenitors—namely, allowing the worldly philosophers to speak for themselves. As is so often the case, there is no substitute for the real thing.

To make that task manageable I have taken two liberties with their words. The first is to limit severely the number of spokesmen for the profession. In place of the nearly one thousand economists whose contributions have warranted mention in the most recent and prestigious overview of the discipline,[2] I have chosen fewer than twenty to represent its historic trajectory. This has required concentrating on a few pivotal figures, such as Adam Smith, John Stuart Mill, Karl Marx, John Maynard Keynes, and a handful more, while relegating to few pages, or even to oblivion, other representatives, some very highly esteemed within the profession. My excuse is that I am interested in presenting an overview and not a catalogue, a book that could actually be read, and not one destined for more or less permanent shelving. I should mention as well that my decision to limit the voices who will be heard allows me to bring my text to an end with John Maynard Keynes and Joseph Schumpeter. This not only rescues me from the invidious task of choosing among many economists whose names are today widely known, but whose historical contributions to economic thought have yet to stand the test of time. First rate analysts we possess by the dozen; worldly philosophers are hard to find.

My second liberty follows from the first. I have permitted myself the liberty of serving as a docent, not merely an editor—appearing briefly before, and often after, each author, and not infrequently between sections of his prose, to point out the significance of the words I have selected. I hope that these interpolations will serve as an Ariadne's thread, helping the reader—

[2] *The New Palgrave: A Dictionary of Economics.* John Eatwell, Murray Milgate, and Peter Newman, eds. New York: Stockton Press, 1987.

whether he or she be browsing or systematically following the text—find the themes that connect and unify ideas whose significance for the larger body of evolving economic thought may not otherwise be evident. I am present, however, only as gallery guide, not as spokesman. The authors of this book are the great economists, and the large-scale narrative is theirs, not mine.

In addition, I should stress that these excerpts make no effort to present in miniature the full accomplishments of their authors. I have left aside many portions of their texts—some of them of considerable importance in themselves—because I did not think they fit into what might be called the Great Scenarios of economic thought. It follows that my principal criterion for inclusion is that my offerings have such a relevance, as well as enough intrinsic interest to tempt some readers to the much more demanding task of looking into the books whence they come. Hence my hope is that my two books together will help advance the understanding of economics in a way that neither could accomplish by itself.

Second, a very important word of thanks. My colleagues William Milberg and Jason Hecht read the manuscript with loving care, providing both encouragement and criticism, both indispensable. My remaining debt takes a little more explaining. When I had finished *The Worldly Philosophers* I was somewhat at a loss for a title. As I have recounted in its last edition:

> I was aware that the word "economics" was death at the box office, and I racked my brains for a substitute. A . . . crucial lunch then took place with Frederick Lewis Allen, editor of *Harper's* magazine, for whom I had done a number of pieces, and who had been extraordinarily kind and helpful to me. I told him about my title difficulties, and said I was thinking of calling the book *The Money Philosophers*, although I knew "money" wasn't quite right. "You mean 'worldly'," he said. I said, "I'll buy lunch."

Rather the same thing happened when the present book was in typescript form. I was having lunch with an old friend, to whom I said that I was thinking of calling it *Lessons from the Worldly Philosophy*, but wasn't quite sure about "lessons." He said, "You mean 'teachings.' " I told him that I would buy lunch, which I did, but did not mention that I now knew what name belonged on the dedication page.

ROBERT HEILBRONER

I

EARLIEST
ECONOMIC
THOUGHT

THE BIBLE

Where is one to begin a search for lessons from the history of economic thought? The title of this chapter gives the answer, but not the reason, to which we will come in due course.

What follows is only a small sampling from the commentaries regarding wealth that we find in "the" Bible—itself a collection of writings that spans at least two hundred years. Nevertheless these first readings will give us a chance to think about a matter that we would certainly consider to be at the heart of economics—the drive to gain wealth. I shall say no more about it until we have looked over this brief, but I think representative, sampling of its many strictures and fewer praises.

DEUTERONOMY

(15:11): [The] poor shall never cease out of the land: therefore I command thee, saying Thou shalt open thine hand wide unto thy brother, to thy poor, and to thy needy in thy land.

(23:20): Unto a stranger thou mayest lend upon usury, but unto thy brother thou shalt not lend upon usury: that the Lord thy God may bless thee in all that thou settest thine hand to in the land whither thou goest to possess it.

ECCLESIASTES

(10:19): A feast is made for laughter, and wine maketh merry; but money answereth all things.

TIMOTHY:

(6:9): [They] that will be rich fall into temptation and a snare, and into many foolish and hurtful lusts, which drown men in destruction and perdition.

(6:10) [T]he love of money is the root of all evil. . . .

PROVERBS

(13:11): Wealth gotten by vanity shall be diminished: but he that gathereth by labour shall increase.

MATTHEW

(19:24): [Again] I say unto you, It is easier for a camel to go through the eye of a needle, than for a rich man to enter into the kingdom of God.*

Now for the relevance of these strictures and praises for our own purposes. One aspect of the matter is immediately apparent. The Bible has little or nothing to say about the social consequences of the actions it holds up for consideration. Usury earns vehement denunciation, but nothing is said about what consequences will ensue, if people charge interest, which is what usury means. In the same fashion, the Bible tells us that the quest for wealth will lead us into temptation and worse, but it does not say why: for example, that one person's wealth necessarily diminishes

*The eye of the needle refers to a narrow portal, probably in the walls of Jerusalem.

another's. In the same vein, why should wealth gotten by vanity diminish, while that gotten by labor increase?

To ask such questions is to get quickly to the root of the matter. Wealth-getting is not considered as an attribute of a particular social order, but only as a private activity whose successful pursuit will come at the expense of the moral character of the pursuer. To put it differently, wealth-seeking is regarded almost exclusively as an ethical, not an "economic" matter—an activity with serious personal consequences, but not one that sets into motion a chain of social consequences, useful or otherwise. So also with the relief of the poor, to whom we are enjoined to hold out our hand for reasons of our own moral well-being (and no doubt their material betterment), but not to initiate changes in social conditions that might alleviate poverty as an omnipresent condition—the poor never ceasing to come out of the land.

The Biblical voices are, in a word, expressions about wealth before it was part of a mechanism that energized and integrated the larger social whole, before something recognizable as an "economy" had become separate from the surrounding society. It is not "economics" but ethics—certainly not a lesser category, but a different one.

Why, then, do the voices nevertheless reverberate in modern ears? The answer is less clear, but I think persuasive once we identify it. It is the ambivalence with which writers from both the Old and New Testaments speak about wealth—at once admiringly and with contempt. Why should this have been? More interesting, why should it continue to be? Why do we "understand" the ambivalence regarding wealth, despite the enormous gulf between that ancient period and our own?

There is no literature on this matter in economics, and for that matter only a scanty one in psychology.* I am myself inclined to view the ambivalence as a consequence of the fact that wealth has always been a proxy for power, which is likewise admired and feared, resisted and worshiped. Whatever its origins the

---

*For those interested, I recommend a remarkable article by Otto Fenichel, a pioneer of psychoanalysis: "The Drive to Amass Wealth." *Psychoanalytic Quarterly* No. 1, 1938.

unease has remained, long after the drive for wealth was considered strictly as a private, morally risky undertaking, and long before that same drive became accepted as a motive that, if not especially honorable, was nonetheless to be accorded its due as the energizing force of a "progressive" social system.

And when does that happen? A social historian would suggest that it arises in the beginning of the sixteenth century as Martin Luther's Protestantism begins to make its peace with an emergent, not yet fully formed social order that will one day be called capitalism. But there is at least a foretaste of the change in the work of that most prescient of all philosophers, Aristotle, to whom we next turn.

ARISTOTLE

(384–322 B.C.)

Aristotle ranks with Plato as one of the timeless philosophical intellects of ancient Greece. As we would expect, he is also deeply
interested in the affairs of "economic" life from a moral viewpoint.
Thus Aristotle divides all buying and selling activity into two sorts:
those having to do with "housekeeping," or the maintenance of a
well-run state, and those having to do with the sheer making of
money for its own sake. The first he calls *œconomia*—whence
"economics"—and the second *chrematistiké*.

More than one economist has suggested that our subject should
be renamed "chrematistics" but for better or worse *œconomia* has
remained its linguistic root. Our first reading, from *The Politics*,
considers the question of what part of money-making can be considered as *œconomia* and what part as *chrematistiké?* The answer,
much in accord with Aristotelean moral principles in general, lies
in the difference between activity that is bounded and therefore
"natural"; and that which is without limit and therefore "unnatural." Given Aristotle's outlook, not surprisingly, *œconomia* is natural and *chrematistiké* is not.

THE POLITICS, BOOK I

Of the art of acquisition then there is one kind which is natural and is a part of the management of a household. Either we must suppose the necessaries of life to exist previously, or the art of household management must provide a store of them for the common use of the family or state. They are the elements of true wealth; for the amount of property which is needed for a good life is not unlimited. . . . [But] there is another variety of the art of acquisition which is commonly and rightly called the art of making money, and has in fact suggested the notion that wealth and property have no limit. Being nearly connected with the preceding, it is often identified with it. But although they are not very different, neither are they the same. . . .

For natural wealth and and the natural art of money-making are a different thing; in their true form they are a part of the management of a household; whereas retail trade is the art of producing wealth, not in every way, but by exchange. And it seems to be concerned with coin; for coin is the starting point and the goal of exchange. And there is no bound to the wealth which springs from this art of money-making. . . . But the art of household management has a limit; the unlimited acquisition of money is not its business. . . .

Of the two sorts of money-making one, as I have just said, is a part of household management, the other is retail trade; the former is necessary and honorable, the latter a kind of exchange which is justly censured; for it is unnatural, and a mode by which men gain from one another. The most hated sort, and with reason, is usury, which makes a gain out of money itself, and not from the natural use of it. For money was intended to be used in exchange, but not to increase at interest. And this term (tokos), which means the breeding of money from money, is applied to the breeding of money because the offspring resembles the parent. Wherefore of all modes of making money it is the most unnatural.

Enough has been said about the theory of money-making; we now proceed to the practical part. The discussion of such matters is not unworthy of philosophy, but to be engaged in them practically is illiberal and irksome.[3]

There now follows some consideration of the activities of money-making that are properly considered as lying within *œconomia*—mainly, farming and husbandry, including beekeeping or the raising of any useful animals or fish. The parts of money-making falling within the concerns of *chrematistiké* are commerce by sea or land, and selling in shops; usury; and offering personal services for hire. Other occupations, such as lumbering and mining, occupy intermediate places between *œconomia* and *chrematistiké*, but as Aristotle comments, "it would be tiresome to dwell upon them at greater length here."

But Aristotle also interests us for another reason. For all his distaste for *chrematistiké*, he is the first of the philosophers to sense that there was an analytical, as well as a moral problem in the conduct of market affairs. We see that new perspective in the selection below, taken from the *Nichomachean Ethics*. It explores the question of the proper ratio of payments to individuals for their work.

THE NICHOMACHEAN ETHICS

Book V

[L]et A represent a builder, B a cobbler, C a house and D a shoe. Then the builder ought to receive from the cobbler some part of his work, and to give him his own work in exchange. If then there is proportionate equality in the first instance, and retaliation or *reciprocity* follows, the result of which we are speaking will be attained. Otherwise the exchange will not be equal or permanent.

. . . It follows that such things as are the subjects of exchange must in some sense be comparable. This is the reason for the invention of money. Money is a sort of medium or mean; for it measures everything and consequently measures among other things excess or defect, e.g., the number of shoes which are equal

[3] From A. E. Monroe, *Early Economic Thought*, Harvard University Press, 1930, pp. 15–20.

to a house or a meal. As a builder then is to a cobbler, so must so many shoes be to a house or a meal; for otherwise there would be no exchange or association. But this will be impossible, unless the shoes and the house or meal are in some sense equalized. Hence arises the necessity of a single universal standard of measurement. . . . This standard is, in truth, the demand for mutual services, which holds society together; for if people had no wants, or their wants were dissimilar, there would be either no exchange, or it would not be the same as it is now. . . .

Money is therefore like a measure that equates things, by making them commensurable; for association would be impossible without exchange, exchange without equality, and equality without commensurability.

Although it is in reality impossible that things which are so widely different should become commensurable, they may become sufficiently so for practical purposes. There must be a single standard, then, and that a standard upon which the world agrees. . . . Let A be a house, B ten minae, C a couch. Now A is half B, if the house is worth, or is equal to, five minae. Again, the couch C is the tenth part of B. It is clear then that the number of couches which are equal to a house is five. It is clear too that this was the method of exchange before the invention of money; for it makes no difference whether it is five couches or the value of five couches that we give in exchange for a house.[4]

Since exchange involves payments for the goods people make or the services they render, the analysis brings Aristotle to confront the question of the rationale behind prices. Under the name of "value," the problem of pricing will become a central question for the economists who arrive on the scene some twenty centuries after Aristotle. For them, value will be important as a means of judging the efficiency of the market mechanism. But Aristotle has addressed the real question: *what division of market gains among its participants will permit exchange to become regularized—that is, a means of social continuity, not social dissatisfaction?*

[4] Monroe, op cit., pp. 27–28.

ST. THOMAS AQUINAS

(1224–1274)

As with Aristotle, St. Thomas Aquinas is not concerned with economics as we know it, but as a locus of perplexing moral issues. By general consensus the greatest of the medieval philosophers, Aquinas wrote some sixty books that attained the same position for later scholarly discourse as did Aristotle's before them. Of these, the *Summa Theologica* was undoubtedly the greatest. The book is divided into three major parts, of which the first and third are devoted to the nature of God and Christ, respectively, while Part II of the *Summa* is directed to a study of the nature and consequences of human actions. It is this volume that interests us.

Aquinas's concerns resemble those of Aristotle with respect to their focus on the moral, not the material results of "economic" behavior. But there is an interesting difference. Aristotle's division between *œconomia* aand *chrematistiké* hinges on the reasoned difference between the "natural" and the "unnatural" aspects of behavior, as Aristotle weighs these attributes. In sharp contrast, Aquinas's scrutiny is not based on his own evaluations of their character so much as on his judgment (never explicitly spelled out) as to the authority that legitimates or delegitimates them. In the extract below we should note how he argues his case, pro and con, by citations from three authorities (including Aristotle, who appears under his medieval pseudonym of "the Philosopher"). In this case, as in others, however, the outcome is not determined on the basis of logical or empirical justification, but on that of the relative moral weights of those on each side. Thus, in the first case below, we find three supporting arguments and only one opposing, but the opposing side wins because it leans on the New Testament.

SUMMA THEOLOGICA, Question LXXVII

On Fraud Committed in Buying and Selling

We have next to consider the sins which have to do with voluntary exchanges; first, fraud committed in buying and selling; second, usury taken on loans. For in the case of other forms of voluntary exchange, no kind of sin is noted which is to be distinguished from rapine or theft.

FIRST ARTICLE
*Whether a man may lawfuly sell a thing for more
than it is worth.*

The first article is analyzed as follows:

1. It seems that a man may lawfully sell a thing for more than it is worth. For in the exchanges of human life, justice is determined by law. But according to this it is lawful for the buyer and seller to deceive each other (Cod., lib IV, tit. 44 *de rescindenda Ventitione*), and this takes place when the seller sells a thing for more than it is worth, or the buyer pays less than it is worth.

2. Furthermore, that which is common to all men seems to be natural and not sinful. But as Augustine relates (13 *de Trin. . .*) the saying of a certain actor was accepted by all: *you wish to buy cheap and sell dear;* which agrees with the saying in Prov-

erbs, xx, 14: *It is naught, it is naught, saith every buyer; and when he is gone away, then he will boast.* Therefore it is legal to sell a thing for more and to buy it for less than it is worth.

3. Furthermore, it does not seem to be unlawful to do by agreement what the claims of honor require. But according to the Philosopher (*Ethics*, VIII, 13) in friendships based on utility, recompense ought to be according to the advantage accruing to the beneficiary; and this sometimes exceeds the value of the thing given, as happens when a man needs something very much, either to escape danger or to obtain some advantage. Therefore in contracts of buying and selling it is lawful to sell a thing for more than it is worth.

But opposed to this is the saying in *Matthew*, vii, 12: *All things whatsoever you would that men should do to you, do you also to them.* But no man wishes to have a thing sold to him for more than it is worth. Therefore no man should sell a thing to another for more than it is worth.

I answer that it is wholly sinful to practice fraud for the express purpose of selling a thing for more than its just price, inasmuch as a man deceives his neighbor to his loss. Hence Cicero says (*de Offic.*, III): *All deception should therefore be eliminated from contracts: the seller should not procure someone to bid up, nor the buyer someone to bid down the price.*[5]

Thus Matthew carries the day, although the final apodictic statement—"I answer that it is wholly sinful. . ." makes Cicero an ally. In all of Aquinas we find a mode of argument that may have its own logic, but it is not that of our time. Hence we will not linger over Aquinas's similar treatment of such questions as *Whether a sale is rendered unlawful by a defect in the thing sold; Whether a seller is bound to declare a defect in a thing sold; Whether in trading it is lawful to sell a thing for more than was paid for it;* or the lengthy consideration of various forms of usury. All the cases per-

[5] Monroe, op. cit., pp. 53–54.

plex us because they are not economic argument as we know it.

What is useful to carry over from this abbreviated consideration is therefore not its mode of analysis, but an appreciation of how differently "economic" questions looked in a period that had not yet rid itself of the ancient notions that gain by trade—not by military victory—was inherently suspicious; that markets were useful, but that the terms of exchange were to be judged by their "justness," not their efficacy; and that commercial intentions counted for more than results. This glimpse of such a world sets the stage for the great evolution to come. The world of economics as a set of problems in virtue must give way to one in which economics becomes the study of an entirely different question—how a market-driven society works—in which Aristotelian and Aquinian problems appear almost unintelligible. In the next section we shall read the first attempts to comprehend such a strange state of affairs.

II

THE
COMMERCIAL
REVOLUTION

INTRODUCTION

The first signs of a market-run society were already apparent in Aquinas's time. Packtrains of merchants had appeared as early as the ninth century, threading their way through a patchwork of fiefdoms and duchies. By then most feudal manors had regular weekly markets where merchants sold goods transported from Italy and even more distant lands, and where peasants sold produce and homespun, or homemade goods.

This was the world to which Aquinas's questions-and-answers had been addressed, but the spread of marketplaces did not come to resemble a market "system"—the precursor of full-fledged capitalism—until the seventeenth century. By then feudalism had evolved into national entitities, at least in England, France, and the Lowlands; the institution of serfdom had begun to give way to a free labor force; and a thousand towns had sprung up, with small guild-run workshops and a considerable commercial flavor.

Three aspects of this rapidly changing social texture will interest the writers in this Part. The first is the increasing recognition that a society in which making money becomes an ever more widespread activity cannot easily apply the precepts of the Church, exemplified in Aquinas's teaching, to the realities of daily life. Second, as foreign trade also begins to occupy a more important place among the considerations of the new nation states, questions emerge for which earlier thinkers had no answer at all—namely, could one buy more from abroad than one sold? Was it acceptable if merchants took gold abroad to exchange it for mere goods? And last, was there some order-bestowing mechanism concealed in the seemingly disorganized life of the marketplace?

BERNARD MANDEVILLE

(1670–1733)

We turn first to a poem published in 1705 by Bernard Mandeville, a native of Holland who studied and practiced medicine in England. Originally entitled *The Grumbling Hive; or Knaves Turned Honest,* the poem was reprinted and enlarged with commentary in 1714 and again in 1724. It immediately created a national scandal; indeed, it was tried by a grand jury and pronounced a "nuisance," and in the popular press its author was referred to as Man-Devil. But Samuel Johnson found it a source of much illumination, and despite, or because of its scandalous message, it was immensely popular.

The message of the *Fable* is blasphemous. It is that fraud, luxury, and waste may be sources of sin in a commercial society, but they are also causes of prosperity. In the poem, Mandeville visits upon such a prosperous society the curse of honesty, with terrible results, as we shall see, in much abbreviated form below:

THE GRUMBLING HIVE

A Spacious Hive well stock'd with Bees,
That lived in Luxury and Ease;

And yet as fam'd for Laws and Arms,
As yielding large and early Swarms;
Was counted the great Nursery
Of Science and Industry. . . .
Vast Numbers thronged the fruitful Hive;
Yet those vast Numbers made 'em thrive;
Millions endeavoring to supply
Each other's Lust and Vanity;
Whilst other Millions were employ'd
To see their Handy-works destroy'd; . . . .
Some with vast Stocks and little Pains
Jump'd into Business of great Gains;
And some were damn'd to Sythes and Spades,
And all those hard laborious Trades;
Where willing Wretches daily sweat,
And wear out Strength and Limb to eat.
Whilst others follow'd Mysteries,
To which few Folks bind 'Prentices; . . . .
As Sharpers, Parasites, Pimps, Players,
Pick-Pockets, Coiners, Quacks, Sooth-Sayers. . . .
These were called Knaves; but bar the Name,
The grave Industrious were the Same.
All Trades and Places knew some Cheat,
No Calling was without Deceit. . . .

 Thus every Part was full of Vice,
Yet the whole Mass a Paradice; . . . .
The Root of evil Avarice,
That damn'd ill-natured baneful Vice,
Was Slave to Prodigality,
That Noble Sin; whilst Luxury
Employ'd a Million of the Poor,
And odious Pride a Million more.
Envy it self, and Vanity
Were Ministers of Industry;
Their darling Folly, Fickleness
In Diet, Furniture, and Dress,
That strange ridic'lous Vice, was made
The very Wheel, that turned the Trade. . . .
 Thus Vice nursed Ingenuity. . . .

To such a Height, the very Poor
Lived better than the Rich before;
And nothing could be added more. . . .

How vain is Mortal Happiness!
Had they but known the Bounds of Bliss;
And, that Perfection here below
Is more than Gods can well bestow. . . .
But they, at every ill Success,
Like Creatures lost without Redress,
Cursed Politicians, Armies, Fleets,
Whilst everyone cry'd Damn the Cheats. . . .
[At last] *Jove*, with Indignation moved,
. . . In Anger swore, he'd rid
The bawling Hive of Fraud, and did.
The very Moment it departs,
And Honesty fills all their Hearts. . . .
Oh, ye Gods! What Consternation,
How vast and sudden was th' Alteration!
In half an Hour, the Nation round,
Meat fell a Penny in the Pound. . . .

Now mind the glorious Hive, and see,
How Honesty and Trade agree:
The Shew is gone, it thins apace;
And looks with quite another Face,
For 'twas not only that they went,
By whom vast Sums were Yearly spent,
But Multitudes, that lived on them,
Were daily forced to do the Same. . . .
The Price of Land and Houses falls;
Mirac'lous Palaces, whose Walls,
Like those of *Thebes*, were raised by Play,
Are to be lett. . . .
The Building Trade is quite destroy'd,
Artificers are not employ'd. . . .
The haughty *Chloe*, to live Great,
Had made her Husband rob the State:
But now she sells her Furniture,
Which th' *Indies* had been ransack'd for. . . .

As Price and Luxury decrease,
So by degrees they leave the Seas.
Not Merchants now; but Companies
Remove whole Manufacturies.
All Arts and Crafts neglected lie;
Content the Bane of Industry,
Makes 'em admire their homely Store,
And neither seek, nor covet more. . . .

The Moral

Then leave Complaints; Fools only strive
To make Great an Honest Hive.
T'enjoy the World's Convencies,
Be famed in War, yet live at Ease
Without great Vices, is a vain
Eutopia seated in the Brain.
Fraud, Luxury and Pride must live
Whilst we the Benefits receive.
Hunger's a dreadful Plague, no doubt,
Yet who digests or thrives without? . . . .
Bare Vertue can't make Nations live
In Splendour; they, that would revive
A Golden Age, must be as free
For Acorns, as for Honesty.[6]

Is there an "answer" to Mandeville? This is a question that modern-day economics tends to avoid. It may be, as Mandeville says, that commercial society has raised the material lot of at least some of the poor to levels not known by the rich of much earlier societies. It may also be, as Mandeville insists, that the use of mild fraud (the blandishments of advertising), the encouragement of luxury, and the appeal to pride are necessary agencies of a busy hive—what we might call a business civilization.

To admit as much is to acknowledge that this civilization rests on motives and behaviors that would not meet the standards of Aristotle or Aquinas. Whether such a civilization could sustain its

[6] Bernard Mandeville, *The Fable of the Bees*, Philip Harth, ed. Penguin Books, 1970, pp. 63–76. Condensed from the original.

material achievements and its considerable political advances on a less invidious and demeaning foundation is a question that lies at the center of our way of life, but it is not one that lies at the center of those problems to which most economists today devote their attention. To turn back to Aristotle for a moment, modern economics has greatly clarified many questions posed by *chrematistiké,* but it can hardly be said to have done the same for *œconomia.*

THOMAS MUN

(1571–1641)

Mandeville's heretical assessment of honesty and chicane in worldly affairs unmistakably announces the radical change of perspective of the seventeenth century. No less significant is the rise of what Adam Smith called a "mercantilist" view of the workings of commercial society. There is no clearcut roster of mercantilist writers, who might best perhaps be regarded as pre-Adamites of many kinds. In England, however, one important group consisted of merchants who wrote about the role of money and foreign trade.

Prior to their writings, the prevailing view was that of Aristotle who, as we have seen, emphasized that the function of money was essentially to provide a medium of exchange. The mercantilists made money much more significant, equating it with "treasure"—a popular mercantilist word. Treasure referred mainly to the hoards of gold that rulers sought to acccumulate, partly to finance their expensive courts, partly to finance the hire of mercenaries. All the more peculiar then, that the mercantilists defended the export of gold as if it were a mere commodity like wool. They argued, of course, that gold would buy imports of goods that, in their turn would be reexported to bring a larger stream of gold back to the home country.

In our first extract, we read an exposition of the rules for gathering treasure written by Thomas Mun, a very successful trader and director of the East India Company. Mun argues for the overriding need for England to pursue a positive balance of trade—that is, to export more than it imports. (How this advice for one nation could be squared with similar advice to others is a question the mercantilists did not consider.) At any rate, with Mun we see a analytical approach to a market economy that is another sign of a period of radical reassessment.

ENGLAND'S TREASURE BY FORRAIGN TRADE

Chapter II

The means to enrich this Kingdom,
and to encrease our Treasure

Although a Kingdom may be enriched by gifts received, or by purchase taken from some other Nations, yet these things are uncertain and of small consideration when they happen. The ordinary means therefore to encrease our wealth and treasure is by *Forraign Trade,* wherein wee must ever observe this rule: to sell more to strangers yearly than we consume of theirs in value. For suppose that when this Kingdom is plentifully served with the Cloth, Lead, Tinn, Iron, Fish and other native commodities, we doe yearly export the overplus to forraign Countries to the value of twenty two hundred thousand pounds; by which means we are enabled beyond the Seas to buy and bring in forraign wares for our use and Consumptions, to the value of twenty hundred thousand pounds; By this order duly kept in our trading, we may rest assured that the Kingdom shall be enriched yearly two hundred thousand pounds, which must be brought to us in so much Treasure; because that part of our stock which is not returned to us in wares must necessarily be brought home in treasure.

For in this case it cometh to pass in the stock of a Kingdom, as in the estate of a private man; who is supposed to have one thousand pounds yearly revenue and two thousand pounds of ready money in his Chest: if such a man through excess shall spend one thousand five hundred pounds *per annum*, all his ready money will be gone in five years; and in the like time his said money will be doubled if he take a Frugal course to spend but five hundred pounds *per annum*; which rule never faileth likewise in the Commonwealth. . . .

Chapter IV

The Exportation of our Moneys in Trade of Merchandise in a means to encrease our Treasure.

This Position is so contrary to the common opinion, that it will require many and strong arguments to prove it before it can be accepted of the Multitude, who bitterly exclaim when they see any monies carried out of the Realm; affirming thereupon that wee have absolutely lost so much Treasure, and that this is an act directly against the long continued laws made and confirmed by the wisdom of this Kingdom in the High Court of Parliament, and that many places, nay *Spain*, it self which is the Fountain of Mony, forbids the exportation thereof, some cases only excepted. To all which I might answer that *Venice, Florence, Genoa*, the *Low Countries* and divers other places permit it, their people applaud it, and find great benefit by it; but all this makes a noise and proves nothing, we must therefore come to reasons which concern the business in question.

First, I will take it for granted which no man of judgment will deny, that we have no means to get Treasure but by forraign trade, for Mines wee have none which do afford it, and how this money is gotten in the managing of our said Trade I have already shewed, that it is done by making our commodities which are exported yearly to over ballance in value the forraign wares which we consume; so that it resteth only to shew how our monyes may be added to our commodities, and being jointly exported may so much the more encrease our Treasure. . . .

I suppose that 100000 *l* being sent in our Shipping to the East Countreys, will buy there one hundred thousand quarters of wheat cleer aboard the Ships, which being after brought into *England* and housed, to export the same at the best time for vent thereof in *Spain* or *Italy*, it cannot yield less in those parts than two hundred thousand pounds to make the Merchant but a saver, yet by this reckoning wee see the Kingdom hath doubled that Treasure.

Again this profit will be far greater when wee trade thus in remote Countreys, as for example, if wee send one hundred thousand pounds into the *East-Indies* to buy Pepper there, and bring it hither, and from hence send it for *Italy* or *Turkey*, it must yield seven hundred thousand pounds at least in those places, in regard of the excessive charge which the Merchant disburseth in those long voyages in Shipping, Wages, Victuals, Insurance, Interest, Customes, Imposts, and the like, all which not withstanding the King and the Kingdom gets. . . .

For it is in the stock of the Kingdom as in the estates of private men, who having store of wares, doe not therefore say they will not venture out or trade with their money (for this were ridiculous) but do also turn that into wares, whereby they multiply their Mony, and so by a continual and orderly change of one into the other grow rich, and when they please turn all their estates into Treasure; for they that have Wares cannot want mony.[7]

It must be clear that the overriding tenet of mercantilism was that Treasure was only to be gained by selling more than one bought in return, and that its underlying philosophy was Devil Take the Hindmost. The central counterthrust against these beliefs was slow in gaining momentum and did not receive its *coup de grace* until David Ricardo published his *Principles of Political Economy* in 1817. Although we cannot follow the history of mercantilism in any detail, it may be useful to close this chapter by glancing at Ricardo's argument.

The argument hinges on what we call the principle of comparative advantage. Suppose, says Ricardo, that England and Portugal both produce two goods—cloth and wine—and suppose that Por-

[7] Thomas Mun, *England's Treasure by Forraign Trade,* from Monroe, op. cit., pp. 171, 179–81.

tugal can produce each of these more efficiently than England. Could there possibly be a profitable exchange between the two countries?

Ricardo answers yes, provided that Portugal's advantage in one commodity is comparatively greater than its advantage in the other—say 50 percent more efficient in cloth and only 25 percent more efficient in wine. For it then follows that if Portugal were to move its working force and capital out of wine production into clothing, and if England were to move *its* labor force and capital from cloth making into wine, the combined production of the two nations would be higher than it was formerly. It follows that the possibility therefore exists for both sides to gain by exchange—Portugal exporting cloth to England, and England exporting wine to Portugal, with both sides enjoying more and cheaper cloth and wine than before!

This basic rationale is still the guide for all who seek to improve economic relations through trade. We should note one thing, however. The argument, as it stands, is stripped of all its real-world entanglements. It does not inquire whether in fact it is possible to move labor from the country to the city. It does not answer questions about whether powerful vested interests do not want the existing pattern of things to change, for whatever reason. As we shall have occasion to see many times as we go along, economic arguments often owe the power of their logic to the omission of, or inattention to, social and political forces and frictions that cast doubt on the *feasibility*—not the logic—of the original argument. That has often been the case with trade arrangements in the real world, and it makes more understandable why mercantilistic arguments aimed at beggaring our neighbors still easily attract the assent of the Multitudes (to use Mun's capitalization), as well as that of their Leaders.

RICHARD CANTILLON

(1680–1734)

We know little about Richard Cantillon's life other than that he was a very successful British merchant with houses in many European cities. His sole work, *Essay on the Nature of Commerce in General,* appears to have been translated into French by its author, but was not published until 1755, twenty-one years after his macabre death—he was murdered in London by his cook. Ignored or unknown for many years, Cantillon has gradually become recognized for his remarkable economic intelligence. Indeed, in 1881 the very critical economist W. Stanley Jevons wrote that Cantillon's *Essay* was "more than any other book I know *the first treatise on economics.*"[8]

Where does Cantillon fit into the early economic thinkers in whom we are interested in this Part? He was not a mercantilist, although he set high store by the importance of a healthy balance of trade. And despite the fact that his book begins with the sentence "The Land is the Source or Matter from whence all Wealth is produced," neither was he a Physiocrat, a member of that

---

[8] "Richard Cantillon and the Nationality of Political Economy," in Henry Higgs, *Essai sur la Nature du Commerce en Général,* New York: Augustus Kelley 1964, p. 342 (italics in original). The Higgs translation is the source of all material in this section.

remarkable group of inquirers whose economic philosophy began from the assumption that land, not labor, was the ultimate source of all wealth. Cantillon's role is better understood as the first attempt to depict the workings of a market-driven society as constituting a "system" with a spontaneous mechanism of self adjustment and a coherent relationship between the supply of money and the prosperity of the society as a whole.

We will catch the flavor of those prescient, and entirely original views in the selections below.

ESSAY ON THE NATURE OF COMMERCE IN GENERAL

Part I, Chapter X

The Price and Intrinsic Value of a Thing in general is the measure of the Land and Labour which enter into its Production.

One Acre of Land produces more Corn or feeds more Sheep than another. The work of one man is dearer than that of another . . . , according to the Skill and Occurrences of the Times. If two Acres of Land are of equal goodness, one will feed as many Sheep and produce as much Wool as the other, supposing the Labour to be the same, and the Wool produced by one Acre will sell at the same Price as that produced by the other.

If the Wool of the one acre is made into a suit of coarse Cloth and the Wool of the other into a suit of fine Cloth, as the latter will require more work and dearer workmanship it will be sometimes ten times dearer, though both contain the same quantity and quality of Wool. . . .

The price of a pitcher of Seine Water is nothing, because there is an immense supply which does not dry up; but in the Streets of Paris people give a sou for it—the price or measure of the Labour of the Water-carrier.

By these examples and inductions it will, I think, be understood that the Price or intrinsic value of a thing is the measure of the quantity of Land and Labour entering into its production, having regard to the fertility or produce of the Land and to the quality of the Labour.

But it often happens that many things which have actually this intrinsic value are not sold on the Market according to that value: that will depend on the Humours and Fancies of men and on their consumption. . . .

There is never a variation in intrinsic values, but the impossibility of proportioning the production of merchandise and produce in a State to their consumptions causes a daily variation, and a perpetual ebb and flow in Market Prices. However in well organized Societies the Market Prices of articles whose consumption is tolerably constant and uniform do not vary much from the intrinsic value; and when there are no years of too scanty or too abundant production the Magistrates of the City are able to fix the Market Prices of many things, like bread and meat, without anyone having cause to complain.

Part II, Chapter II

Of *Market Prices*

Suppose the Butchers on one side and the Buyers on the other. The price of Meat will be settled after some altercations, and a pound of Beef will be in value to a piece of silver pretty nearly as the whole Beef to all the silver brought there to buy Beef.

This proportion is come at by bargaining. The Butcher keeps up his Price according to the number of Buyers he sees; the Buyers, on their side, offer less according as they think the Butcher will have less sale: the Price set by some is usually followed by others. Some are more clever in puffing up their wares, others in running them down. Though this method of fixing Market prices has no exact or geometrical foundation, since it often depends upon the eagerness or easy temperament of a few Buyers or Sellers, it does seem that it could be done in any more convenient way. It is clear that the quantity of Produce or Merchandise offered for sale, in proportion to the demand or number of Buyers, is the basis on which is fixed or always supposed to be fixed the actual market Prices; and that in general these prices do not vary much from the intrinsic value.

Chapter VI

Of the increase and decrease in the quantity of hard money in a State

If mines of gold or silver be found in a State and considerable quantities of minerals drawn from them, the Proprietor of these Mines, the Undertakers,* and all those who work there, will not fail to increase their expenses in proportion to the wealth and profit they make: they will have over and above what they need to spend.

All this money, whether lent or spent, will enter into circulation and will not fail to raise the price of products and merchandise in all the channels of circulation which it enters. Increased money will bring about increased expenditure and this will cause an increase in Market prices in the highest years of exchange and gradually in the lowest. . . .

Mr. Locke lays it down as a fundamental maxim that the quantity of produce and merchandise in proportion to the quantity of money serves as the regulator of Market price . . . ; but he has not considered how it does so. . . . I may therefore venture to offer a few observations on the subject, even though I may not be able to give an account which is exact and precise.

If the increase in actual money comes from Mines or gold or silver in the State the Owner of these Mines, the Adventurers, the Smelters, Refiners, and all other workers will increase their expenses in proportion to their gains. They will consume in their households more Meat, Wine, or Beer than before, will accustom themselves to wear better cloaths, finer linen, to have better furnished Houses and other choicer commodities. They will consequently give employment to several Mechanicks who had not so much to do before and who for the same reason will increase their expenses: all this increase in Meat, Wine, Wool, etc. . . .

*We might note that this is the first use of the term *entrepreneur:* see Higgs, pp. 388–89.

diminishes of necessity the share of the other inhabitants of the State who do not participate at first in the wealth of the Mines in question. The altercations of the market, or the demand for Meat, Wine, Wool, etc., being more intense than usual, will not fail to raise their prices. These high prices will determine the Farmers to employ more land to produce them in another year: these same Farmers will profit by this rise of prices and will increase the expenditure of their Families like the others.

Those then who suffer from the dearness and increased consumption will be first of all Landowners, during the term of their Leases, then their Domestic Servants and all the Workmen or fixed Wage-earners who support their families on their wages. All these must diminish their expenditure in proportion to the new consumption, which will compel a large number of them to emigrate or seek a living elsewhwre. The Landowners will dismiss many of them, and the rest will demand an increase of wages to enable them to live as before. It is thus, approximately, that a considerable increase in Money from the Mines increases consumption, and by diminishing the number of inhabitants entails a greater expense among those who remain. . . .[9]

I will not pursue further this extraordinary analysis, so far ahead of its time, but let me quote one last Cantillonian bit. Here he speaks of the consequences of an increase in the supply of money:

I conclude that by doubling the quantity of money in a State the prices of products and merchandise are not always doubled. A River which runs and winds about in its bed will not flow with double the speed when the amount of water is doubled. . . .

The proportion of the dearness which the increased quantity of money brings about in the State will depend on the turn which the money will give to consumption and circulation. . . . It will be directed more or less to certain products or merchandise according to the idea of those who acquire the money. Market

[9] Higgs, pp. 159, 161, 163, 165.

prices will rise more for certain things than for others, however abundant the money may be. (pp. 177, 179)

_____

All these observations strike us as testimony to Cantillon's keen analytic capability. They testify as well to something else. That is his vision that markets, still in his time regarded as elements that disturbed the presumed peaceful setting of a society regulated by tradition and authority, were in fact mechanisms by which another kind of order was established—a much more dynamic order to be sure, but an order nonetheless. Think back to the outcome of the altercations of the housewives and the butchers!

Let me once again turn to William Stanley Jevons for a summary judgment: "After reading well over one thousand economic writings of earlier date than 1734 I would put Cantillon's analysis of the circulation of wealth, trite as it may appear, on the same level of priority as Harvey's study of the circulation of the blood."[10]

[10] Higgs, op. cit., p. 388.

FRANÇOIS QUESNAY

(1694–1774)

With François Quesnay we introduce an odd group of French reformers who sought to rationalize the rickety economic system of France in the years before the French Revolution. Quesnay himself was physician to no less famous a personage than Mme. de Pompadour, mistress to His Majesty Louis XV. His small but prestigious circle included the renowned Marquis de Mirabeau, who had published Cantillon's work in 1755; Anne Robert Jacques Turgot, Controleur Général des Finances under Louis XVI in 1774, whose remarkable work we shall meet in the next chapter; and du Pont de Nemours, a talented young scholar who eventually emigrated to America where he opened a gunpowder plant. Adam Smith would have dedicated *The Wealth of Nations* to Quesnay had not the doctor died before its publication.

Quesnay's circle called its approach to political economy Physiocracy. The word means "order of nature," and it refers to the central belief that land alone yields a surplus because nature labors with man, whereas man working with machines can do no more than reshape the material that had originally been wrested from the fecund soil. Strange as it sounds to modern ears, there is a *prima facie* rationale for this belief: Did not 100 bushels of wheat yield a crop of 300 or 400 bushels? Whence came these additional bushels if not from nature's generosity?

Thus Quesnay and his followers called all agricultural work "productive," because it seemed to yield a tangible surplus of wealth over the labor that was expended on it, whereas industrial work was more severely described as "sterile," insofar as its products, however useful, did not evidence an unambiguous and tangible increase in wealth comparable to the contrast between the corn sowed and the corn reaped. Here is how Quesnay describes matters in his article "Men," written for Diderot's Encyclopedia.

EXTRACT FROM 'MEN'

. . . Those who make manufactured commodities do not produce wealth, because their labour increases the value of commodities only by an amount equal to the wages which are paid to them and which are drawn from the product of landed property. The manufacturer who makes cloth, the tailor who makes clothes, the cobbler who makes shoes, do not produce wealth any more than do the cook who makes his master's dinner, the worker who saws wood, or the musicians who give a concert. They are all paid out of one and the same fund, in proportion to the rate of reward fixed for their work, and they spend their receipts in order to obtain their subsistence. Thus they consume as much as they produce; the product of their labour is equal to the cost of their labour, and no surplus of wealth results from it. Thus it is only those who cause to be generated from landed property products whose value exceeds their costs who produce weath or annual revenue.[11]

What is the fallacy in this analysis? We will come to that shortly. But first let us look at an unusually interesting aspect of Physiocracy which anticipates a direction in which economic analysis would be moving a hundred years later. This is its famous "zigzag" diagram (or *Tableau Économique*) which first appeared in Quesnay's manuscript in 1758, and thereafter in many printed

[11] From Ronald Meek, *The Economics of Physiocracy* Cambridge, Massachusetts: Harvard University Press, 1973, p. 96.

editions. Recall Cantillon's comment that there seemed to be no "exact or geometrical" way of determining prices (see page 31). The Physiocratic zigzags do not illumine how prices are determined, but they illustrate something even more interesting—how a commercial society renews and replenishes itself. Let us therefore look at one of many zigzags, from Quesnay's Third edition.[12]

PRODUCTIVE CLASS	PROPRIETORS	STERILE CLASS
Annual advances required to produce a revenue of 600ˡ are 600ˡ	Annual revenue	Annual advances for the works of sterile expenditure are
600ˡ reproduce net ·········· 600ˡ		600ˡ
Products one-half goes here	one-half goes here	Works, etc.
300ˡ reproduce net ·········· 300ˡ	one-half	one-half ·········· 300ˡ
one-half goes here		goes here
150 reproduce net ·········· 150	one-half, etc.	150
75 reproduce net ·········· 75		75
37 ..10ˢ reproduce net ·········· 37 ..10		37 ..10
18 ..15 reproduce net ·········· 18 ..15		18 ..15
9 ... 7 ... 6ᵈ reproduce net ·········· 9 ... 7 ... 6ᵈ		9 ... 7 ... 6ᵈ
4 ..13 ... 9 reproduce net ·········· 4 ..13 ... 9		4 ..13 ... 9
2 ... 6 ..10 reproduce net ·········· 2 ... 6 ..10		2 ... 6 ..10
1 ... 3 ... 5 reproduce net ·········· 1 ... 3 ... 5		1 ... 3 ... 5
0 ..11 ... 8 reproduce net ·········· 0 ..11 ... 8		0 ..11 ... 8
0 ... 5 ..10 reproduce net ·········· 0 ... 5 ..10		0 ... 5 ..10
0 ... 2 ..11 reproduce net ·········· 0 ... 2 ..11		0 ... 2 ..11
0 ... 1 ... 5 reproduce net ·········· 0 ... 1 ... 5		0 ... 1 ... 5

One cannot actually read this bizarre diagram without benefit of the notes and explanations that Quesnay adds to the figure itself. Once we take these into account, however, we begin to see the rationale behind the presentation.

[12] From Steven Pressman, *Quesnay's Tableau Économique* Fairfield, New Jersry, Augustus M. Kelley, 1994, p. 22.

Let us begin with the three designations at the top: Productive class, Proprietors, and Sterile class. We should note that the first and last are not actually social classes, insofar as they include employers as well as workmen, and that the Proprietors include very large numbers of servants along with a much smaller number of seigneurs. Hence, the three columns are better thought of as "sectors." Equally important is Quesnay's allocation of population among these sectors, also not shown on the zigzag: the Productives number half the population, the Proprietors (including their large retinues) one quarter, and the Steriles comprise the last quarter.

Last, and emphatically not least, is an assumption about the size of the "gift of nature," also discussed elsewhere in the *Tableau:* it is assumed that the wealth gained from working with the soil will be worth double the value of the work itself: if a year's payroll for agriculture is 100 *livres* (abbreviated as *l*), the crop produced will be worth 200 *l*.

We are now ready to tackle the zigzag. We note at the top left that the Productive class transfers 600 *l* of "produce net" to the Proprietors: this is its annual payment of rent; and the zigs and zags will depict how this rent is redistributed by the flow of production to replenish both classes and to start a second year's accrual of rent.

We next see that the Proprietors spend half their income on the Sterile sectors, purchasing outputs of every kind except those grown on the soil, and the other half on the output of the Productive class, for which they receive grains, meat, caviar, and plovers' eggs. Having performed their function, the Proprietors play no further role, and the action devolves to the activities of the Productives and Steriles. Here, both sectors follow the lead of the Proprietors, dividing their incomes equally between expenditures on Productive and Sterile outputs—but with very different consequences. Note that every expenditure that goes to the Productive class results in a dotted horizontal line, whereas there are no such lines resulting from expenditures to the Sterile sector. This is, of course, a depiction of the gift of nature, and we should take a moment to pursue Quesnay's analysis further.

We begin with the Productive sector which has just received 300 from the Proprietors. The Productive sector now spends one-half its receipts for purchases—clothes, tools, and the like—from the Sterile sector and uses the other half to pay for the work of its labor force (although maddeningly this is not shown on Quesnay's diagram).* Thus the value of the total "inputs" into agriculture consists of 150 *l* of the foods needed by its workers, plus 150 *l* worth of clothes and tools, bought from the Sterile sector. This comes to 300 *l* of total input which, thanks to the bounty of nature, yields 600 *l* of output.

Following down the zigs and zags we see this pattern repeated: the Steriles and Productives exchange half of the receipts they get from the other class, and use half for the payment of their own work forces. But with each exchange, the Productives gather a gift from nature, which will be paid as rent, whereas the Steriles do not. In the end, the total of the rental amounts comes to 600 *livres,* and each sector has likewise received the amounts needed to sustain its own activity.

The zigzag shows us several things—for example, that the required size of the productive sector depends on the leverage of the gift of nature. In our example, if that leverage—which Quesnay knew to depend greatly on the use of farm machinery—were less than 2 to 1, the productive sector would have to be *more* than half the population to generate a stable flow of output over time.

Moreover, the diagram shows that the ratio of expenditure between the two sectors is crucial, given the allocation of population among the sectors. In our zigzag, the proprietors in our diagram must spend at least half their incomes for productive output to maintain things as they are. On the other hand, if they spent more than half on agriculture, the gift of nature will enlarge the total output of society, including their own rents. If they spend less than half, all incomes will shrink, after a few rounds. What is novel and interesting here is the first demonstration of a systemic

---

*Anyone wishing to penetrate further into the zigzag, which bewilders as much as it clarifies, should consult the books by Ronald Meek and Steven Pressman cited above.

relationship between expenditure and income in a commercial society.

Last, the diagram shows that only one class can be taxed without interfering with the production of wealth. It is certainly not the productive class, which is the source of its growth. It is not the sterile class, which just balances its books. Hence the only group that can be safely taxed consists of the Proprietors. This leads to Quesnay's famous recommendation that the hopeless tax situation of pre-revolutionary France be replaced by a Single Tax on rents. One can imagine the enthusiasm with which it was greeted by the land-owning nobility at Versailles.

Finally, in the face of so much brilliance and insight, what was the fatal Physiocratic fallacy? Essentially it lay in the deception that arises when the final product of a labor process is the same as its original input. To the naive eye, the corn that emerges from a crop is the same as the corn that goes into the ground, and the increase in volume therefore appears as a "gift" from nature—the only visible force at work. By way of contrast, the pots made from clay or the planks made from a tree trunk do not seem to grow in value, because their form changes: the pots do not appear as "more" than the clay in the way that a harvested crop is manifestly larger than its original seed.

Yet, with the crop as well as with the pot, final output requires that labor be applied to the input. Further, the unchanged nature of corn input into corn output hides the fact that the additional bushels of crop may not be net gain. They are required to sustain the labor of "sterile" makers of agricultural implements, as well as of husbandmen. Depending on how generously these needs are met, larger or smaller amounts of output will be left over as a gift from nature. Moreover, take away the agricultural implements made by the sterile sector, and there may not be any increase of corn output over corn input. Physiocracy thus builds its analysis on a misconstrued conception of productivity, restricting it to increases in the output of unchanged commodities, and ignoring the very real increases in wealth produced by machines, not to mention cooks or lumbermen.

ANNE ROBERT JACQUES TURGOT

(1727–1781)

Physiocracy has long interested economists because it is a bridge between the past and the present. Adam Smith, who would usher in that present, said of the Physiocratic school that "with all its imperfections," it was, "the nearest approximation to the truth that has yet been published upon the subject of political economy."[13]

Of all the representatives of the school, the most "modern" is surely Anne Robert Jacques Turgot. For the focus of Turgot's extraordinary sketch is not just the productivity of land. *Capital* becomes a moving force in Turgot's reconstruction to a degree never before seen in Physiocratic writings. Moreover, although Turgot is unable to shake the Physiocratic fallacy (as we will see), his is surely the most lucid and interesting of the pre-Smithian reconstructions of history, in that it includes the rise and function of commercial society.

Finally, the *Réflections* are very short, divided into 101 sections, many no longer than a brief paragraph, preceded with an italicized sentence or two. I have used only as much of the text as is needed to convey its main thrust, omitting subjects, such as the

---

[13] *Wealth*, op. cit., p. 642.

nature of money, that are not vital to that end, and condensing many excerpts.

I have also inserted myself at a number of places where I felt a word of explication or warning might be helpful. Indeed I shall start with such a word before we begin. The *Réflections* falls into a small, but intriguing category of social literature that might be called conjectural history. The seventeenth century philosopher Giambattista Vico composed such a history, in which he described the original communication among humans as taking place by song, not talk; Thomas Hobbes and John Locke are famous expositors of their own such histories—"nasty, brutish and short" for the first; "social compact" for the second. Turgot begins his own such history by tracing how property and class differentiation arose "naturally" in prehistory to form the basis for a stratified, commercial society.

REFLECTIONS ON THE FORMATION AND DISTRIBUTION OF WEALTH

I

The impossibility of Commerce on the assumption of an equal division of land, where each man would have only what was necessary for his own support.

If land were distributed among all the inhabitants of a country in such a way that each of them had precisely the quantity needed for his support, and nothing more, it is evident that, all being equal, no one would be willing to work for others. . . .

III

The products of the land require long and difficult preparations in order to render them suitable to men's needs.

The produce which the land yields . . . must be subjected to various changes and be prepared by means of art. Wheat must be converted into flour and then into bread. . . . If the same man who caused [things] to be produced from his land. . . . were also obliged to subject them to all these intermediate preparations, it is certain that the result would turn out very badly.

IV

The necessity for these preparations leads to the exchange of products for labour.

The same motive which brought about the exchange of one kind of produce for another as between Cultivators of soils of different qualities was bound to lead also to the exchange of produce for labour as between the Cultivators and another part of society, which had come to prefer the occupation of preparing and working up the products of the soil to growing them. Every one gained as a result of this arrangement, for each man, by devoting himself to a single kind of work succeeded much better in it. . . .

I call attention to the word "prefer" above, which now permits Turgot to introduce the appearance of first two, then three new socioeconomic classes.

V

Pre-eminence of the Husbandman who produces over the Artisan who prepares . . . It is he who causes the land to produce the wages of all Artisans.

It must however be noted that the Husbandman, who supplies everyone with the most important and considerable articles of their consumption (I mean their food and also the materials of almost all manufactures), has the advantage of a greater degree of independence. . . . What we have here is a primacy arising not from honour or dignity, but from *physical necessity*. The Husbandman, generally speaking, can get on without the labour of the other Workmen, but no Workman can labour if the Husbandman does not support him . . . Whatever his labour causes the land to produce over and above his personal needs is the unique fund from which are paid the wages all other members of society receive. . . .

VII

The Husbandman is the only one whose labour produces anything over and above the wage of labour. He is therefore the unique source of all wealth.

. . . As soon as the labour of the Husbandman produces something over and above his needs, he is able, with this surplus over and above the reward for his toil which nature allows him as a pure gift, to purchase the labour of other members of the society.

VIII

Primary Division of society into two classes: first, the productive class, or the Cultivator; and second, the stipendiary class or the Artisans.

Here then we have the whole society divided, as a result of a necessity founded on the nature of things, into two classes, both of which are occupied in work. But one of these, through its labour, produces or rather extracts from the land wealth which is continually renascent. . . . [T]he other, engaged in preparing the produced materials, . . . sells its labour to the first and receives its subsistence in exchange. . . .

XIII

. . . The cultivator distinguished from the Proprietor

[Now] we have landed estates as objects of commerce, being bought and sold. The portion of the Proprietor who is extravagant or unfortunate serves to increase that of the Proprietor who is luckier or more prudent. . . . [I]t is natural enough that a wealthy man should wish to enjoy his wealth in peace, and that instead of employing all his time in arduous labour, he should prefer to give a part of his surplus to people who will work for him.

XIV

Division of the product between the Cultivator and the Proprietor.

According to this new arrangement, the product of land is divided into two parts. One comprises the subsistence and profits of the Husbandman, which are the reward for his labour. . . . What remains is that independent and disposable part which the land gives as a pure gift to the one who cultivates it, over and above his advances and the wages of his toil. [T]his is the share of the Proprietor, or the *revenue*, with which the latter is able to live without working and which he takes wherever he wishes.

XV

[There is now a] New Division of Society Into three Classes, the Cultivators, the Artisans, and the Proprietors, or the 'productive' class, the 'stipendiary' class, and the 'disposable' class.

. . . [T]he class of Proprietors, the only one which, not being bound by the need for subsistence to one particular kind of work, may be employed to meet the general needs of the Society, for example in war and the administration of justice, whether through personal services, or through the payment of a part of its revenue with which the State or Society may hire men to discharge these functions. The name which for this reason suits it best is the *disposable class*.

———————

Turgot has presented a brilliant apologia for Physiocracy, although we should note that there are some very dubious historical assumptions in his reconstruction of society. Thus the origins of social classes remain veiled to Turgot himself, as well, I am sure, to his readers. Nonetheless, although this sets the stage for a Physiocratic view of the economic process, Turgot takes us by surprise in Section XIX below, when he turns from a review of different ways of generating a revenue to a consideration of capital itself. It will come as no surprise that these new uses treat the employment of money capital as a means of generating a "revenue," comparable to that of land.

XIX

Of Capitals in general, and of the revenue of money

There is another way of being wealthy without working and without possessing land of which I have not yet spoken. . . . This way consists in living on what is called the revenue of one's money, or on the interest which is derived from money put out on loan.

XLIX

Of the reserve of annual produce, accumulated to form capitals

As soon as men were found whose ownership of land assured them of an annual revenue more than sufficient to meet all their needs, there were bound to be men who, either because they were anxious about the future or merely because they were prudent, put into reserve a portion of what they gathered in each year. . . . When the produce which they gathered in was difficult to keep, they must have sought to obtain for themselves in exchange objects of a more durable nature whose value would not be lost with time. . . .

L

Moveable wealth; accumulation of money

Possessions of this kind, resulting from the accumulation of unconsumed annual produce, are known by the name of *moveable wealth*. . . . [A]s soon as it became known . . . that money was the most imperishable of objects of Commerce, it could not fail to be sought above all other things by anyone who wanted to accumulate. . . .

LVIII

Every capital in the form of money . . . is the equivalent of a piece of land producing a revenue equal to a particular fraction of this sum.

. . . Anyone, who, whether in the form of revenue from his land, or of wages from his labour or his industry, receives each year more value than he needs to spend, can put his surplus into reserve and accumulate it: these accumulated values are what is called *a capital*. . . . The Possessor of a *capital* may, therefore, in the first place, employ it in the purchase of land, but there are also other courses open to him.

LX

Further points about the use of capitals in industrial enterprises. . . .

. . . Here then another advance is indispensable. Who . . . will collect together the materials for the work, and the ingredients and tools necessary for their preparation? Who will get canals, markets, and buildings of all kinds constructed? Who will make it possible for this great number of Workmen to live until [their product] is sold? . . . It will be one of those Possessors of *capitals* or of moveable accumulated values, who will use them, partly as advances . . . , and partly as the daily wages of the Workmen who work them up. . . .

LXI

Subdivision of the industrial stipendiary Class into capitalist Entrepreneurs and ordinary Workmen

Thus the whole Class which is engaged in meeting the different needs of society with the vast variety of industrial products finds itself, so to speak, subdivided into two orders: that of Entrepreneurs, Manufacturers, and Masters who are all possessors of large capitals which they turn to account by setting to work, through the medium of their advances, the second order, which consists of ordinary Artisans who possess no property but their own hands, and who advance nothing but their daily labour, and who receive no profit but their wages.

LXVIII

True idea of the circulation of money

We see, from what has just been said, how the cultivation of land, manufactures of all kinds, and all the branches of commerce depend upon a mass of capitals, or moveable accumulated wealth, which, having been first advanced by the Entrepreneurs in each of these different classes of work, must return to them every year a regular profit; that is, the capital to be reinvested and newly advanced in the continuation of the same enterprises, and the profit to provide for the more or less comfortable subsistence of the Entrepreneur. It is this continual advance and return of capitals which constitutes *what ought to be called the circulation of money* . . . which is with good reason compared to the circulation of blood in the animal body. For if, through any disarrangement . . , the Entrepreneurs cease to get back their advances together with the profit which they have a right to expect from them, it is obvious that they will be obliged to reduce their enterprises; that the amount of labour, the amount of consumption of the fruits of the earth, and the amount of production and of revenue will be reduced in like measure; that poverty will take the place of wealth, and that the ordinary Workmen, ceasing to find employment, will sink into the most extreme destitution.

LXXXI

Employment of capitals: the loan at interest . . .

The possessors of money balance the risk which their capital may run if the enterprise should not succeed, against the advantage if enjoying a regular profit without any labour. . . . Here is another outlet which is open to the Possessor of money, the loan at interest, or trade in money. For there must be no mistake about it: the loan at interest is nothing but a trading transaction in which the Lender is a man who sells the use of his money, and the Borrower a man who buys it, in exactly the same way as the Proprietor of a piece of land and a Farmer respectively sell and buy the use of an estate which is being leased.

LXXXVIII

Nevertheless, the products of these different employments [of money] mutually limit one another, and in spite of their inequality are kept in a kind of equilibrium.

. . . In a word, as soon as the profits resulting from one employment of money, whatever it may be, increase or diminish, capitals either turn in its direction or are withdrawn from the other employments; and this necessarily alters in each of these employments the ratio between the capital and the annual product. . . . [W]hatever the manner in which money is employed, its product cannot increase or diminish without all the other employments experiencing a proportionate increase or diminution.

LXXXIX

The Current interest on money is the thermometer by which one may judge of the abundance or scarcity of capitals; it is a measure of the extent to which a Nation can carry its agricultural, manufacturing, and commercial enteprises.

XCVI

Interest on money is not disposable in this sense, that the State can without any disadvantage appropriate part of it for its own needs.

. . . In a word, the capitalist lender of money ought to be considered as one who trades in a commodity which is absolutely necessary for the production of wealth, and which cannot be at too low a price. It is as unreasonable to burden this trade with a tax as to put a tax on the dung which serves to manure the land. . .

Having described in some detail various aspects of the use of capital, Turgot takes us by surprise once again. Here, at the end of his conjectural history, Physiocratic promptings again come to the fore in the extraordinary sections to follow.

XCIX

There exists no truly disposable revenue in a State except the net product of land.

We can see from what has been said that interest on money placed at loan is taken out of the revenue of land or out of the profits of agricultural, industrial, or commercial enterprises. But we have already shown that these profits themselves are only a part of the product of land; that the product of land is divided into two portions; that one is earmarked for the wages of the cultivator, for his profits, and for the return of the advances and interest on them; and that the other is the share of the proprietor. . . . Whether these profits are distributed in the form of workmen's wages, entpreneurs' profits, or interest on advances, they do not change their nature, and do not increase at all the amount of revenue produced by the productive class . . . in which the industrial class shares only to the extent of the price of its labour.

It still remains true, therefore, that there is no revenue except the net product of land, and that all other annual profit is either paid out of the revenue, or forms part of the expenditure which serves to produce revenue.

C

The land has also provided for the whole amount of moveable wealth or capitals in existence, and these are formed only as the result of a portion of its product being put into reserve each year.

Not only is it the case that there neither exists nor can exist any revenue other than the net product of land, but it is also the land which has provided all the capitals which constitute the totality of all the advances in cultivation and commerce. Land offered, without being cultivated, the first rude advances which were indispensable for the first labors; all the rest is the accumulated fruit of the economy of the centuries which have followed since man began to cultivate the land.... [A]lthough capitals are formed in part by means of savings from the profits of the industrious classes, yet, as these always come from the land ... it is obvious that capitals come from the land just as the revenue does, or rather, that they are simply the accumulation of that part of the values produced by land which the proprietors of the land, or those who share it with them, can put into reserve each year without using it to meet their needs.

CI

Although money is the direct object of saving, and is so to speak the raw material of capitals in the processes of their formation, specie constitutes only an almost imperceptible part of the sum total of capitals.

We have seen that money counts for almost nothing in the sum total of existing capitals; but it counts for a good deal in the formation of capitals. ... In fact, almost all savings are made in the form of money; it is in the form of money that revenues are returned to proprietors, and that advances and profits are returned to entrepreneurs. ... [Thus] the annual increase of capitals comes about in the form of money; but none of the entrepreneurs make any other use of it than to convert it immediately into different kinds of effects upon which the enterprise depends. Thus this money comes back into circulation, and the greater part of capitals exists only in the form of effects of different kinds, as has already been explained above.[14]

"Profit on capital in the true sense, of which rent is itself only an offshoot, ... does not exist for the Physiocrats."[15] Thus did Karl Marx criticize the school which, having come so close to perceiving the centrality of capital as stored-up labor, shied away at the end to attribute capital to the "gifts" of land.

[14]From Ronald L. Meek, *Turgot on Progress, Sociology and Economics*, London: Cambridge University Press, 1973, pp. 119 ff.

[15]Karl Marx, *Theories of Surplus Value* Moscow: Progress Publishers, 1969, Part I, p. 47.

One need not be a Marxist to see the value of Marx's criticism. The Physiocratic fallacy is, at root, a failure to see that the generative powers of the soil, which are indeed a gift, are of no greater importance than the gifts of the gravity that turns a water wheel, the elasticity of steam that powers the steam engine, the solubility, rigidity, and other physical and chemical properties of the world on which humanity depends for its sustenance. To put it more precisely, Turgot does not perceive that the *economic* significance of capital and "land" lie in their social, not their natural attributes— above all in the social arrangements that award to the owners of land and other property the money revenues that these "gifts" bring, ignoring the hands and backs of the laborers who were midwives at their birth.

That myopia will persist long after Physiocracy was only a fading chapter in the history of economic thought. But perhaps it is only in retrospect that we can see what a difference that chapter made. Before Quesnay, Turgot, and their fellow *économistes,* the commercial world presented moral perplexities, but no sense of a comprehensible internal order. When the brief moment of Physiocracy was finished—the school disappeared with the French Revolution—the stage was set for the work of the classical economists. Moral confusions vanish or recede; but a vitally important sense of order comes to the fore.

III

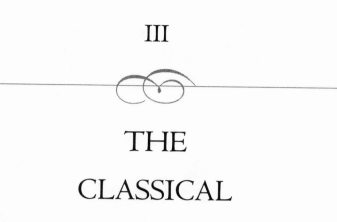

THE
CLASSICAL
ECONOMISTS

ADAM SMITH

(1723–1790)

Let us start with a very few words about Smith's life, not an eventful one. Born in the small town of Kirkcaldy, Scotland, he grew up in a country then half-wild, although Edinburgh was home to a remarkable group of first rate minds, including that of David Hume, perhaps England's greatest philosopher. Smith soon displayed his own scholarly talents and was awarded a scholarship to Oxford. There he passed his time in solitary reading—there was very little formal education in the Oxford of those days, and indeed Smith was nearly expelled when a copy of Hume's *Treatise of Human Nature* was found in his rooms.

On his return to Scotland Smith secured a teaching post at Glasgow, and in 1859 published his first book, *The Theory of Moral Sentiments.* The book made a considerable impression and little busts of Smith appeared in shop windows. More important, it won for Smith an invitation to be the personal companion to the young son of the Duke of Buccleuch on a tour of the continent. In Paris Smith met Quesnay and began serious work on what was to be his magnum opus, *The Weath of Nations.* When it appeared in 1776, Hume wrote: "Euge! Belle! Dear Mr. Smith I am much pleas'd with your performance." Later, when Smith was awarded a sinecure that made him financially secure, Hume wrote him again:

Dear Sir

Among the strange reports, which are every day circulating in this wide town, I heard one to-day so very extraordinary, that I do not know how to give credit to it. I was informed that a place of Commissioner of Customs of Scotland had been given to a Philosopher who for his own glory and for the benefit of mankind had enlightened the world by the most profound and systematic treatise on the great objects of trade and revenue which had ever been published in any age or any country. But as I was told that this Philosopher was my particular friend, I found myself forcible [sic] inclined to believe, what I most sincerely wished and desired.[16]

Smith died in 1790, to be buried under a simple tombstone saying, "Here Lies the Author of *The Wealth of Nations.*"

Everyone knows that Adam Smith is a pivotal as well as towering figure in the development of economic thought. Precisely what he contributed to economics is less well known, as is his moral appraisal of the social order to which his analysis was addressed—the order we would call preindustrial capitalism. Smith called it a Society of Perfect Liberty, the word capitalism not yet having been invented—it would not be, until a century after the publication of the *Wealth.*

Two things strike us with respect to that appraisal. First, the words "perfect liberty" suggest that the attribute of early capitalism most attractive to Smith was political, not economic. It is the liberty of its members to pursue their own freely chosen ends that Smith celebrates, because this liberty will redound to the general good of society. The centrality of this orientation emerges most clearly when we compare it with that of an *Inquiry into the Princi-*

---

[16] *The Correspondence of Adam Smith.* Ernest Campbell Mossner and Ian Simpson Ross, eds. Oxford: Clarendon Press, 1977, p. 228.

ples of Political Oeconomy, published in 1766 by another commentator of his day, Sir James Steuart. Steuart's political theme, sounded many times in his book, is this:

> The best way to govern society, and to engage every one to conduct himself according to a plan, is for the statesman to form a system of administration, the most consistent possible with the interest of every individual, and never to flatter himself that his people will be brought to act in general, and in matters which purely regard the public, from any other principle than private interest.[17]

The "statesman" personifies Steuart's general belief that economic growth and distribution must be entrusted to strong governmental guidance, not to the seemingly uncoordinated and unpredictable forces of individual aggrandizement. What Smith thought of this view is shown by his treatment of Steuart in *The Wealth:* he never mentions him.

Second, Smith's appraisal of the economic engine of a Society of Perfect Liberty was not one of unmixed admiration. While recognizing and saluting the productive impetus of a society driven by the drive for private wealth, Smith was far from an uncritical celebrant of the source of that impetus—namely, the drive to amass wealth. As we read selections from the two books that made his fame we shall see that Smith is always the philosopher, never a mere propagandist.

We start with the *Theory of Moral Sentiments*[18] (1759), not merely because it precedes the *Wealth,* but because it lays the basis on which the second book rests. This basis is behavior—more exactly, the inner feelings (sympathy) that determine much of behavior, not only in ordinary life, but in the exercise of one

[17] *Sir James Steuart, An Inquiry into the Principles of Political Oeconomy.* Andrew Skinner, ed. Edinburgh & London, 1966, p. 143.

[18] I am using the definitive Clarendon Press, Oxford edition, edited by D. D. Raphael and A. L. MacFie, 1976, adding a few italicized sideheads, and some additional indentations, for ease of reading. A reader seeking a condensed, more readily available source might consult my own *The Essential Adam Smith,* New York: W. W. Norton, 1986.

passion of great importance in a Society of Perfect Liberty—
namely, seeking to make money.

In such a society we are free to act as we will. What then saves
us from anarchy and disorder? The answer is that sympathy—we
would call it empathy—leads us to make our behavior conform
with prevailing norms. Slowly, however, we come to seek a
higher level of approval than that of the outside world. This is the
approval of a demanding judge within ourselves whom Smith
calls the "Impartial Spectator." We would call it the approval of
our conscience; if we will, our superego.

I shall again play a docent's role with a few words of guidance
or emphasis before or after—occasionally in the midst of—the
chapters to come. Once again, therefore, I begin with a word of
guidance. Smith's style is leisurely, a little homiletic, lit with illus-
trations from daily life. It may help to bear in mind that these
words were originally lectures, delivered to a teen-aged audience
of students. Although they do not make for light reading, I believe
they make a lasting impression—a commentary from the 1750s
whose contemporaneity is still evident.

THE THEORY OF MORAL SENTIMENTS

Part I; Sec. I; Chapter I

Of Sympathy

How selfish soever man may be supposed, there are evidently
some principles in his nature, which interest him in the fortune
of others, and render their happiness necessary to him, though
he derives nothing from it except the pleasure of seeing it. Of
this kind is pity or compassion, the emotion which we feel for the
misery of others, when we either see it, or are made to conceive it
in a very lively manner. That we often derive sorrow from the
sorrow of others, is a matter of fact too obvious to require any
instances to prove it; for this sentiment, like all the other original
passions of human nature, is by no means confined to the virtuous and humane, though they perhaps may feel it with the most

exquisite sensibility. The greatest ruffian, the most hardened vio-
lator of the laws of society, is not altogether without it.

As we have no immediate experience of what other men feel,
we can form no idea of the manner in which they are affected,
but by conceiving what we ourselves should feel in the like situation. Though our brother is upon the rack, as long as we ourselves are at our ease, our senses will never inform us of what he
suffers. They never did, and never can, carry us beyond our own
person, and it is by the imagination only that we can form any
conception of what are his sensations. Neither can that faculty
help us to this any other way, than by representing to us what
would be our own, if we were in his case. It is the impressions
of our own senses only, not those of his, which our imaginations
copy. By the imagination we place ourselves in his situation, we
conceive ourselves enduring all the same torments, we enter as
it were into his body, and become in some measure the same
person with him, and thence form some idea of his sensations,
and even feel something which, though weaker in degree, is not
altogether unlike them. . . .

That this is the source of our fellow-feeling for the misery of
others, that it is by changing places in fancy with the sufferer,
that we come either to conceive or to be affected by what he
feels, may be demonstrated by many obvious observations, if it
should not be thought sufficiently evident of itself. When we see
a stroke aimed and just ready to fall upon the leg or arm of
another person, we naturally shrink and draw back our own leg
or our own arm; and when it does fall, we feel it in some measure, and are hurt by it as well as the sufferer. The mob, when
they are gazing at a dancer on the slack rope, naturally writhe
and twist and balance their own bodies, as they see him do, and
as they feel that they themselves must do if in his situation. Persons of delicate fibres and a weak constitution of body complain,
that in looking on the sores and ulcers which are exposed by
beggars in the streets, they are apt to feel an itching or uneasy
sensation in the correspondent part of their own bodies. The horror which they conceive at the misery of those wretches affects
that particular part in themselves more than any other; because

that horror arises from conceiving what they themselves would suffer, if they really were the wretches whom they are looking upon, and if that particular part in themselves was actually affected in the same miserable manner. . . .

[Pity and Compassion] Pity and compassion are words appropriated to signify our fellow-feeling with the sorrow of others. Sympathy, though its meaning was, perhaps, originally the same, may now, however, without much impropriety, be made use of to denote our fellow-feeling with any passion whatever.

Upon some occasions sympathy may seem to arise merely from the view of a certain emotion in another person. The passions, upon some occasions, may seem to be transfused from one man to another, instantaneously, and antecedent to any knowledge of what excited them in the person principally concerned. Grief and joy, for example, strongly expressed in the look and gestures of any one, at once affect the spectator with some degree of a like painful or agreeable emotion. A smiling face is, to every body that sees it, a cheerful object; as a sorrowful countenance, on the other hand, is a melancholy one.

This, however, does not hold universally, or with regard to every passion. There are some passions of which the expressions excite no sort of sympathy, but before we are acquainted with what gave occasion to them, serve rather to disgust and provoke us against them. The furious behaviour of an angry man is more likely to exasperate us against himself than against his enemies. As we are unacquainted with his provocation, we cannot bring his case home to ourselves, nor conceive any thing like the passions which it excites. But we plainly see what is the situation of those with whom he is angry, and to what violence they may be exposed from so enraged an adversary. We readily, therefore, sympathize with their fear or resentment, and are immediately disposed to take part against the man from whom they appear to be in so much danger.

If the very appearances of grief and joy inspire us with some degree of the like emotions, it is because they suggest to us the general idea of some good or bad fortune that has befallen the person in whom we observe them: and in these passions this is sufficient to have some little influence upon us. The effects of grief and joy terminate in the person who feels those emotions, of which the expressions do not, like those of resentment, suggest to us the idea of any other person for whom we are concerned, and whose interests are opposite to his. The general idea of good or bad fortune, therefore, creates some concern for the person who has met with it, but the general idea of provocation excites no sympathy with the anger of the man who has received it. Nature, it seems, teaches us to be more averse to enter into this passion, and, till informed of its cause, to be disposed rather to take part against it.

Even our sympathy with the grief or joy of another, before we are informed of the cause of either, is always extremely imperfect. General lamentations, which express nothing but the anguish of the sufferer, create rather a curiosity to inquire into his situation, along with some disposition to sympathize with him, than any actual sympathy that is very sensible. The first question which we ask is, What has befallen you? Till this be answered, though we are uneasy both from the vague idea of his misfortune, and still more from torturing ourselves with conjectures about what it may be, yet our fellow-feeling is not very considerable.

Sympathy, therefore, does not arise so much from the view of the passion, as from that of the situation which excites it. We sometimes feel for another, a passion of which he himself seems to be altogether incapable; because, when we put ourselves in his case, that passion arises in our breast from the imagination, though it does not in his from the reality. We blush for the impudence and rudeness of another, though he himself appears to have no sense of the impropriety of his own behaviour; because we cannot help feeling with what confusion we ourselves should be covered, had we behaved in so absurd a manner. . . .

[How we judge one another]

Philosophers have, of late years, considered chiefly the tendency of affections, and have given little attention to the relation which they stand in to the cause which excites them. In common life, however, when we judge of any person's conduct, and of the sentiments which directed it, we constantly consider them under both these aspects. When we blame in another man the excesses of love, of grief, of resentment, we not only consider the ruinous effects which they tend to produce, but the little occasion which was given for them. The merit of his favourite, we say, is not so great, his misfortune is not so dreadful, his provocation is not so extraordinary, as to justify so violent a passion. We should have indulged, we say; perhaps, have approved of the violence of his emotion, had the cause been in any respect proportioned to it.

When we judge in this manner of any affection, as proportioned or disproportioned to the cause which excites it, it is scarce possible that we should make use of any other rule or canon but the correspondent affection in ourselves. If, upon bringing the case home to our own breast, we find that the sentiments which it gives occasion to, coincide and tally with our own, we necessarily approve of them as proportioned and suitable to their objects; if otherwise, we necessarily disapprove of them, as extravagant and out of proportion.

Every faculty in one man is the measure by which he judges of the like faculty in another. I judge of your sight by my sight, of your ear by my ear, of your reason by my reason, of your resentment by my resentment, of your love by my love. I neither have, nor can have, any other way of judging about them.

These charming observations serve an important purpose. They remind us that Smith is not seeking for the roots of "sympathy" in some bland, sentimental meaning of the word, but as a term that refers to our ability to understand actions and emotions of many kinds, disreputable as well as unimpeachable. This leads him into a considerable quandary—namely, how to justify the drive to amass wealth that evoked the contempt of the Biblical writers, Aristotle and Aquinas.

Rather like them, Smith is uneasy about the moral foundations of the drive for riches considered in itself, and he is therefore placed in an awkward position with respect to the appropriate estimation in which that drive should be held in a society where acquisitiveness plays a vital role. In the six editions of *The Moral Sentiments,* his unease becomes progressively more visible, although he is always able to extricate himself from an untenable position by virtue of two saving beliefs: that in moments of great crisis we consult sentiments other than those of self interest; that the micromotives of a Society of Perfect Liberty would in the end be redeemed by the outcome to which they led.

In our next selection, from Sections II and III of Chapter II, we see his outspoken description of the "corruption of our moral sentiments" that arises from the temptation to admire the rich and powerful. In subsequent selections we will read about the remedies for this state of affairs—such as they are.

Chapter II

Of the origin of Ambition, and of the distinction of Ranks

It is because mankind are disposed to sympathize more entirely with our joy than with our sorrow, that we make parade of our riches, and conceal our poverty. Nothing is so mortifying as to be obliged to expose our distress to the view of the public, and to feel, that though our situation is open to the eyes of all mankind, no mortal conceives for us the half of what we suffer. Nay, it is chiefly from this regard to the sentiments of mankind, that we pursue riches and avoid poverty. For to what purpose is all the toil and bustle of this world? what is the end of avarice and ambition, of the pursuit of wealth, of power, and preheminence? Is it to supply the necessities of nature? The wages of the meanest labourer can supply them. We see that they afford him food and clothing, the comfort of a house, and of a family. If we examined his œconomy with rigour, we should find that he spends a great part of them upon conveniencies, which may be regarded as superfluities, and that, upon extraordinary occasions, he can give something even to vanity and distinction.

What then is the cause of our aversion to his situation, and why should those who have been educated in the higher ranks of life, regard it as worse than death to be reduced to live, even without labour, upon the same simple fare with him, to dwell under the same lowly roof, and to be clothed in the same humble attire? Do they imagine that their stomach is better, or their sleep sounder in a palace than in a cottage? The contrary has been so often observed, and, indeed, is so very obvious, though it had never been observed, that there is nobody ignorant of it.

From whence, then, arises that emulation which runs through all the different ranks of men, and what are the advantages which we propose by that great purpose of human life which we call bettering our condition? To be observed, to be attended to, to be taken notice of with sympathy, complacency, and approbation, are all the advantages which we can propose to derive from it. It is the vanity, not the ease, or the pleasure, which interests us. But vanity is always founded upon the belief of our being the object of attention and approbation. The rich man glories in his riches, because he feels that they naturally draw upon him the attention of the world, and that mankind are disposed to go along with him in all those agreeable emotions with which the advantages of his situation so readily inspire him. At the thought of this, his heart seems to swell and dilate itself within him, and he is fonder of his wealth, upon this account, than for all the other advantages it procures him.

The poor man, on the contrary, is ashamed of his poverty. He feels that it either places him out of the sight of mankind, or, that if they take any notice of him, they have, however, scarce any fellow-feeling with the misery and distress which he suffers. He is mortified upon both accounts; for though to be overlooked, and to be disapproved of, are things entirely different, yet as obscurity covers us from the daylight of honour and approbation, to feel that we are taken no notice of, necessarily damps the most agreeable hope, and disappoints the most ardent desire, of human nature. The poor man goes out and comes in unheeded, and when in the midst of a crowd is in the same obscurity as if shut up in his own hovel. Those humble cares and painful attentions which occupy those in his situation, afford no amusement to the dissipated and the gay. They turn away their eyes from him, or if the extremity of his distress forces them to look at him, it is only to spurn so disagreeable an object from among them. The fortunate and the proud wonder at the insolence of human wretchedness, that it should dare to present itself before them, and with the loathsome aspect of its misery presume to disturb the serenity of their happiness.

The man of rank and distinction, on the contrary, is observed by all the world. Every body is eager to look at him, and to conceive, at least by sympathy, that joy and exultation with which his circumstances naturally inspire him. His actions are the objects of the public care. Scarce a word, scarce a gesture, can fall from him that is altogether neglected. In a great assembly he is the person upon whom all direct their eyes; it is upon him that their passions seem all to wait with expectation, in order to receive that movement and direction which he shall impress upon them; and if his behaviour is not altogether absurd, he has, every moment, an opportunity of interesting mankind, and of rendering himself the object of the observation and fellow-feeling of every body about him. It is this, which, notwithstanding the restraint it imposes, notwithstanding the loss of liberty with which it is attended, renders greatness the object of envy, and compensates, in the opinion of mankind, all that toil, all that anxiety, all those mortifications which must be undergone in the pursuit of it; and what is of yet more consequence, all that leisure, all that ease, all that careless security, which are forfeited for ever by the acquisition. . . . *[The pleasures of vanity]*

Upon this disposition of mankind, to go along with all the passions of the rich and the powerful, is founded the distinction of ranks, and the order of society. Our obsequiousness to our superiors more frequently arises from our admiration for the advantages of their situation, than from any private expectations of benefit from their good-will. Their benefits can extend but to a few; but their fortunes interest almost every body. We are eager to assist them in completing a system of happiness that approaches so near to perfection; and we desire to serve them for their own sake, without any other recompense but the vanity or the honour of obliging them. Neither is our deference to their inclinations founded chiefly, or altogether, upon a regard to the utility of such submission, and to the order of society, which is best supported by it. Even when the order of society seems to require that we should oppose them, we can hardly bring ourselves to do it.

Chapter III

Of the corruption of our moral sentiments, which is occasioned by this disposition to admire the rich and the great, and to despise or neglect persons of poor and mean condition

This disposition to admire, and almost to worship, the rich and the powerful, and to despise, or, at least, to neglect persons of poor and mean condition, though necessary both to establish and to maintain the distinction of ranks and the order of society, is, at the same time, the great and most universal cause of the corruption of our moral sentiments. That wealth and greatness are often regarded with the respect and admiration which are due only to wisdom and virtue; and that the contempt, of which vice and folly are the only proper objects, is often most unjustly bestowed upon poverty and weakness, has been the complaint of moralists in all ages.

We desire both to be respectable and to be respected. We dread both to be contemptible and to be contemned. But, upon coming into the world, we soon find that wisdom and virtue are by no means the sole objects of respect; nor vice and folly, of contempt. We frequently see the respectful attentions of the world more strongly directed towards the rich and the great, than towards the wise and the virtuous. We see frequently the vices and follies of the powerful much less despised than the poverty and weakness of the innocent. To deserve, to acquire, and to enjoy the respect and admiration of mankind, are the great objects of ambition and emulation. Two different roads are presented to us, equally leading to the attainment of this so much desired object; the one, by the study of wisdom and the practice of virtue; the other, by the acquisition of wealth and greatness. Two different characters are presented to our emulation; the one, of proud ambition and ostentatious avidity; the other, of humble modesty and equitable justice. Two different models, two different pictures, are held out to us, according to which we may fashion our own character and behaviour; the one more gaudy and glittering in its colouring; the other more correct and more exquisitely beautiful in its outline: the one forcing itself upon the notice of every wandering eye; the other, attracting the attention of scarce any body but the most studious and careful observer. They are the wise and the virtuous chiefly, a select, though, I am afraid, but a small party, who are the real and steady admirers of wisdom and virtue. The great mob of mankind are the admirers and worshippers, and, what may seem more extraordinary, most frequently the disinterested admirers and worshippers, of wealth and greatness. . . .

How does Smith extricate himself from the awkward fact that the motive on which the Society of Perfect Liberty depends is also a principal source of its corruption? In part it is the recognition, already voiced at the end of Chapter II above, that "Upon this disposition of mankind, to go along with the passions of the rich and powerful, is founded the distinction of ranks, and the order of society." Thus whatever its morally corrupting effect, our tendency to identify with our superiors imparts to society a stability it would not otherwise have. Smith, the supremely realistic political observer, accepts this as a necessary condition for social order.

But I made reference earlier to two other saving considerations. The first is that in moments of great humanitarian importance, we do not consult our self interest, but remount to a higher court—the man within the breast, our conscience, our sense of right and wrong. Here is that saving propensity in one of my favorite passages in *The Theory of Moral Sentiments,* Part II, Chapter III

On the Influence and Authority of Conscience

Let us suppose that the great empire of China, with all its myriads of inhabitants, was suddenly swallowed up by an earthquake, and let us consider how a man of humanity in Europe, who had no sort of connexion with that part of the world, would be affected upon receiving intelligence of this dreadful calamity. He would, I imagine, first of all, express very strongly his sorrow for the misfortune of that unhappy people, he would make many melancholy reflections upon the precariousness of human life, and the vanity of all the labours of man, which could thus be annihilated in a moment. He would too, perhaps, if he was a man of speculation, enter into many reasonings concerning the effects which this disaster might produce upon the commerce of Europe, and the trade and business of the world in general. And when all this fine philosophy was over, when all these humane sentiments had been once fairly expressed, he would pursue his business or his pleasure, take his repose or his diversion, with the same ease and tranquillity, as if no such accident had happened. The most frivolous disaster which could befal himself would occasion a more real disturbance. If he was to lose his little finger to-morrow, he would not sleep to-night; but, provided he never saw them, he will snore with the most profound security over the ruin of a hundred millions of his brethren, and the destruction of that immense multitude seems plainly an object less interesting to him, than this paltry misfortune of his own.

To prevent, therefore, this paltry misfortune to himself, would a man of humanity be willing to sacrifice the lives of a hundred millions of his brethren, provided he had never seen them? Human nature startles with horror at the thought, and the world, in its greatest depravity and corruption, never produced such a villain as could be capable of entertaining it. But what makes this difference? When our passive feelings are almost always so sordid and so selfish, how comes it that our active principles should often be so generous and so noble? When we are always so much more deeply affected by whatever concerns ourselves, than by whatever concerns other men; what is it which prompts the generous, upon all occasions, and the mean upon many, to sacrifice their own interests to the greater interests of others?

It is not the soft power of humanity, it is not that feeble spark of benevolence which Nature has lighted up in the human heart, that is thus capable of counteracting the strongest impulses of self-love. It is a stronger power, a more forcible motive, which exerts itself upon such occasions. It is reason, principle, conscience, the inhabitant of the breast, the man within, the great judge and arbiter of our conduct. It is he who, whenever we are about to act so as to affect the happiness of others, calls to us, with a voice capable of astonishing the most presumptuous of our passions, that we are but one of the multitude, in no respect better than any other in it; and that when we prefer ourselves so shamefully and so blindly to others, we become the proper objects of resentment, abhorrence, and execration. It is from him only that we learn the real littleness of ourselves, and of whatever relates to ourselves, and the natural misrepresentations of self-love can be corrected only by the eye of this impartial spectator. It is he who shows us the propriety of generosity and the deformity of injustice; the propriety of resigning the greatest interests of our own, for the yet greater interests of others, and the deformity of doing the smallest injury to another, in order to obtain the greatest benefit to ourselves. It is not the love of our neighbour, it is not the love of mankind, which upon many occasions prompts us to the practice of those divine virtues. It is a stronger love, a more powerful affection, which generally takes place upon such occasions; the love of what is honourable and noble, of the grandeur, and dignity, and superiority of our own characters.

Now what of the second safeguard? It concerns, not the inner workings of conscience, but the outer workings of economics. Smith looks to the dynamics of a Society of Perfect Liberty to bring about from its acquisitive drive, blunted by competition, a distribution of outputs little different from that which would meet with our moral approval. "The rich," he writes, "only select from the heap what is most precious and agreeable. They consume little more than the poor"—for which, incidentally, they have paid dearly in worry and concern.

There is more apologism in this passage than in all the rest of Smith put together, but the rather uncharacteristic hypocrisy—for hypocrisy it surely is—must be viewed in the light of Smith's perception of the Society of Perfect Liberty directing its efforts toward social betterment, "as if guided by an invisible hand."

The workings of that hand will not be adumbrated until we reach *The Wealth of Nations* in our next major reading. But these pages from *The Moral Sentiments,* Part IV, Chapter 1, in which we follow the career of a "poor man's son," struck with ambition, serve as a perfect introduction to that masterwork.

The poor man's son, whom heaven in its anger has visited with ambition, when he begins to look around him, admires the condition of the rich. He finds the cottage of his father too small for his accommodation, and fancies he should be lodged more at his ease in a palace. He is displeased with being obliged to walk a-foot, or to endure the fatigue of riding on horseback. He sees his superiors carried about in machines, and imagines that in one of these he could travel with less inconveniency. He feels himself naturally indolent, and willing to serve himself with his own hands as little as possible; and judges, that a numerous retinue of servants would save him from a great deal of trouble. He thinks if he had attained all these, he would sit still contentedly, and be quiet, enjoying himself in the thought of the happiness and tranquillity of his situation. He is enchanted with the distant idea of this felicity. It appears in his fancy like the life of some superior rank of beings, and, in order to arrive at it, he devotes himself for ever to the pursuit of wealth and greatness.

To obtain the conveniencies which these afford, he submits in the first year, nay in the first month of his application, to more fatigue of body and more uneasiness of mind than he could have suffered through the whole of his life from the want of them. He studies to distinguish himself in some laborious profession. With the most unrelenting industry he labours night and day to acquire talents superior to all his competitors. He endeavours next to bring those talents into public view, and with equal assiduity solicits every opportunity of employment. For this purpose he makes his court to all mankind; he serves those whom he hates, and is obsequious to those whom he despises. Through the whole of his life he pursues the idea of a certain artificial and elegant repose which he may never arrive at, for which he sacrifices a real tranquillity that is at all times in his power, and which, if in the extremity of old age he should at last attain to it, he will find to be in no respect preferable to that humble security and contentment which he had abandoned for it.

It is then, in the last dregs of life, his body wasted with toil and diseases, his mind galled and ruffled by the memory of a thousand injuries and disappointments which he imagines he has met with from the injustice of his enemies, or from the perfidy and ingratitude of his friends, that he begins at last to find that wealth and greatness are mere trinkets of frivolous utility, no more adapted for procuring ease of body or tranquillity of mind than the tweezer-cases of the lover of toys; and like them too, more troublesome to the person who carries them about with him than all the advantages they can afford him are commodious. There is no other real difference between them, except that the conveniencies of the one are somewhat more observable than those of the other. . . .

But in the languor of disease and the weariness of old age, the pleasures of the vain and empty distinctions of greatness disappear. To one, in this situation, they are no longer capable of recommending those toilsome pursuits in which they had formerly engaged him. In his heart he curses ambition, and vainly regrets the ease and the indolence of youth, pleasures which are fled for ever, and which he has foolishly sacrificed for what, when he has got it, can afford him no real satisfaction. In this miserable aspect does greatness appear to every man when reduced either by spleen or disease to observe with attention his own situation, and to consider what it is that is really wanting to his happiness. Power and riches appear then to be, what they are, enormous and operose machines contrived to produce a few trifling conveniencies to the body, consisting of springs the most nice and delicate, which must be kept in order with the most anxious attention, and which in spite of all our care are ready every moment to burst into pieces, and to crush in their ruins their unfortunate possessor. They are immense fabrics, which it requires the labour of a life to raise, which threaten every moment to overwhelm the person that dwells in them, and which while they stand, though they may save him from some smaller inconveniencies, can protect him from none of the severer inclemencies of the season. They keep off the summer shower, not the winter storm, but leave him always as much, and sometimes more exposed than before, to anxiety, to fear, and to sorrow; to diseases, to danger, and to death. . . .

The Invisible Hand

And it is well that nature imposes upon us in this manner. It is this deception which rouses and keeps in continual motion the industry of mankind. It is this which first prompted them to cultivate the ground, to build houses, to found cities and commonwealths, and to invent and improve all the sciences and arts, which ennoble and embellish human life; which have entirely changed the whole face of the globe, have turned the rude forests of nature into agreeable and fertile plains, and made the trackless and barren ocean a new fund of subsistence, and the great high road of communication to the different nations of the earth. The earth by these labours of mankind has been obliged to redouble her natural fertility, and to maintain a greater multitude of inhabitants. It is to no purpose, that the proud and unfeeling landlord views his extensive fields, and without a thought for the wants of his brethren, in imagination consumes himself the whole harvest that grows upon them.

The homely and vulgar proverb, that the eye is larger than the belly, never was more fully verified than with regard to him. The capacity of his stomach bears no proportion to the immensity of his desires, and will receive no more than that of the meanest peasant. The rest he is obliged to distribute among those, who prepare, in the nicest manner, that little which he himself makes use of, among those who fit up the palace in which this little is to be consumed, among those who provide and keep in order all the different baubles and trinkets, which are employed in the oeconomy of greatness; all of whom thus derive from his luxury and caprice, that share of the necessaries of life, which they would in vain have expected from his humanity or his justice. The produce of the soil maintains at all times nearly that number of inhabitants which it is capable of maintaining. The rich only select from the heap what is most precious and agreeable. They consume little more than the poor, and in spite of their natural

selfishness and rapacity, though they mean only their own con-
veniency, though the sole end which they propose from the
labours of all the thousands whom they employ, be the gratification of their own vain and insatiable desires, they divide with
the poor the produce of all their improvements. They are led by
an invisible hand* to make nearly the same distribution of the
necessaries of life, which would have been made, had the earth
been divided into equal portions among all its inhabitants, and
thus without intending it, without knowing it, advance the interest of the society, and afford means to the multiplication of the
species. When Providence divided the earth among a few lordly
masters, it neither forgot nor abandoned those who seemed to
have been left out in the partition. These last too enjoy their share
of all that it produces. In what constitutes the real happiness of
human life, they are in no respect inferior to those who would
seem so much above them. In ease of body and peace of mind,
all the different ranks of life are nearly upon a level, and the
beggar, who suns himself by the side of the highway, possesses
that security which kings are fighting for.

That last sentence is certainly not Smith at his best, and indeed
accords with a stereotyped view of him as a great "conservative"
economic thinker. All the more reason to turn to *The Wealth of
Nations,* where I think most readers will discover a worldly philosopher very different from what they expect.

THE WEALTH OF NATIONS

The Wealth of Nations is a marvelous work, but not an easy one
to present in capsule form.† The reason is that the treatise is
divided into five Books, each devoted to a different, although inte-
gral, aspect of the workings of a Society of Perfect Liberty.

*Nota bene!
†I have used the definitive Oxford edition, with some additional paragraphing and
sideheads. Those wishing a more easily obtainable (and much cheaper) edition might
well look to the excellent Modern Library *Wealth* which contains the very helpful
sidenotes added by Edwin Cannan in 1904. My own *The Essential Adam Smith,* mentioned on page 57 n.18, may be useful for someone wishing a condensed version of
the book and more explicit discussion of its themes.

I shall focus first on Book I. After a brief overview of Smith's grand subject—what makes some nations rich and powerful—we proceed to a justly famous examination of the reason: the Division of Labor. There is no need for a guide in these pages. They are clear and even vivid; very interesting; and in the final peroration about how the provision of an "industrious and frugal peasant" exceeds the "accommodation . . . of many an African king" they set the stage for what is to follow.

Introduction and Plan of the Work

The annual labour of every nation is the fund which originally supplies it with all the necessaries and conveniences of life which it annually consumes, and which consist always, either in the immediate produce of that labour, or in what is purchased with that produce from other nations.

According therefore, as this produce, or what is purchased with it, bears a greater or smaller proportion to the number of those who are to consume it, the nation will be better or worse supplied with all the necessaries and conveniences for which it has occasion.

But this proportion must in every nation be regulated by two different circumstances; first, by the skill, dexterity, and judgment with which its labour is generally applied; and, secondly, by the proportion between the number of those who are employed in useful labour, and that of those who are not so employed. Whatever be the soil, climate, or extent of territory of any particular nation, the abundance or scantiness of its annual supply must, in that particular situation, depend upon those two circumstances.

The abundance or scantiness of this supply too seems to depend more upon the former of those two circumstances than upon the latter. Among the savage nations of hunters and fishers, every individual who is able to work, is more or less employed in useful labour, and endeavours to provide, as well as he can, the necessaries and conveniencies of life, for himself, for such of his family or tribe as are either too old, or too young, or too infirm to go a hunting and fishing. Such nations, however, are so miserably poor, that, from mere want, they are frequently reduced, or, at least, think themselves reduced, to the necessity sometimes of directly destroying, and sometimes of abandoning their infants, their old people, and those afflicted with lingering diseases, to perish with hunger, or to be devoured by wild beasts. Among civilized and thriving nations, on the contrary, though a great number of people do not labour at all, many of whom consume the produce of ten times, frequently of a hundred times more labour than the greater part of those who work; yet the produce of the whole labour of the society is so great, that all are often abundantly supplied, and a workman, even of the lowest and poorest order, if he is frugal and industrious, may enjoy a greater share of the necessaries and conveniences of life than it is possible for any savage to acquire.

Chapter I

Of the Division of Labour

The greatest improvement in the productive powers of labour, and the greater part of the skill, dexterity, and judgment with which it is any where directed, or applied, seem to have been the effects of the division of labour.

The effects of the division of labour, in the general business of society, will be more easily understood, by considering in what manner it operates in some particular manufactures. It is commonly supposed to be carried furthest in some very trifling ones; not perhaps that it really is carried further in them than in others of more importance: but in those trifling manufactures which are destined to supply the small wants of but a small number of people, the whole number of workmen must necessarily be small; and those employed in every different branch of the work can often be collected into the same workhouse, and placed at once under the view of the spectator. In those great manufactures, on the contrary, which are destined to supply the great wants of the great body of the people, every different branch of the work employs so great a number of workmen that it is impossible to collect them all into the same workhouse. We can seldom see more, at one time, than those employed in one single branch. Though in such manufactures, therefore, the work may really be divided into a much greater number of parts, than in those of a more trifling nature, the division is not near so obvious, and has accordingly been much less observed.

[The pin factory]

To take an example, therefore, from a very trifling manufacture; but one in which the division of labour has been very often taken notice of, the trade of the pin-maker; a workman not educated to this business (which the division of labour has rendered a distinct trade), nor acquainted with the use of the machinery employed in it (to the invention of which the same division of labour has probably given occasion), could scarce, perhaps, with his utmost industry, make one pin in a day, and certainly could not make twenty. But in the way in which this business is now carried on, not only the whole work is a peculiar trade, but it is divided into a number of branches, of which the greater part are likewise peculiar trades. One man draws out the wire, another straights it, a third cuts it, a fourth points it, a fifth grinds it at the top for receiving the head; to make the head requires two or three distinct operations; to put it on, is a peculiar business, to whiten the pins is another; it is even a trade by itself to put them into the paper; and the important business of making a pin is, in this manner, divided into about eighteen distinct operations, which, in some manufactories, are all performed by distinct hands, though in others the same man will sometimes perform two or three of them. I have seen a small manufactory of this kind where ten men only were employed, and where some of them consequently performed two or three distinct operations. But though they were very poor, and therefore but indifferently accommodated with the necessary machinery, they could, when they exerted themselves, make among them about twelve pounds of pins in a day. There are in a pound upwards of four thousand pins of a middling size. Those ten persons, therefore, could make among them upwards of forty-eight thousand pins in a day. Each person, therefore, making a tenth part of forty-eight thousand pins, might be considered as making four thousand eight hundred pins in a day. But if they had all wrought separately and independently, and without any of them having been educated to this peculiar business, they certainly could not each of them have made twenty, perhaps not one pin in a day; that is, certainly, not the two hundred and fortieth, perhaps not the four thousand eight hundredth part of what they are at present capable of performing, in consequence of a proper division and combination of their different operations. . . .

This great increase of the quantity of work, which, in consequence of the division of labour, the same number of people are capable of performing, is owing to three different circumstances; first, to the increase of dexterity in every particular workman; secondly, to the saving of the time which is commonly lost in passing from one species of work to another; and lastly, to the invention of a great number of machines which facilitate and abridge labour, and enable one man to do the work of many.

[Effect of the Division of Labour]

First, the improvement of the dexterity of the workman necessarily increases the quantity of the work he can perform, and the division of labour, by reducing every man's business to some one simple operation, and by making this operation the sole employment of his life, necessarily increases very much the dexterity of the workman. A common smith, who, though accustomed to handle the hammer, has never been used to make nails, if upon some particular occasion he is obliged to attempt it, will scarce, I am assured, be able to make above two or three hundred nails in a day, and those too very bad ones. A smith who has been accustomed to make nails, but whose sole or principal business has not been that of a nailer, can seldom with his utmost diligence make more than eight hundred or a thousand nails in a day. I have seen several boys under twenty years of age who had never exercised any other trade but that of making nails, and who, when they exerted themselves, could make, each of them, upwards of two thousand three hundred nails in a day. The making of a nail, however, is by no means one of the simplest operations. The same person blows the bellows, stirs or mends the fire as there is occasion, heats the iron, and forges every part of the nail: In forging the head too he is obliged to change his tools. The different operations into which the making of a pin, or of a metal button, is subdivided, are all of them much more simple, and the dexterity of the person, of whose life it has been the sole business to perform them, is usually much greater. The rapidity with which some of the operations of those manufactures are performed, exceeds what the human hand could, by those who had never seen them, be supposed capable of acquiring.

Secondly, the advantage which is gained by saving the time commonly lost in passing from one sort of work to another, is much greater than we should at first view be apt to imagine it. It is impossible to pass very quickly from one kind of work to another, that is carried on in a different place, and with quite different tools. A country weaver, who cultivates a small farm, must lose a good deal of time in passing from his loom to the field, and from the field to his loom. When the two trades can be carried on in the same workhouse, the loss of time is no doubt much less. It is even in this case, however, very considerable. A man commonly saunters a little in turning his hand from one sort of employment to another. When he first begins the new work he is seldom very keen and hearty; his mind, as they say, does not go to it, and for some time he rather trifles than applies to good purpose. The habit of sauntering and of indolent careless application, which is naturally, or rather necessarily acquired by every country workman who is obliged to change his work and his tools every half hour, and to apply his hand in twenty different ways almost every day of his life; renders him almost always slothful and lazy, and incapable of any vigorous application even on the most pressing occasions. Independent, therefore, of his deficiency in point of dexterity, this cause alone must always reduce considerably the quantity of work which he is capable of performing.

[On Ma-
chinery]

Thirdly, and lastly, every body must be sensible how much labour is facilitated and abridged by the application of proper machinery. It is that the invention of all those machines by which labour is so much facilitated and abridged, seems to have been originally owing to the division of labour. Men are much more likely to discover easier and readier methods of attaining any object, when the whole attention of their minds is directed towards that single object, than when it is dissipated among a great variety of things. But in consequence of the division of labour, the whole of every man's attention comes naturally to be directed towards some one very simple object. It is naturally to be expected, therefore, that some one or other of those who are employed in each particular branch of labour should soon find out easier and readier methods of performing their own particular work, wherever the nature of it admits of such improvement.

A great part of the machines made use of in those manufactures in which labour is most subdivided, were originally the inventions of common workmen, who, being each of them employed in some very simple operation, naturally turned their thoughts towards finding out easier and readier methods of performing it. Whoever has been much accustomed to visit such manufactures, must frequently have been shewn very pretty machines, which were the inventions of such workmen, in order to facilitate and quicken their own particular part of the work. In the first fire-engines, a boy was constantly employed to open and shut alternately the communication between the boiler and the cylinder, according as the piston either ascended or descended. One of those boys, who loved to play with his companions, observed that, by tying a string from the handle of the valve, which opened this communication, to another part of the machine, the valve would open and shut without his assistance, and leave him at liberty to divert himself with his play-fellows. One of the greatest improvements that has been made upon this machine, since it was first invented, was in this manner the discovery of a boy who wanted to save his own labour.

All the improvements in machinery, however, have by no means been the inventions of those who had occasion to use the machines. Many improvements have been made by the ingenuity of the makers of the machines, when to make them became the business of a peculiar trade; and some by that of those who are called philosophers or men of speculation, whose trade it is, not to do any thing, but to observe every thing; and who, upon that account, are often capable of combining together the powers of the most distant and dissimilar objects. In the progress of society, philosophy or speculation becomes, like every other employment, the principal or sole trade and occupation of a particular class of citizens. Like every other employment too, it is subdivided into a great number of different branches, each of which affords occupation to a peculiar tribe or class of philosophers; and this subdivision of employment in philosophy, as well as in every other business, improves dexterity, and saves time. Each individual becomes more expert in his own peculiar branch, more work is done upon the whole, and the quantity of science is considerably increased by it.

It is the great multiplication of the productions of all the different arts, in consequence of the division of labour, which occasions, in a well-governed society, that universal opulence which extends itself to the lowest ranks of the people. Every workman has a great quantity of his own work to dispose of beyond what he himself has occasion for; and every other workman being exactly in the same situation, he is enabled to exchange a great quantity of his own goods for a great quantity, or, what comes to the same thing, for the price of a great quantity of theirs. He supplies them abundantly with what they have occasion for, and they accommodate him as amply with what he has occasion for, and a general plenty diffuses itself through all the different ranks of the society.

[Gains from Productivity] Observe the accommodation of the most common artificer or day-labourer in a civilized and thriving country, and you will perceive that the number of people of whose industry a part, though but a small part, has been employed in procuring him this accommodation, exceeds all computation. The woollen coat, for example, which covers the day-labourer, as coarse and rough as it may appear, is the produce of the joint labour of a great multitude of workmen. The shepherd, the sorter of the wool, the wool-comber or carder, the dyer, the scribbler, the spinner, the weaver, the fuller, the dresser, with many others, must all join their different arts in order to complete even this homely production.

How many merchants and carriers, besides, must have been employed in transporting the materials from some of those workmen to others who often live in a very distant part of the country! How much commerce and navigation in particular, how many ship-builders, sailors, sail-makers, rope-makers, must have been employed in order to bring together the different drugs made use of by the dyer, which often come from the remotest corners of the world! What a variety of labour too is necessary in order to produce the tools of the meanest of those workmen! To say nothing of such complicated machines as the ship of the sailor, the mill of the fuller, or even the loom of the weaver, let us consider only what a variety of labour is requisite in order to form that very simple machine, the shears with which the shepherd clips the wool. The miner, the builder of the furnace for smelting the ore, the feller of the timber, the burner of the charcoal to be made use of in the smelting-house, the brick-maker, the brick-layer, the workmen who attend the furnace, the mill-wright, the forger, the smith, must all of them join their different arts in order to produce them.

Were we to examine, in the same manner, all the different parts of his dress and household furniture, the coarse linen shirt which he wears next his skin, the shoes which cover his feet, the bed which he lies on, and all the different parts which compose it, the kitchen-grate at which he prepares his victuals, the coals which he makes use of for that purpose, dug from the bowels of the earth, and brought to him perhaps by a long sea and a long land carriage, all the other utensils of his kitchen, all the furniture of his table, the knives and forks, the earthen or pewter plates upon which he serves up and divides his victuals, the different hands employed in preparing his bread and his beer, the glass window which lets in the heat and the light, and keeps out the wind and the rain, with all the knowledge and art requisite for preparing that beautiful and happy invention, without which these northern parts of the world could scarce have afforded a very comfortable habitation, together with the tools of all the different workmen employed in producing those different conveniencies; if we examine, I say, all these things, and consider what a variety of labour is employed about each of them, we shall be sensible that without the assistance and cooperation of many thousands, the very meanest person in a civilized country could not be provided, even according to, what we very falsely imagine, the easy and simple manner in which he is commonly accommodated. Compared, indeed, with the more extravagant luxury of the great, his accommodation must no doubt appear extremely simple and easy; and yet it may be true, perhaps, that the accommodation of an European prince does not always so much exceed that of an industrious and frugal peasant , is the accommodation of the latter exceeds that of many an African king, the absolute master of the lives and liberties of ten thousand naked savages.

We pass now from economics to psychology, from a consideration of the effects of the division of labor to an inquiry into its behavioral origins. Smith proposes a "propensity to truck, barter and exchange" discoverable in no creature save humankind. It is this propensity that gives rise to the mode of production characteristic of a Society of Perfect Liberty.

This last phrase is not unimportant. If there is a propensity of the kind that Smith describes, we might well ask why it did not manifest itself early in human history? I would think that Smith's answer—he never deeply considers the question—is that the propensity requires a certain institutional framework to flourish, and this framework consists in the transfer of the arrangements of production out from under the heavy hands of tradition and command—the great shaping forces of production in earlier times—to the peculiar arrangements of private property, free labor, and market organization that we call capitalism.

Chapter II

Of the Principle which gives occasion to the Division of Labour

This division of labour, from which so many advantages are derived, is not originally the effect of any human wisdom, which foresees and intends that general opulence to which it gives occasion. It is the necessary, though very slow and gradual consequence of a certain propensity in human nature which has in view no such extensive utility; the propensity to truck, barter, and exchange one thing for another.

Whether this propensity be one of those original principles in human nature, of which no further account can be given; or whether, as seems more probable, it be the necessary consequence of the faculties of reason and speech, it belongs not to our present subject to enquire. It is common to all men, and to be found in no other race of animals, which seem to know neither this nor any other species of contracts. Two greyhounds, in running down the same hare, have sometimes the appearance of acting in some sort of concert. Each turns her towards his companion, or endeavours to intercept her when his companion turns her towards himself. This, however, is not the effect of any contract, but of the accidental concurrence of their passions in the same object at that particular time. Nobody ever saw a dog make a fair and deliberate exchange of one bone for another with another dog. Nobody ever saw one animal by its gestures and natural cries signify to another, this is mine, that yours; I am willing to give this for that. When an animal wants to obtain something either of a man or of another animal, it has no other means of persuasion but to gain the favour of those whose service it requires. A puppy fawns upon its dam, and a spaniel endeavours by a thousand attractions to engage the attention of its master who is at dinner, when it wants to be fed by him.

Man sometimes uses the same arts with his brethren, and when he has no other means of engaging them to act according to his inclinations, endeavours by every servile and fawning attention to obtain their good will. He has not time, however, to do this upon every occasion. In civilized society he stands at all times in need of the cooperation and assistance of great multitudes, while his whole life is scarce sufficient to gain the friendship of a few persons. In almost every other race of animals each individual, when it is grown up to maturity, is intirely independent, and in its natural state has occasion for the assistance of no other living creature. But man has almost constant occasion for the help of his brethren, and it is in vain for him to expect it from their benevolence only. He will be more likely to prevail if he can interest their self-love in his favour, and shew them that it is for their own advantage to do for him what he requires of them. Whoever offers to another a bargain of any kind, proposes to do this. Give me that which I want, and you shall have this which you want, is the meaning of every such offer; and it is in this manner that we obtain from one another the far greater part of those good offices which we stand in need of.

It is not from the benevolence of the butcher, the brewer, or the baker, that we expect our dinner, but from their regard to their own interest. We address ourselves, not to their humanity but to their self-love, and never talk to them of our own necessities but of their advantages. Nobody but a beggar chuses to depend chiefly upon the benevolence of his fellow-citizens. Even a beggar does not depend upon it entirely. The charity of well-disposed people, indeed, supplies him with the whole fund of his subsistence. But though this principle ultimately provides him with all the necessaries of life which he has occasion for, it neither does nor can provide him with them as he has occasion for them. The greater part of his occasional wants are supplied in the same manner as those of other people, by treaty, by barter, and by purchase. With the money which one man gives him he purchases food. The old cloaths which another bestows upon him he exchanges for other old cloaths which suit him better, or for lodging, or for food, or for money, with which he can buy either food, cloaths, or lodging, as he has occasion.

The next step in the argument must be obvious. It is to consider the relation between the extent of the division of labor and the extent of the market to which it caters. As we might expect, the larger that market, the more finely detailed becomes the degree to which labor can be specialized and divided, largely with the use of machinery.

Chapter III

That the Division of Labour is limited by the Extent of the Market

As it is the power of exchanging that gives occasion to the division of labour, so the extent of this division must always be limited by the extent of that power, or, in other words, by the extent of the market. When the market is very small, no person can have any encouragement to dedicate himself entirely to one employment, for want of the power to exchange all that surplus part of the produce of his own labour, which is over and above his own consumption, for such parts of the produce of other men's labour as he has occasion for.

There are some sorts of industry, even of the lowest kind, which can be carried on no where but in a great town. A porter, for example, can find employment and subsistence in no other place. A village is by much too narrow a sphere for him; even an ordinary market town is scarce large enough to afford him constant occupation. In the lone houses and very small villages which are scattered about in so desert a country as the Highlands of Scotland, every farmer must be butcher, baker and brewer for his own family. In such situations we can scarce expect to find even a smith, a carpenter, or a mason, within less than twenty miles of another of the same trade. The scattered families that live at eight or ten miles distance from the nearest of them, must learn to perform themselves a great number of little pieces of work, for which, in more populous countries, they would call in the assistance of those workmen. Country workmen are almost every where obliged to apply themselves to all the different branches of industry that have so much affinity to one another as to be employed about the same sort of materials. A country carpenter deals in every sort of work that is made of wood: a country smith in every sort of work that is made of iron. The former is not only a carpenter, but a joiner, a cabinet-maker, and even a carver in wood, as well as a wheelwright, a plough-wright, a cart and waggon maker. The employments of the latter are still more various. It is impossible there should be such a trade as even that of a nailer in the remote and inland parts of the Highlands of Scotland. Such a workman at the rate of a thousand nails a day, and three hundred working days in the year, will make three hundred thousand nails in the year. But in such a situation it would be impossible to dispose of one thousand, that is, of one day's work in the year. . . .

We pass next to a quite different but equally important subject. It is a consideration of the question to which, as we have seen, both Aristotle and Cantillon directed their attention—whether there was some "just" or "intrinsic" price in market exchanges, and whether such a price would in some mysterious fashion emerge spontaneously from the workings of the market itself.

Earlier thinkers had no answer to this question (which, incidentally, never bothered the Physiocrats at all.) But Smith did have an answer, and in its general approach it prefigures what later economists—a hundred years later—would give us in the form of "supply and demand schedules." The answer lies in the relation between "market prices," which are whatever prices obtain on a market at any time, and "natural" prices—prices that would just balance the amount of any good that buyers sought (what Smith called "effectual demand") and the amount of the good forthcoming to meet that demand. (Today we call natural prices equilibrium prices, a term Smith did not use.) The crucial element in this balancing process is competition, which drives both sellers and buyers to find a price that satisfies them. In some ways, the chapter to follow is the first real exercise in what we would call "modern economics."

Chapter VII

Of the natural and market Price of Commodities

. . . The market price of every particular commodity is regulated by the proportion between the quantity which is actually brought to market, and the demand of those who are willing to pay the natural price of the commodity, or the whole value of the rent, labour, and profit, which must be paid in order to bring it thither. Such people may be called the effectual demanders, and their demand the effectual demand, since it may be sufficient to effectuate the bringing of the commodity to market. It is different from the absolute demand. A very poor man may be said in some sense to have a demand for a coach and six; he might like to have it; but his demand is not an effectual demand, as the commodity can never be brought to market in order to satisfy it.

When the quantity of any commodity which is brought to market falls short of the effectual demand, all those who are willing to pay the whole value of the rent, wages, and profit, which must be paid in order to bring it thither, cannot be supplied with the quantity which they want. Rather than want it altogether, some of them will be willing to give more. A competition will immediately begin among them, and the market price will rise more or less above the natural price, according as either the greatness of the deficiency, or the wealth and wanton luxury of the competitors, happen to animate more or less the eagerness of the competition. Among competitors of equal wealth and luxury the same deficiency will generally occasion a more or less eager competition, according as the acquisition of the commodity happens to be of more or less importance to them. Hence the exorbitant price of the necessaries of life during the blockade of a town or in a famine.

When the quantity brought to market exceeds the effectual demand, it cannot be all sold to those who are willing to pay the whole value of the rent, wages and profit, which must be paid in order to bring it thither. Some part must be sold to those who are willing to pay less, and the low price which they give for it must reduce the price of the whole. The market price will sink more or less below the natural price, according as the greatness of the excess increases more or less the competition of the sellers, or according as it happens to be more or less important to them to get immediately rid of the commodity. The same excess in the importation of perishable, will occasion a much greater competition than in that of durable commodities; in the importation of oranges, for example, than in that of old iron.

[Natural
Prices]
When the quantity brought to market is just sufficient to supply the effectual demand and no more, the market price naturally comes to be either exactly, or as nearly as can be judged of, the same with the natural price. The whole quantity upon hand can be disposed of for this price, and cannot be disposed of for more. The competition of the different dealers obliges them all to accept of this price, but does not oblige them to accept of less.

The quantity of every commodity brought to market naturally suits itself to the effectual demand. It is the interest of all those who employ their land, labour, or stock, in bringing any commodity to market, that the quantity never should exceed the effectual demand; and it is the interest of all other people that it never should fall short of that demand.

If at any time it exceeds the effectual demand, some of the component parts of its price must be paid below their natural rate. If it is rent, the interest of the landlords will immediately prompt them to withdraw a part of their land; and if it is wages or profit, the interest of the labourers in the one case, and of their employers in the other, will prompt them to withdraw a part of their labour or stock from this employment. The quantity brought to market will soon be no more than sufficient to supply the effectual demand. All the different parts of its price will rise to their natural rate, and the whole price to its natural price.

If, on the contrary, the quantity brought to market should at any time fall short of the effectual demand, some of the component parts of its price must rise above their natural rate. If it is rent, the interest of all other landlords will naturally prompt them to prepare more land for the raising of this commodity; if it is wages or profit, the interest of all other labourers and dealers will soon prompt them to employ more labour and stock in preparing and bringing it to market. The quantity brought thither will soon be sufficient to supply the effectual demand. All the different parts of its price will soon sink to their natural rate, and the whole price to its natural price.

The natural price, therefore, is, as it were, the central price, to which the prices of all commodities are continually gravitating. Different accidents may sometimes keep them suspended a good deal above it, and sometimes force them down even somewhat below it. But whatever may be the obstacles which hinder them from settling in this center of repose and continuance, they are constantly tending towards it. . . .

The concept of natural, equilibrating prices concludes Smith's analysis of the market as an order-bestowing mechanism. We next move to the question of what determines the incomes of laborers, entrepreneurs, and landlords. This is a question that will become a major issue for Smith's great successor, David Ricardo, whom we will meet in our next set of readings. But the matter to which Ricardo directs his attention—the threat that landlords' rents will squeeze out capitalists' profits—is not in Smith's mind. Nor is he particularly interesting when he comes to the determination of profits: they will be the return necessary to induce capitalists to shoulder the risks of enterprise.

Where Smith *is* interesting—indeed, astonishing—will be found a few paragraphs down in this somewhat abbreviated version of his chapter, beginning: "Is not, however, difficult to foretell . . ." That paragraph and the one following will put an end to any lingering doubts as to whether Smith was indifferent to, or ignorant of the state of England's working class in the 1770s. Despite his occasional hypocrisies—we recall the happy beggar lying in the sun, on page 73 above—Smith's judgment concerning all three classes is anything but unaware of the plight of the working man and woman, and never in the slightest degree uncritically admiring of landlords or capitalists. In Chapter XI, the finale of Book I, Smith discusses, one by one, the respective abilities of the three great classes to form disinterested policy judgments concerning England. I will not give away what is his most shocking finding here—the reader must patiently wait until the last sentence line of this reading.

Chapter VIII

Of the Wages of Labour

The produce of labour constitutes the natural recompence or wages of labour.

In that original state of things, which precedes both the appropriation of land and the accumulation of stock, the whole produce of labour belongs to the labourer. He has neither landlord nor master to share with him. . . .

But this original state of things, in which the labourer enjoyed the whole produce of his own labour, could not last beyond the first introduction of the appropriation of land and the accumulation of stock. It was at an end, therefore, long before the most considerable improvements were made in the productive powers of labour, and it would be to no purpose to trace farther what might have been its effects upon the recompence or wages of labour.

As soon as land becomes private property, the landlord demands a share of almost all the produce which the labourer can either raise, or collect from it. His rent makes the first deduction from the produce of the labour which is employed upon land.

It seldom happens that the person who tills the ground has wherewithal to maintain himself till he reaps the harvest. His maintenance is generally advanced to him from the stock of a master, the farmer who employs him, and who would have no interest to employ him, unless he was to share in the produce of his labour, or unless his stock was to be replaced to him with a profit. This profit makes a second deduction from the produce of the labour which is employed upon land.

The produce of almost all other labour is liable to the like deduction of profit. In all arts and manufactures the greater part of the workmen stand in need of a master to advance them the materials of their work, and their wages and maintenance till it be compleated. He shares in the produce of their labour, or in the value which it adds to the materials upon which it is bestowed; and in this share consists his profit. . . .

What are the common wages of labour depends every where upon the contract usually made between those two parties, whose interests are by no means the same. The workmen desire to get as much, the masters to give as little as possible. The former are disposed to combine in order to raise, the latter in order to lower the wages of labour.

It is not, however, difficult to foresee which of the two parties must, upon all ordinary occasions, have the advantage in the dispute, and force the other into a compliance with their terms. The masters, being fewer in number, can combine much more easily; and the law, besides, authorises, or at least does not prohibit their combinations, while it prohibits those of the workmen. We have no acts of parliament against combining to lower the price of work; but many against combining to raise it. In all such disputes the masters can hold out much longer. A landlord, a farmer, a master manufacturer, or merchant, though they did not employ a single workman, could generally live a year or two upon the stocks which they have already acquired. Many workmen could not subsist a week, few could subsist a month, and scarce any a year without employment. In the long-run the workman may be as necessary to his master as his master is to him; but the necessity is not so immediate. [Contest Between the Parties]

We rarely hear, it has been said, of the combinations of masters; though frequently of those of workmen. But whoever imagines, upon this account, that masters rarely combine, is as ignorant of the world as of the subject. Masters are always and every where in a sort of tacit, but constant and uniform combination, not to raise the wages of labour above their actual rate. To violate this combination is every where a most unpopular action, and a sort of reproach to a master among his neighbours and equals. We seldom, indeed, hear of this combination, because it is the usual, and one may say, the natural state of things which nobody ever hears of. Masters too sometimes enter into particular combinations to sink the wages of labour even below this rate. These are always conducted with the utmost silence and secrecy, till the moment of execution, and when the workmen yield, as they sometimes do, without resistance, though severely felt by them, they are never heard of by other people. Such combinations, however, are frequently resisted by a contrary defensive combination of the workmen; who sometimes too, without any provocation of this kind, combine of their own accord to raise the price of their labour. Their usual pretences are, sometimes the high price of provisions, sometimes the great profit which their masters make by their work. But whether their combinations be offensive or defensive, they are always abundantly heard of. In order to bring the point to a speedy decision, they have always recourse to the loudest clamour, and sometimes to the most shocking violence and outrage. They are desperate, and act with the folly and extravagance of desperate men, who must either starve, or frighten their masters into an immediate compliance with their demands. The masters upon these occasions are just as clamorous upon the other side, and never cease to call aloud for the assistance of the civil magistrate, and the rigorous execution of those laws which have been enacted with so much severity against the combinations of servants, labourers, and journeymen. The workmen, accordingly, very seldom derive any advantage from the violence of those tumultuous combinations, which, partly from the interposition of the civil magistrate, partly from the superior steadiness of the masters, partly from the necessity which the greater part of the workmen are under of submitting for the sake of present subsistence, generally end in nothing, but the punishment or ruin of the ringleaders. . . .

Conclusion of Chapter XI

The whole annual produce of the land and labour of every country, or what comes to the same thing, the whole price of that annual produce, naturally divides itself, it has already been observed, into three parts; the rent of land, the wages of labour, and the profits of stock; and constitutes a revenue to three different orders of people; to those who live by rent, to those who live by wages, and to those who live by profit. These are the three great, original and constituent orders of every civilized society, from whose revenue that of every other order is ultimately derived.

The interest of the first of those three great orders, it appears [*The Landlord's View*] from what has been just now said, is strictly and inseparably connected with the general interest of the society. Whatever either promotes or obstructs the one, necessarily promotes or obstructs the other. When the publick deliberates concerning any regulation of commerce or police, the proprietors of land never can mislead it, with a view to promote the interest of their own particular order; at least, if they have any tolerable knowledge of that interest. They are, indeed, too often defective in this tolerable knowledge. They are the only one of the three orders whose revenue costs them neither labour nor care, but comes to them, as it were, of its own accord, and independent of any plan or project of their own. That indolence, which is the natural effect of the ease and security of their situation, renders them too often, not only ignorant, but incapable of that application of mind which is necessary in order to foresee and understand the consequences of any publick regulation.

The interest of the second order, that of those who live by wages, is as strictly connected with the interest of the society as that of the first. The wages of the labourer, it has already been shewn, are never so high as when the demand for labour is continually rising, or when the quantity employed is every year increasing considerably. When this real wealth of the society becomes stationary, his wages are soon reduced to what is barely enough to enable him to bring up a family, or to continue the race of labourers. When the society declines, they fall even below this. The order of proprietors may, perhaps, gain more by the prosperity of the society, than that of labourers: but there is no order that suffers so cruelly from its decline. But though the interest of the labourer is strictly connected with that of the society, he is incapable either of comprehending that interest, or of understanding its connection with his own. His condition leaves him no time to receive the necessary information, and his education and habits are commonly such as to render him unfit to judge even though he was fully informed. In the publick deliberations, therefore, his voice is little heard and less regarded, except upon some particular occasions, when his clamour is animated, set on, and supported by his employers, not for his, but their own particular purposes.

[The Master's View]

His employers constitute the third order, that of those who live by profit. It is the stock that is employed for the sake of profit, which puts into motion the greater part of the useful labour of every society. The plans and projects of the employers of stock regulate and direct all the most important operations of labour, and profit is the end proposed by all those plans and projects. But the rate of profit does not, like rent and wages, rise with the prosperity, and fall with the declension of the society. On the contrary, it is naturally low in rich, and high in poor countries, and it is always highest in the countries which are going fastest to ruin. The interest of this third order, therefore, has not the same connection with the general interest of the society as that of the other two. Merchants and master manufacturers are, in this order, the two classes of people who commonly employ the largest capitals, and who by their wealth draw to themselves the greatest share of the publick consideration. As during their whole lives they are engaged in plans and projects, they have frequently more acuteness of understanding than the greater part of country gentlemen. As their thoughts, however, are commonly exercised rather about the interest of their own particular branch of business, than about that of the society, their judgment, even when given with the greatest candour (which it has not been upon every occasion) is much more to be depended upon with regard to the former of those two objects, than with regard to the latter. Their superiority over the country gentleman is, not so much in their knowledge of the publick interest, as in their having a better knowledge of their own interest than he has of his. It is by this superior knowledge of their own interest that they have frequently imposed upon his generosity, and persuaded him to give up both his own interest and that of the publick, from a very simple but honest conviction, that their interest, and not his, was the interest of the publick.

The interest of the dealers, however, in any particular branch of trade or manufactures, is always in some respects different from, and even opposite to, that of the publick. To widen the market and to narrow the competition, is always the interest of the dealers. To widen the market may frequently be agreeable enough to the interest of the publick; but to narrow the competition must always be against it, and can serve only to enable the dealers, by raising their profits above what they naturally would be, to levy, for their own benefit, an absurd tax upon the rest of their fellow-citizens. The proposal of any new law or regulation of commerce which comes from this order, ought always to be listened to with great precaution, and ought never to be adopted till after having been long and carefully examined, not only with the most scrupulous, but with the most suspicious attention. It comes from an order of men, whose interest is never exactly the same with that of the publick, who have generally an interest to deceive and even to oppress the publick, and who accordingly have, upon many occasions, both deceived and oppressed it.

Thus Book I concludes with the finding that the interests of the landlord may coincide with those of the nation (Ricardo will vehemently dissent), but because rent comes to the landowner without any active participation on his part, he will be "not only ignorant, but incapable of that application of mind" needed to become an intelligent advisor to the country. The laborer, too, finds his interests tied directly into those of the larger society, but he has neither the education, nor the leisure needed to gain the needed information. And as for the last order—"those who live by profit"—the concluding sentence above delivers the devastating judgment I announced. Where does that leave us? With the government. Let us see what Smith has to say about it.

Books II–V

Government lies in Book V of the *Wealth,* but we must first look at Books II through IV. This is not quite so Procrustian a move as it may seem, for there is not a great deal in these chapters that is needed to flesh out the larger Smithian scenario. Book II, for instance, considers the process by which stock—we would say

capital—is accumulated, by parsimony (saving) and investment.
As Smith puts it in Chapter III:

... [T]he principle which prompts to save is the desire of bettering our condition, a desire which though generally calm and
dispassionate, comes with us from the womb, and never leaves
us till we go into the grave ... An augmentation of fortune is the
means by which the greater part of men propose and wish to
better their fortune ... and the most likely way of augmenting
their fortune is to save and accumulate some part of what they
acquire....

Smith's tone is so matter-of-fact that we feel there will be little
here to think about, until we recall an earlier remark in Chapter
IX, Book I, where Smith raises the intriguing possibility that accumulation might have a limit:

In a country fully stocked in proportion to all the business it had
to transact, as great a quantity of capital would be employed in
every particular branch as the nature and extent of the trade
would permit. The competition, therefore, would everywhere be
as great, and consequently the ordinary profit as low as possible.

This seems like a remarkable premonition of what we would
call economic stagnation, but it is better seen as reflecting the preindustrial age in which Smith lived. Smith's pins were not, in his
opinion, the forerunners of safety pins, then zippers, then Velcro.
In the technologically quiescent environment of his time the possibility of a country being "fully stocked" with capital was more
imaginable than in our day. But it does add a note of sobriety to
Smith's larger historic prospect. The Society of Perfect Liberty, as
he foresaw it, was not only burdened with a work force rendered
"stupid and ignorant" by the numbing routines of the mechanized
division of labor, but threatened with the prospect of an eventual
end to accumulation, after which would come decline.

Book III gives us a sketch of economic history, tracing the evolution of the Society of Perfect Liberty from the social disarray that

followed the fall of the Roman Empire: in Chapter IV Smith recounts how itinerant merchants brought commercial life into the feudal world by catering to the luxury consumption of its great lords. As we would imagine, the invisible hand is once again at work. In Smith's words:

To gratify the most childish vanity was the sole motive of the great proprietors. The merchants and artificers, much less ridiculous, acted merely from a view to their own interest and in pursuit of their own pedlar principle of turning a penny wherever a penny was to be got. Neither had either knowledge or foresight of that great revolution which the folly of the one and the the industry of the other was gradually bringing about.

In similar fashion, Book IV tells us about systems of political economy, mostly mercantilism and Physiocracy, the first of which Smith hated, the second of which, as we know, he criticized but admired. But here too, a brief excerpt from the last pages of Chapter IX sums up the whole:

All systems either of preference or of restraint, therefore, being thus completely taken away, the obvious and simple system of natural liberty establishes itself of its own accord. Every man, as long as he does not violate the laws of justice, is left perfectly free to pursue his own interest his own way, and to bring both his industry and capital into competition with those of any other man, or order of men. The sovereign is completely discharged from a duty, in the attempting to perform which he must always be exposed to numerous delusions, and for the proper performance of which no human wisdom or knowledge could ever be sufficient; the duty of superintending the industry of private people, and of directing it towards the employments most suitable to the interest of the society. According to the system of natural liberty, the sovereign has only three duties to attend to; three duties of great importance, indeed, but plain and intelligible to common understandings: first, the duty of protecting the society from the violence and invasion of other independent societies; secondly, the duty of protecting, as far as possible, every member of the society from the injustice or oppression of every other member of it, or the duty of establishing an exact administration of justice; and, thirdly, the duty of erecting and maintaining certain public works and certain public institutions, which it can never be for the interest of any individual, or small number of individuals to erect and maintain; because the profit could never repay the expense to any individual or small number of individuals, though it may frequently do much more than repay it to a great society.

It remains now for us to examine in some more detail this last, and obviously very important part of Smith's vision. We begin with warnings about the mounting costs of the sovereign's first duty—defense:

Book V

CHAPTER I

Of the Expences of the Sovereign or Commonwealth

OF THE EXPENCE OF DEFENCE

The first duty of the sovereign, that of protecting the society from the violence and invasion of other independent societies, can be performed only by means of a military force. But the expence both of preparing this military force in time of peace, and of employing it in time of war, is very different in the different states of society, in the different periods of improvement.

Among nations of hunters, the lowest and rudest state of society, such as we find it among the native tribes of North America, every man is a warrior as well as a hunter. When he goes to war, either to defend his society, or to revenge the injuries which have been done to it by other societies, he maintains himself by his own labour, in the same manner as when he lives at home. His society, for in this state of things there is properly neither sovereign nor commonwealth, is at no sort of expence, either to prepare him for the field, or to maintain him while he is in it.

Among nations of shepherds, a more advanced state of society, such as we find it among the Tartars and Arabs, every man is, in the same manner, a warrior. Such nations have commonly no fixed habitation, but live, either in tents, or in a sort of covered waggons which are easily transported from place to place. The whole tribe or nation changes its situation according to the different seasons of the year, as well as according to other accidents. When its herds and flocks have consumed the forage of one part of the country, it removes to another, and from that to a third. In the dry season, it comes down to the banks of the rivers; in the wet season it retires to the upper country. When such a nation goes to war, the warriors will not trust their herds and flocks to the feeble defence of their old men, their women and children; and their old men, their women and children, will not be left behind without defence and without subsistence. The whole nation, besides, being accustomed to a wandering life, even in time of peace, easily takes the field in time of war.

In a more advanced state of society, two different causes contribute to render it altogether impossible that they, who take the field, should maintain themselves at their own expence. Those two causes are, the progress of manufactures, and the improvement in the art of war. . . .

The first duty of the sovereign, therefore, that of defending the society from the violence and injustice of other independent societies, grows gradually more and more expensive, as the society advances in civilization. The military force of the society, which originally cost the sovereign no expence either in time of peace or in time of war, must, in the progress of improvement, first be maintained by him in time of war, and afterwards even in time of peace.

A similar warning attends the second duty of the sovereign—that of establishing a system of justice.

OF THE EXPENCE OF JUSTICE

The second duty of the sovereign, that of protecting, as far as possible, every member of the society from the injustice or oppression of every other member of it, or the duty of establishing an exact administration of justice, requires too very different degrees of expence in the different periods of society.

Among nations of hunters, as there is scarce any property, or at least none that exceeds the value of two or three days labour; so there is seldom any established magistrate or any regular administration of justice. Men who have no property can injure one another only in their persons or reputations. But when one man kills, wounds, beats, or defames another, though he to whom the injury is done suffers, he who does it receives no benefit. It is otherwise with the injuries to property. The benefit of the person who does the injury is often equal to the loss of him who suffers it. Envy, malice, or resentment, are the only passions which can prompt one man to injure another in his person or reputation. But the greater part of men are not very frequently under the influence of those passions; and the very worst men are so only occasionally. As their gratification too, how agreeable soever it may be to certain characters, is not attended with any real or permanent advantage, it is in the greater part of men commonly restrained by prudential considerations. Men may live together in society with some tolerable degree of security, though there is no civil magistrate to protect them from the injustice of those passions. But avarice and ambition in the rich, in the poor the hatred of labour and the love of present ease and enjoyment, are the passions which prompt to invade property, passions much more steady in their operation, and much more universal in their influence. Wherever there is great property, there is great inequality. For one very rich man, there must be at least five hundred poor, and the affluence of the few supposes the indigence of the many. The affluence of the rich excites the indignation of the poor, who are often both driven by want, and prompted by envy, to invade his possessions. It is only under the shelter of the civil magistrate that the owner of that valuable property, which is acquired by the labour of many years, or perhaps of many successive generations, can sleep a single night in security. He is at all times surrounded by unknown enemies, whom, though he never provoked, he can never appease, and from whose injustice he can be protected only by the powerful arm of the civil magistrate continually held up to chastise it. The acquisition of valuable and extensive property, therefore, necessarily requires the establishment of civil government. Where there is no property, or at least none that exceeds the value of two or three days labour, civil government is not so necessary.

Civil government supposes a certain subordination. But as the necessity of civil government gradually grows up with the acquisition of valuable property, so the principal causes which naturally introduce subordination gradually grow up with the growth of that valuable property. . . . The rich, in particular, are necessarily interested to support that order of things, which can alone secure them in the possession of their own advantages. Men of inferior wealth combine to defend those of superior wealth in the possession of their property, in order that men of superior wealth may combine to defend them in the possession of theirs. . . . Civil government, so far as it is instituted for the security of property, is in reality instituted for the defence of the rich against the poor, or of those who have some property against those who have none at all. . . .

Finally, we turn to education, by no means so bland a question as might be expected. Smith's stinging analysis once again expresses his concern over the degrading effects of routinized labor, for which the necessary remedy, as he sees it, is government-financed schooling.

Part III

OF THE EXPENCE OF PUBLICK WORKS AND PUBLICK INSTITUTIONS

The third and last duty of the sovereign or commonwealth is that of erecting and maintaining those publick institutions and those publick works, which, though they may be in the highest degree advantageous to a great society, are, however, of such a nature, that the profit could never repay the expence to any individual or small number of individuals, and which it, therefore, cannot be expected that any individual or small number of individuals should erect or maintain. The performance of this duty requires too very different degrees of expence in the different periods of society. . . .

In the progress of the division of labour, the employment of the far greater part of those who live by labour, that is, of the great body of the people, comes to be confined to a few very simple operations; frequently to one or two. But the understandings of the greater part of men are necessarily formed by their ordinary employments. The man whose whole life is spent in performing a few simple operations, of which the effects too are, perhaps, always the same, or very nearly the same, has no occasion to exert his understanding, or to exercise his invention in finding out expedients for removing difficulties which never occur. He naturally loses, therefore, the habit of such exertion, and generally becomes as stupid and ignorant as it is possible for a human creature to become. The torpor of his mind renders him, not only incapable of relishing or bearing a part in any rational conversation, but of conceiving any generous, noble, or tender sentiment, and consequently of forming any just judgment concerning many even of the ordinary duties of private life. Of the great and extensive interests of his country, he is altogether incapable of judging; and unless very particular pains have been taken to render him otherwise, he is equally incapable of defending his country in war. The uniformity of his stationary life naturally corrupts the courage of his mind, and makes him regard with abhorrence the irregular, uncertain, and adventurous life of a soldier. It corrupts even the activity of his body, and renders him incapable of exerting his strength with vigour and perseverance, in any other employment than that to which he has been bred. His dexterity at his own particular trade seems, in this manner, to be acquired at the expence of his intellectual, social, and martial virtues. But in every improved and civilized society this is the state into which the labouring poor, that is, the great body of the people, must necessarily fall, unless government takes some pains to prevent it.

It is otherwise in the barbarous societies, as they are commonly called, of hunters, of shepherds, and even of husbandmen in that rude state of husbandry which precedes the improvement of manufactures, and the extension of foreign commerce. In such societies the varied occupations of every man oblige every man to exert his capacity, and to invent expedients for removing difficulties which are continually occurring. Invention is kept alive, and the mind is not suffered to fall into that drowsy stupidity, which, in a civilized society, seems to benumb the understanding of almost all the inferior ranks of people. In those barbarous societies, as they are called, every man, it has already been observed, is a warrior. Every man too is in some measure a statesman, and can form a tolerable judgment concerning the interest of the society, and the conduct of those who govern it. . . .

In a civilized state, on the contrary, though there is little variety in the occupations of the greater part of individuals, there is an almost infinite variety in those of the whole society. These varied occupations present an almost infinite variety of objects to the contemplation of those few, who, being attached to no particular occupation themselves, have leisure and inclination to examine the occupations of other people. The contemplation of so great a variety of objects necessarily exercises their minds in endless comparisons and combinations, and renders their understandings, in an extraordinary degree, both acute and comprehensive. Unless those few, however, happen to be placed in some very particular situations, their great abilities, though honourable to themselves, may contribute very little to the good government or happiness of their society. Notwithstanding the great abilities of those few, all the nobler parts of the human character may be, in a great measure, obliterated and extinguished in the great body of the people.

The education of the common people requires, perhaps, in a civilized and commercial society, the attention of the publick more than that of people of some rank and fortune. People of some rank and fortune are generally eighteen or nineteen years of age before they enter upon that particular business, profession, or trade, by which they propose to distinguish themselves in the world. They have before that full time to acquire, or at least to fit themselves for afterwards acquiring, every accomplishment which can recommend them to the publick esteem, or render them worthy of it. . . .

It is otherwise with the common people. They have little time to spare for education. Their parents can scarce afford to maintain them even in infancy. As soon as they are able to work, they must apply to some trade by which they can earn their subsistence. That trade too is generally so simple and uniform as to give little exercise to the understanding; while, at the same time, their labour is both so constant and so severe, that it leaves them little leisure and less inclination to apply to, or even to think of any thing else.

But though the common people cannot, in any civilized society, be so well instructed as people of some rank and fortune, the most essential parts of education, however, to read, write, and account, can be acquired at so early a period of life, that the greater part even of those who are to be bred to the lowest occupations, have time to acquire them before they can be employed in those occupations. For a very small expence the publick can facilitate, can encourage, and can even impose upon almost the whole body of the people, the necessity of acquiring those most essential parts of education.

As we can see, Smith has sketched out a large, not a small role for government to play—always keeping in mind that government is not itself supposed to carry on the tasks of production or distribution. As the distinguished economist Herbert Stein has pointed out, Smith explicitly accords to government the following powers:

- Protecting the merchant marine and giving bounties to defense-related manufactures.
- Imposing tariffs to obtain reciprocal reductions from other countries.
- Taking measures against dishonesty, violence, and fraud.
- Establishing quality indicators, such as the sterling silver mark.
- Requiring employers to pay wages in cash rather than kind.
- Regulating banking.

- Providing public goods, such as highways, canals, and the like.
- Running a postal service.
- Granting patents and copyrights.
- According temporary monopoly rights to trading companies developing commerce in new or risky regions.
- Requiring that children attain a certain level of schooling.
- Providing protection against communicable disease.
- Requiring public hygiene, such as clean streets.
- Imposing taxation to discourage improper or luxurious behavior.
- Establishing ceilings on interest rates.

Referring to an emblem of the Reagan years, Stein comments: "Adam Smith did not wear a Smith necktie".[19]

[19] *Wall Street Journal*, April 6, 1994.

THOMAS ROBERT MALTHUS

(1766–1834)

and

DAVID RICARDO

(1772–1823)

Adam Smith is the great tutelary figure of economics as a moral philosophy; David Ricardo its first great analytical observer. Smith saw the underlying psychological and political sources of the dynamics of the economic process; Ricardo the structural consequences of these dynamics. It is curious, however, that the element at the center of the great Ricardian scenario was, as its author always acknowledged, discovered not by himself, but by someone of a quite different cast of mind, and certainly of occupation.

That someone was Thomas Robert Malthus, an ordained clergyman whose calling could hardly have been further removed from Ricardo's career as a brilliantly successful trader in securities. Malthus's name was already associated with views on population growth for which he was to become famous (or infamous) as the opponent of any hopes for social improvement in the face of the relentless tendency of population growth to outpace production. Ricardo's appreciation of Malthus was not, however, based on the population issue, but rather on an obscure paper entitled "Inquiry into the Nature and Progress of Rent." As Ricardo wrote in the Preface of his quickly famous *On the Principles of Political Economy and Taxation,* published in 1818:

In 1815 Mr. Malthus, in his "Inquiry into the Nature and Progress of Rent," and a Fellow of University College Oxford* . . .
presented to the world, nearly at the same moment, the true
doctrine of rent; without a knowledge of which it is impossible
to understand the effect of the progress of wealth on profits and
wages, or to trace satisfactorily the influence of taxation on different classes of the community. . . ."

How shall we give voice to the views of these two central figures, at once interdependent and independent? I propose to do so
by beginning with two overall statements: Malthus's views on population, which hover in the background of Ricardo's scenario; and
Ricardo's own overview of what that scenario was to be.

First, then, a few often quoted pages from Chapters I, II, and VII
of Malthus's *An Essay on the Principle of Population.* The essay
was originally written as a wholly private dissent from the views
of one William Godwin who believed that population growth cast
no shadows on the future, insofar as one could expect a diminution of the "passions," once universal well-being was achieved.
Published anonymously in 1798, at the urging of his father, Malthus's *Essay* made an immediate impact, for reasons that this brief
excerpt will make clear:

AN ESSAY ON THE PRINCIPLE OF POPULATION

Chapter 1

The great and unlooked for discoveries that have taken place of
late years in natural philosophy, the increasing diffusion of general knowledge from the extension of the art of printing, the
ardent and unshackled spirit of inquiry that prevails throughout
the lettered and even unlettered world, the new and extraordinary lights that have been thrown on political subjects which
dazzle and astonish the understanding, and particularly that tremendous phenomenon in the political horizon, the French revolution, which, like a blazing comet, seems destined either to

---

*Edward West, an obscure but brilliant scholar.

inspire with fresh life and vigour, or to scorch up and destroy the shrinking inhabitants of the earth, have all concurred to lead many able men into the opinion that we were touching on a period big with the most important changes, changes that would in some measure be decisive of the future fate of mankind.

It has been said that the great question is now at issue, whether man shall henceforth start forwards with accelerated velocity towards illimitable and hitherto unconceived improvement or be aware of the tremendous obstacles that threaten, even in theory, to oppose the progress of man towards perfection. . . .

I think I may fairly make two postulata.

First, That food is necessary to the existence of man.

Secondly, That the passion between the sexes is necessary and will remain nearly in its present state.

These two laws, ever since we have had any knowledge of mankind, appear to have been fixed laws of our nature, and, as we have not hitherto seen any alteration in them, we have no right to conclude that they will ever cease to be what they now are, without an immediate act of power in that Being who first arranged the system of the universe, and for the advantage of his creatures, still executes, according to fixed laws, all its various operations.

I do not know that any writer has supposed that on this earth man will ultimately be able to live without food. But Mr. Godwin has conjectured that the passion between the sexes may in time be extinguished. As, however, he calls this part of his work a deviation into the land of conjecture, I will not dwell longer upon it at present than to say that the best arguments for the perfectibility of man are drawn from a contemplation of the great progress that he has already made from the savage state and the difficulty of saying where he is to stop. But towards the extinction of the passion between the sexes, no progress whatever has hitherto been made. It appears to exist in as much force at present as it did two thousand or four thousand years ago. There are individual exceptions now as there always have been. But, as these exceptions do not appear to increase in number, it would surely be a very unphilosophical mode of arguing, to infer merely from the existence of an exception, that the exception would, in time, become the rule, and the rule the exception.

Assuming then, my postulata as granted, I say that the power of population is indefinitely greater than the power in the earth to produce subsistence for man.

Population, when unchecked, increases in a geometrical ratio. Subsistence increases only in an arithmetical ratio. A slight acquaintance with numbers will shew the immensity of the first power in comparison of the second.

By that law of our nature which makes food necessary to the life of man, the effects of these two unequal powers must be kept equal.

This implies a strong and constantly operating check on population from the difficulty of subsistence. This difficulty must fall some where and must necessarily be severely felt by a large portion of mankind. . . .

Chapter II

. . . [To] make the argument more general and less interrupted by partial views of emigration, let us take the whole earth, instead of one spot, and suppose that the restraints to population were universally removed. If the subsistence for man that the earth affords was to be increased every twenty-five years by a quantity equal to what the whole world at present produces, this would allow the power of production in the earth to be absolutely unlimited and its ratio to increase much greater than we can conceive that any possible exertions of mankind could make it.

Taking the population of the world at any number, a thousand millions, for instance, the human species would increase in the ratio of—1, 2, 4, 8, 16, 32, 64, 128, 256, 512, &c. and subsistence as—1, 2, 3, 4, 5, 6, 7, 8, 9, 10, &c. In two centuries and a quarter, the population would be to the means of subsistence as 512 to 10, in three centuries as 4096 to 13, and in two thousand years the difference would be almost incalculable, though the produce in that time would have increased to an immense extent. . . .

Chapter VII

. . . Famine seems to be the last, the most dreadful resource of nature. The power of population is so superior to the power in earth to produce subsistence for man, that premature death must in some shape or other visit the human race. The vices of mankind are active and able ministers of depopulation. They are the precursors in the great army of destruction, and often finish the dreadful work themselves. But should they fail in this war of extermination, sickly seasons, epidemics, pestilence, and plague, advance in terrific array and sweep off their thousands and ten thousands. Should success be still incomplete, gigantic inevitable famine stalks in the rear, and with one mighty blow, levels the population with the food of the world.

Must it not then be acknowledged by an attentive examiner of the histories of mankind, that in every age and in every State in which man has existed, or does now exist,

That the increase of population is necessarily limited by the means of subsistence.

That population does invariably increase when the means of subsistence increase. And that the superior power of population is repressed, and the actual population kept equal to the means of subsistence, by misery and vice.[20]

RICARDO'S PRINCIPLES

Malthus's reputation as the father of an "iron law" of wages had a long, infamous, and largely undeserved life. His view was clearly incompatible with Utopian hopes for rapidly improving living conditions for the great masses, but he was sufficiently uneasy with respect to the uncompromising tone of his *Essay* to get to work on a second edition that would not appear until 1803. In that edition, the tone was considerably softened. Population

[20] Thomas Robert Malthus, *An Essay on the Principle of Population*, Philip Appleman, ed. New York: W.W. Norton, 1976, pp. 15f.

growth was still seen as the great enemy of rising living standards, but now Malthus was careful to state that it took a while before a newborn crop of children actually increased the supply of workers enough to depress wages, and he conceded that habit and custom played a role in determining the "subsistence" wage, offering a chance for a slow upward drift of workers' standards. What he did not advocate was birth control—a subject quite taboo in that era. Instead, he urged delayed marriage as a means of curbing the birth rate.

As a result, the second edition was much less powerful than the first: Walter Bagehot, the brilliant English banker and essayist, was to write: "In its first form the *Essay on Population* was conclusive as to argument, only it was based on untrue facts; in its second form it was based on true facts, but it was inconclusive as to argument."[21]

Let me therefore move to the work of David Ricardo, mentioned above as depending crucially on Malthus's powerful pronunciamento. I do so by first presenting the first three paragraphs of the Preface to Ricardo's *Principles*,[22] published in 1817, seemingly light-years removed from Malthus's impassioned declaration.

PRINCIPLES OF POLITICAL ECONOMY AND TAXATION

David Ricardo

Preface

The produce of the earth—all that is derived from its surface by the united application of labour, machinery, and capital, is divided among three classes of the community; namely, the proprietor of the land, the owner of the stock or capital necessary for its cultivation, and the labourers by whose industry it is cultivated.

[21] Thomas Robert Malthus, *On Population*, Gertrude Himmelfarb, ed. New York: Modern Library, 1960, p. xxxiii.
[22] David Ricardo, *The Works and Correspondence of David Ricardo*, Piero Sraffa, ed. Vol. 1. *On the Principles of Political Economy and Taxation*, New York: Cambridge University Press, 1951.

But in different stages of society, the proportions of the whole produce of the earth which will be allotted to each of these classes, under the names of rent, profit, and wages, will be essentially different; depending mainly on the actual fertility of the soil, on the accumulation of capital and population, and on the skill, ingenuity, and instruments employed in agriculture.

To determine the laws which regulate this distribution, is the principal problem in Political Economy: much as the science has been improved by the writings of Turgot, Stuart, Smith, Say, Sismondi, and others, they afford very little satisfactory information respecting the natural course of rent, profit, and wages.

Unlike Malthus, Ricardo's style is terse and matter of fact—a rhetoric much befitting his extraordinarily analytic approach to economics. A few comments on the paragraphs above may therefore help prepare us for the chapter to follow.

First, we note that Ricardo speaks primarily about distribution, not production. This does not mean that he is uninterested in the latter. On the contrary, in the very next paragraph he gives Malthus credit for presenting the first "true doctrine" of rent, by directly linking that payment not to the "gifts" of nature to which the Physiocrats (and even Adam Smith, on occasion) had turned, but to its increasing stinginess, as we move to lands of lesser productivity. Malthus's insight was that *differences in fertility* from one tract of land to the next are what give rise to rent—differences that create larger yields, and therefore lower costs, in some lands than in others.

A Ricardian scholar might protest that the real fulcrum of Ricardo's analysis lies in his analysis of value—the underlying rationale of price—which he links almost exclusively to labor. The objection is well founded, but for non-scholars I think rent is the more interesting point of entry into the Ricardian scenario.

To compress his contribution into a paragraph, Ricardo links a growing population to an increasing need for food, and an increasing need for food to a need to have recourse to lands of progressively less fertility. The result is a steady rise of the comparative advantage in physical output of all lands above those at the margin that just pay their way, and therefore the growing share of the value of output attributable to rent. In the chapter below, we see that process at work.

Chapter II

On Rent

... Rent is that portion of the produce of the earth, which is paid to the landlord for the use of the original and indestructible powers of the soil. It is often, however, confounded with the interest and profit of capital, and, in popular language, the term is applied to whatever is annually paid by a farmer to his landlord. If, of two adjoining farms of the same extent, and of the same natural fertility, one had all the conveniences of farming buildings, and, besides, were properly drained and manured, and advantageously divided by hedges, fences and walls, while the other had none of these advantages, more remuneration would naturally be paid for the use of one, than for the use of the other; yet in both cases this remuneration would be called rent. But it is evident, that a portion only of the money annually to be paid for the improved farm, would be given for the original and indestructible powers of the soil; the other portion would be paid for the use of the capital which had been employed in ameliorating the quality of the land, and in erecting such buildings as were necessary to secure and preserve the produce. ...

On the first settling of a country, in which there is an abundance of rich and fertile land, a very small proportion of which is required to be cultivated for the support of the actual population, or indeed can be cultivated with the capital which the population can command, there will be no rent; for no one would pay for the use of land, when there was an abundant quantity not yet appropriated, and, therefore, at the disposal of whosoever might choose to cultivate it.

On the common principles of supply and demand, no rent could be paid for such land, for the reason stated why nothing is given for the use of air and water, or for any other of the gifts of nature which exist in boundless quantity. With a given quantity of materials, and with the assistance of the pressure of the atmosphere, and the elasticity of steam, engines may perform work, and abridge human labour to a very great extent; but no charge is made for the use of these natural aids, because they are inexhaustible, and at every man's disposal. In the same manner the brewer, the distiller, the dyer, make incessant use of the air and water for the production of their commodities; but as the supply is boundless, they bear no price. If all land had the same properties, if it were unlimited in quantity, and uniform in quality, no charge could be made for its use, unless where it possessed peculiar advantages of situation. It is only, then, because land is not unlimited in quantity and uniform in quality, and because in the progress of population, land of an inferior quality, or less advantageously situated, is called into cultivation, that rent is ever paid for the use of it. When in the progress of society, land of the second degree of fertility is taken into cultivation, rent immediately commences on that of the first quality, and the amount of that rent will depend on the difference in the quality of these two portions of land.

When land of the third quality is taken into cultivation, rent immediately commences on the second, and it is regulated as before, by the difference in their productive powers. At the same time, the rent of the first quality will rise, for that must always be above the rent of the second, by the difference between the produce which they yield with a given quantity of capital and labour. With every step in the progress of population, which shall oblige a country to have recourse to land of a worse quality, to enable it to raise its supply of food, rent, on all the more fertile land, will rise.

Thus suppose land—No. 1, 2, 3,—to yield, with an equal employment of capital and labour, a net produce of 100, 90, and 80 quarters of corn. In a new country, where there is an abundance of fertile land compared with the population, and where therefore it is only necessary to cultivate No. 1, the whole net produce will belong to the cultivator, and will be the profits of the stock which he advances. As soon as population had so far increased as to make it necessary to cultivate No. 2, from which ninety quarters only can be obtained after supporting the labourers, rent would commence on No. 1; for either there must be two rates of profit on agricultural capital, or ten quarters, or the value of ten quarters must be withdrawn from the produce of No. 1, for some other purpose. Whether the proprietor of the land, or any other person, cultivated No. 1, these ten quarters would equally constitute rent; for the cultivator of No. 2 would get the same result with his capital, whether he cultivated No. 1, paying ten quarters for rent, or continued to cultivate No 2, paying no rent. In the same manner it might be shown that when No. 3 is brought into cultivation, the rent of No. 2 must be ten quarters, or the value of ten quarters, whilst the rent of No. 1 would rise to twenty quarters; for the cultivator of No. 3 would have the same profits whether he paid twenty quarters for the rent of No. 1, ten quarters for the rent of No. 2, or cultivated No. 3 free of all rent.

. . . The reason then, why raw produce rises in comparative value, is because more labour is employed in the production of the last portion obtained, and not because a rent is paid to the landlord. The value of corn is regulated by the quantity of labour bestowed on its production on that quality of land, or with that portion of capital, which pays no rent. Corn is not high because a rent is paid, but a rent is paid because corn is high; and it has been justly observed, that no reduction would take place in the price of corn, although landlords should forego the whole of their rent. Such a measure would only enable some farmers to live like gentlemen, but would not diminish the quantity of labour necessary to raise raw produce on the least productive land in cultivation.

Nothing is more common than to hear of the advantages which the land possesses over every other source of useful produce, on account of the surplus which it yields in the form of rent. Yet when land is most abundant, when most productive, and most fertile, it yields no rent; and it is only when its powers decay, and less is yielded in return for labour, that a share of the original produce of the more fertile portions is set apart for rent. It is singular that this quality in the land, which should have been noticed as an imperfection, compared with the natural agents by which manufacturers are assisted, should have been pointed out as constituting its peculiar preeminence. If air, water, the elasticity of steam, and the pressure of the atmosphere, were of various qualities; if they could be appropriated, and each quality existed only in moderate abundance, they, as well as the land, would afford a rent, as the successive qualities were brought into use. With every worse quality employed, the value of the commodities in the manufacture of which they were used, would rise, because equal quantities of labour would be less productive. Man would do more by the sweat of his brow, and nature perform less; and the land would be no longer preeminent for its limited powers. . . .

The rise of rent is always the effect of the increasing wealth of the country, and of the difficulty of providing food for its augmented population. It is a symptom, but it is never a cause of wealth; for wealth often increases most rapidly while rent is either stationary, or even falling. Rent increases most rapidly, as the disposable land decreases in its productive powers. Wealth increases most rapidly in those countries where the disposable land is most fertile, where importation is least restricted, and where through agricultural improvements, productions can be multiplied without any increase in the proportional quantity of labour, and where consequently the progress of rent is slow.

Perhaps the reader has noted the phrase "where importation is least restricted" in the last sentence of the preceding excerpt. The words are significant, for they underlie a political position to which Ricardo's analysis has forced him. It is that the rising aggregate of rents implies a steady shift of incomes into the hands of landlords.

A shift at whose expense? Not that of the laborer whose wages are seen by Ricardo, as well as by Smith or Malthus, as essentially those of subsistence. As the banker Alexander Baring said in Parliament, the worker will get "his dry bread in one case and his dry bread in the other."[23] Nor will the shift in incomes come at the landlord's expense because, as we have just seen, population growth swells the rents accruing to the owners of all higher-than-marginal tracts. Hence the share of national income paid out as rent rises, and this growing share will, of necessity, come from a squeeze on the incomes of the only remaining class of income receivers—the movers and drivers of the system that we would call its capitalists.

In Ricardo's day there was one obvious remedy for this problem. It was the repeal of the Corn Laws that sought to protect land-holders' interests by prohibiting the import of grains until home prices had reached very high levels. Of all people, Malthus now defended these interests. In his *Principles of Political Economy,* published in 1820, he wrote that rents would be difficult to defend if rent-yielding lands remained always with the immediate descendants of their first possessors. "But happily," he added, "the benefit is attached to the soil, not to any particular proprietors. Rents are the reward of present valour and wisdom, as well as of past strength and cunning. Every day lands are purchased with the fruits of industry."[24]

Indeed, here Malthus adds a footnote:

Mr. Ricardo himself is an instance of what I am stating. He is now become, by his talents and industry, a considerable land-holder, and a more honorable and excellent man. . . . I could not point out in the whole circle of landholders.

It is somewhat singular that Mr. Ricardo, a considerable receiver of rents, should have so much underrated their national importance; while I, who never received, nor expect to receive any, shall probably be accused of overrating their importance. Our different situations and opinions may at least serve to shew our mutual sincerity, and afford a strong presumption, that to

---

[23] The comment by Baring is quoted in Wesley Mitchell, *Types of Economic Theory,* New York: Augustus Kelley, 1987, Vol. I.
[24] *Notes on Malthus's Principles of Political Economy,* in *Works of David Ricardo,* P. Sraffa ed., op. cit., Vol II., pp. 222–23.

whatever bias our minds may have been subjected in the doc-trines we have laid down, it has not been that, against which it is perhaps most difficult to guard, the insensible bias of situation and interest.[25]

The comment is given additional interest because in 1919 a great grandson of Ricardo's discovered a bundle of paper casually stored in the lumber room of the former residence of Ricardo's eldest son. The bundle consisted of over two hundred loose sheets covered on both sides with Ricardo's commentaries on Malthus's book, all carefully keyed to the passages in question. To the passage above, in which Malthus defends the virtues of landholders and landholding, Ricardo adds this comment:

There is a surplus produce from the land from which profits and rents are taken. I am of the opinion that the interests of society are best promoted by allowing the free importation of corn, the consequence of which is that the surplus produce from the land in cultivation at home will be divided in proportions more favorable to the farmer and capitalist, and less favorable to the landholder. Mr. Malthus appears to differ from me, but instead of shewing that society would be benefited by taking from the capitalist and giving to the landlord, he considers rent a clear gain and accuses me of underrating its value because I am not willing to allow that the surplus produce increases or diminishes as rent rises or falls.

We need not linger over the colloquy: the Ricardian view of rents prevailed over that of Malthus. But the intellectual give and take between these best of friends now turned in a different direction. For in his *Principles,* Malthus advanced a view of much greater significance, and certainly of much greater boldness, than that of defending the Corn Laws whose eventual fate was already becoming clear. His heresy lay in espousing an idea that had previously flourished only in the underground of near-seditious

[25] *Ibid.,* pp. 222–23n.

views, where it had always been greeted by the more respectable spokesmen for political economy with disbelief and disdain. At stake was the question of whether there could be a general "glut" of commodities.

In his *Principles* Malthus wrote:

It has been thought by some very able writers, that although there may easily be a glut of particular commodities, there cannot possibly be a glut of commodities in general; because, according to their view of the subject, commodities being always exchanged for commodities, one half will furnish the market for the other half, and production being the only source of demand, an excess in the supply of one article merely proves a deficiency in the supply of some other, and a general excess is impossible. M. Say,[26] in his distinguished work on political economy, has indeed gone so far as to state that the consumption of a commodity by taking it out of the market diminishes demand, and the production of a commodity proportionally increases it.

This doctrine, however . . . , appears to me to be utterly unfounded and completely to contradict the great principles which regulate supply and demand.[27]

Malthus's argument essentially makes three points: first, the proponents of the anti-glut doctrine, whom he identifies as Say, James Mill, and Ricardo, "consider commodities as if they were so many mathematical figures, or arithmetical characters, the relations of which were to be compared, instead of articles of consumption, which must of course be referred to the numbers and wants of the consumers"; second, that they fail to take into consideration "the influence of so general and important a principle of human nature, as indolence or the love of ease"; and third, that they assume that "accumulation ensures demand," or that the consumption of the laborers hired by capitalists will encourage a continued increase of production.

[26] Jean Baptiste Say, *Treatise on Political Economy*, 1803.
[27] *Notes on Malthus's Principles of Political Economy*, op. cit., pp. 303–06 (Malthus's text).

Ricardo replies to the charges with equanimity. He writes on his note attached to Malthus's objection:

Mistakes may be made, and commodities not suited to the market may be produced—of these there may be a glut; they may not sell at their usual price; but this then is owning to the mistake and not to the want of demand for production. For every thing produced there must be a proprietor. Either it is the master, the landlord, or the labourer. Whoever is possessed of a commodity is necessarily a demander, either he wishes to consume the commodity himself, and then no purchaser is wanted; or he wishes to sell it, and purchase some other thing with the money, which shall either be consumed by him or made instrumental to future production. The commodity he possesses will either obtain this or it will not. If it will, the object is accomplished, and his commodity has found a market. If it will not, what does it prove? That he has not adapted his means well to his end, he has miscalculated. . . . What I wish to impress on the reader's mind is that it is at all times the bad adaptation of the commodities produced to the wants of mankind which is the specific evil, and not the abundance of commodities. Demand is only limited by the will and power to purchase.[28]

In another note referring to Malthus's suggestion that "indolence" may be a cause of a general glut, Ricardo answers:

We do not say that indolence may not be preferred to luxuries. I think it may and therefore if the question was respecting the motives to produce, there would be no difference between us. But Mr. Malthus supposes the motive strong enough to produce the commodities and then contends there would be no demand for them. It is this proposition we deny. We do not say the commodities will under all circumstances be produced, but if they are produced there will always be some who have the will and power to consume them, or in other words there will always be

[28] For the above citations see op. cit., pp. 305, 307, 309, 314.

a demand for them. Mr. Malthus brings forward a case of a society not accumulating, preferring indolence to luxuries, not demanding labour. . . . Men will prefer indolence to luxuries! Luxuries will not then be produced, because they cannot be produced without labour, the opposite of indolence. If not produced they cannot want a market, there can be no glut of them.[29]

Thus, wherever Malthus's argument can be countered with logic, Ricardo has the best of him: Malthus remarks in passing that "Many a merchant has made a large fortune, although during the acquisition of this fortune, there was perhaps hardly a single year in which he did not increase rather than diminish his expenditure in objects of luxury, enjoyment, and liberality," to which Ricardo replies: "True, but a brother merchant who avoided an increased expenditure on objects of luxury, enjoyment and liberality, would get rich faster than him."[30]

Yet, at another level, Ricardo sometimes fails to catch the drift of his friend's misgivings. This applies particularly to Malthus's first objection—that the opponents of the possibility of general gluts tended to disregard the particularities of commodities in favor of the abstractions of mathematics. As we have already seen with Cantillon, the level of abstraction vitally affects our "vision" of economic reality, which in turn directly affects our analytic approach to it. Ricardo's vision was peculiarly prone to what Joseph Schumpeter was to call the Ricardian Vice—the habit of theorizing at such a stratospheric level of refinement that "nothing lacks save sense."[31]

In 1819 the unorthodox journalist/economist J-C-L Simonde de Sismondi, a declared admirer of Ricardo, spotted one such example. It lies in Chapter 26 of the *Principles* where Ricardo writes:

To an individual with a capital of £20,000 per annum, it would be a matter quite indifferent whether his capital would employ

[29] Op. cit., pp. 314–15.
[30] Op cit., pp. 376, 377.
[31] Joseph A. Schumpeter, *History of Economic Analysis*, Oxford University Press, 1954, p. 473.

a hundred or a thousand men . . . , provided . . . his profits were not diminished below £2000. Is not the real interest of the nation similar? Provided its net income, its rent and profits be the same, it is of no importance whether the nation consists of ten or twelve million inhabitants.

"Indeed," comments Sismondi; "Wealth is everything, men are absolutely nothing? What? Wealth itself is only something in relation to taxes? In truth, there is nothing more to wish for than that the king, remaining alone on his island, by constantly turning a crank, might produce, through automata, all the output of England?"[32]

There remains one last surprising twist to Ricardo's work. It is his own apostasy with respect to an issue that was as ill-understood, and potentially just as damaging, as the possibility that general gluts might be a recurrent problem for a capitalist economy. The issue concerned the effect of machinery on employment.

The first two editions of Ricardo's *Principles*, dated 1817 and 1819, contain no special mention of machinery. But in the third edition, published in 1821, a new chapter appears: *On Machinery*. It contains the following remarkable statement:

[T]he opinion of the labouring class, that the employment of machinery is frequently detrimental to their interests, is not founded on prejudice and error, but conforms to the correct principles of political economy.[33]

The words should have been a bombshell, but they were not. The argument, as the reader will see in the coming excerpt, is not easy to follow, but essentially it depends on the possibility that by investing its "wage-fund"—the cash it had formerly used to pay wages—in machinery a firm may be able to maintain, even to increase its profit, but would have less capital available for payrolls. Ricardo asks, of what interest is that to the capitalist? He

[32] Sismondi, *New Principles of Political Economy* (1819). Richard Hyse, trans. and ed. Transaction Publishers, Rutgers University, 1991, p. 563n.
[33] Ricardo, op. cit., p. 392.

might have inquired of what interest it would be to economists? The answer, alas, is that the heretical chapter was overlooked, dismissed, or simply forgotten, to be rediscovered only in rather recent years, when the question of automation-related unemployment has come to the fore.

Chapter XXXI

On Machinery

In the present chapter I shall enter into some enquiry respecting the influence of machinery on the interests of the different classes of society, a subject of great importance, and one which appears never to have been investigated in a manner to lead to any certain or satisfactory results. It is more incumbent on me to declare my opinion on this question, because they have, on further reflection, undergone a considerable change; and although I am not aware that I have ever published any thing respecting machinery which it is necessary for me to retract, yet I have in other ways given my support to doctrines which I now think erroneous; it, therefore, becomes a duty in me to submit my present views to examination, with my reasons for entertaining them.

Ever since I first turned my attention to questions of political economy, I have been of opinion, that such an application of machinery to any branch of production, as should have the effect of saving labour, was a general good, accompanied only with that portion of inconvenience which in most cases attends the removal of capital and labour from one employment to another. It appeared to me, that provided the landlords had the same money rents, they would be benefited by the reduction in the prices of some of the commodities on which those rents were expended, and which reduction of price could not fail to be the consequence of the employment of machinery. The capitalist, I thought, was eventually benefited precisely in the same demand for labour as before, and that wages would be no lower, I thought that the labouring class would, equally with the other classes, participate in the advantage, from the general cheapness of commodities arising from the use of machinery.

These were my opinions, and they continue unaltered, as far as regards the landlord and the capitalist; but I am convinced, that the substitution of machinery for human labour, is often very injurious to the interests of the class of labourers.

My mistake arose from the supposition, that whenever the net income of a society increased, its gross income would also increase; I now, however, see reason to be satisfied that the one fund, from which landlords and capitalists derive their revenue, may increase, while the other, that upon which the labouring class mainly depend, may diminish, and therefore it follows, if I am right, that the same cause which may increase the net revenue of the country, may at the same time render the population redundant, and deteriorate the condition of the labourer.

A capitalist we will suppose employs a capital of the value of 20,000*l.* and that he carries on the joint business of a farmer, and a manufacturer of necessaries. We will further suppose, that 7000*l.* of this capital is invested in fixed capital, viz. in buildings, implements, &c. &c. and that the remaining 13,000*l.* is employed as circulating capital in the support of labour. Let us suppose, too, that profits are 10 per cent., and consequently that the capitalist's capital is every year put into its original state of efficiency, and yields a profit of 2000*l.*

Each year the capitalist begins his operations, by having food and necessaries in his possession of the value of 13,000*l.*, all of which he sells in the course of the year to his own workmen for that sum of money, and, during the same period, he pays them the like amount of money for wages: at the end of the year they replace in his possession food and necessaries of the value of 15,000*l.*, 2000*l.* of which he consumes himself, or disposes of as may best suit his pleasure and gratification. As far as these products are concerned, the gross produce for that year is 15,000*l.*, and the net produce 2000*l.* Suppose now, that the following year the capitalist employs half his men in constructing a machine, and the other half in producing food and necessaries as usual. During that year he would pay the sum of 13,000*l.* in wages as usual, and would sell food and necessaries to the same amount to his workmen; but what would be the case the following year?

While the machine was being made, only one-half of the usual quantity of food and necessaries would be obtained, and they would be only one-half the value of the quantity which was produced before. The machine would be worth 7500*l.*, and the food and necessaries 7500*l.*, and, therefore, the capital of the capitalist would be as great as before; for he would have besides these two values, his fixed capital worth 7000*l.*, making in the whole 20,000*l.* capital, and 2000*l.* profit. After deducting this latter sum for his own expenses, he would have a no greater circulating capital than 5500*l.* with which to carry on his subsequent operations; and, therefore, his means of employing labour, would be reduced in the proportion of 13,000*l.* to 5500*l.*, and, consequently, all the labour which was before employed by 7500*l.*, would become redundant.

The reduced quantity of labour which the capitalist can employ, must, indeed, with the assistance of the machine, and after deductions for its repairs, produce a value equal to 7500*l.*, it must replace the circulating capital with a profit of 2000*l.* on the whole capital; but if this be done, if the net income be not diminished, of what importance is it to the capitalist, whether the gross income be of the value of 3000*l.*, of 10,000*l.*, or of 15,000*l.?*

In this case, then, although the net produce will not be diminished in value, although its power of purchasing commodities may be greatly increased, the gross produce will have fallen from a value of 15,000*l.* to a value of 7500*l.*, and as the power of supporting a population, and employing labour, depends always on the gross produce of a nation, and not on its net produce, there will necessarily be a diminution in the demand for labour, population will become redundant, and the situation of the labouring classes will be that of distress and poverty.

As, however, the power of saving from revenue to add to capital, must depend on the efficiency of the net revenue, to satisfy the wants of the capitalist, it could not fail to follow from the reduction in the price of commodities consequent on the introduction of machinery, that with the same wants he would have increased means of saving,—increased facility of transferring revenue into capital. But with every increase of capital he would employ more labourers; and, therefore, a portion of the people thrown out of work in the first instance, would be subsequently employed; and if the increased production, in consequence of the employment of the machine, was so great as to afford, in the shape of net produce, as great a quantity of food and necessaries as existed before in the form of gross produce, there would be the same ability to employ the whole population, and, therefore, there would not necessarily be any redundancy of people.

All I wish to prove, is, that the discovery and use of machinery may be attended with a diminution of gross produce; and whenever that is the case, it will be injurious to the labouring class, as some of their number will be thrown out of employment, and population will become redundant, compared with the funds which are to employ it. . . .

The statements which I have made will not, I hope, lead to the inference that machinery should not be encouraged. To elucidate the principle, I have been supposing, that improved machinery is *suddenly* discovered, and extensively used; but the truth is, that these discoveries are gradual, and rather operate in determining the employment of the capital which is saved and accumulated, than in diverting capital from its actual employment.

———————

A last word. Much still remains for anyone who wishes to mine the full *Principles*—there is the famous Ricardian explanation of free trade, his brilliant chapter *On Sudden Changes in the Channels of Trade,* on *Value and Riches,* and a great deal more. But the machinery chapter has a contemporary relevance that makes it a fitting adieu to an economist's economist, which includes the courage to put forward unpopular opinions.

JOHN STUART MILL

⟨∞⟩

(1806–1873)

I will begin this chapter by borrowing a paragraph from *The Worldly Philosophers:*

> John Stuart Mill was born in 1806. In 1809 (not 1819) he began to learn Greek. At age seven he had read most of the dialogues of Plato. The next year he began Latin, having meanwhile digested Herodotus, Xenophon, Diogenes Laërtius, and part of Lucian. Between eight and twelve he finished Virgil, Horace, Livy, Sallust, Ovid, Terence, Lucretius, Sophocles, and Aristophanes; had mastered geometry, algebra, and the differential calculus; written a Roman History, an Abridgement of the Ancient Universal History, a History of Holland and a few verses. "I never composed at all in Greek, even in prose, and but little in Latin," he wrote in his famous *Autobiography,*[34] "Not that my father was indifferent to the value of the practice ... but because there really was not the time for it."

The miracle, as more than one commentator has noted, is not that he learned so much, but that he survived thereafter as a

---

[34] *Collected Works of John Stuart Mill,* Vol. I, Toronto: University of Toronto Press, 1965, p. 39.

human being. At the cost of considerable turmoil, and perhaps only with the help of one Harriet Taylor—first as an inspiring collaborator; later, after her husband's death, as his wife—Mill did become a remarkable human being whose humanity pervades his contribution to political economy, and as we shall see, gives it its special character. It would, however, be an injustice to begin straight away with these writings. Mill's works stretch over a very large domain, and unless we are at least aware of their breadth, our study of him will be too cramped. A paragraph, then, to indicate the scope of what is surely one of the most remarkable intellects ever to work in the field.

Mill's father, James Mill, was a close acquaintance of Ricardo and a strong supporter of both Ricardian economics and of utilitarian philosophy, then embodied in the formidable person and teachings of Jeremy Bentham which we will discuss later. One of the young Mill's later works was a re-presentation of the Benthamite philosophy that had placed man under the guidance of two "sovereign masters," pleasure and pain, leaving it to them alone "to point out what we ought to do, as well as to determine what we shall do." Characteristically, Mill's version did not abandon Bentham's central teaching, but qualified it by insisting that there were higher as well as lower pleasures, and that in the end only a view of pleasure that associates it with justice will win the approval of *conscience,* Mill's word for the approval of the "inhabitant of the breast" to whom Adam Smith turned.[35]

Utilitarianism is, however, less significant in taking the measure of Mill than his *Logic,* (1843), or the treatise on *The Subjection of Women* (1869), and most of all, his tract *On Liberty,* published in 1859 after Harriet Taylor's death, with a lengthy dedication attributing to her "all that is best in my writing." Because the message of *Liberty* permeates much of his political economy, here is a paragraph from it that warrants reproduction:

The object of this Essay is to assert one very simple principle, as entitled to govern absolutely the dealings of society with the

[35] For Smith, see the excerpt from *The Theory of Moral Sentiments,* p. 69 above; for Mill, see *Utilitarianism,* Chapter III.

individual in the way of compulsion and control, whether the means used be physical force in the form of legal penalties, or the moral coercion of public opinion. That principle is, that the sole end for which mankind are warranted, individually or collectively, in interfering with the liberty of action of any of their number, is self-protection. That the sole purpose for which power can be rightfully exercised over any member of a civilized community, against his will, is to prevent harm to others. His own good, either physical or moral, is not a sufficient warrant. He cannot rightfully be compelled to do or forbear because it will be better for him to do so, because it will make him happier, because, in the opinions of others, to do so would be wise, or even right. These are good reasons remonstrating with him, or persuading him, or entreating him, but not for compelling him, or visiting him with any evil in case he do otherwise. To justify that, the conduct from which it is desired to deter him must be calculated to produce evil in some one else. The only part of the conduct of any one, for which he is amendable to society, is that which concerns others. In the part which merely concerns himself, his independence is, of right, absolute. Over himself, over his own body and mind, the individual is sovereign.[36]

Mill is thus, first and foremost, a fervent libertarian, taking that word to denote the practical realization of the ideal described above. How does this affect his views as an economist? That will be the central object of our readings to come.

PRINCIPLES OF POLITICAL ECONOMY

Published in 1848, Mill's *Principles* dominated political economy for a generation, earning at first the admiration, then gradually the impatience of subsequent writers who grew up in its shadow. The book itself is long, and much of it will not be of interest, but there is a fascinating text-within-the-text that I hope to bring out.

[36]John Stuart Mill, *On Liberty*, in *Utilitarianism, Liberty, Representative Government*, London and New York: E.P. Dutton, 1929.

That inner text is, in fact, signaled at the very outset of the *Principles,* where Mill discusses the nature of wealth. In its concluding paragraph, that chapter lays out the distinction between production and distribution that will then be taken up in its full ramifications one hundred and seventy pages later.

The opening chapter is well worth a glance:

Preliminary Remarks

In every department of human affairs, Practice long precedes Science: systematic enquiry into the modes of action of the powers of nature, is the tardy product of a long course of efforts to use those powers for practical ends. The conception, accordingly, of Political Economy as a branch of science is extremely modern; but the subject with which its enquiries are conversant has in all ages necessarily constituted one of the chief practical interests of mankind, and, in some, a most unduly engrossing one.

That subject is Wealth. Writers on Political Economy profess to teach, or to investigate, the nature of Wealth, and the laws of its production and distribution: including, directly or remotely, the operation of all the causes by which the condition of mankind, or of any society of human beings, in respect to this universal object of human desire, is made prosperous or the reverse. Not that any treatise on Political Economy can discuss or even enumerate all these causes; but it undertakes to set forth as much as is known of the laws and principles according to which they operate.

Every one has a notion, sufficiently correct for common purposes, of what is meant by wealth. The enquiries which relate to it are in no danger of being confounded with those relating to any other of the great human interests. All know that it is one thing to be rich, another thing to be enlightened, brave, or humane; that the questions how a nation is made wealthy, and how it is made free, or virtuous, or eminent in literature, in the fine arts, in arms, or in polity, are totally distinct enquiries. Those things, indeed, are all indirectly connected, and react upon one another. A people has sometimes become free, because it had first grown wealthy; or wealthy, because it had first become free. The creed and laws of a people act powerfully upon their economical condition; and this again, by its influence on their mental development and social relations, reacts upon their creed and laws. But though the subjects are in very close contact, they are essentially different, and have never been supposed to be otherwise.

. . . In so far as the economical condition of nations turns upon the state of physical knowledge, it is a subject for the physical sciences, and the arts founded on them. But in so far as the causes are moral or psychological, dependent on institutions and social relations, or on the principles of human nature, their investigation belongs not to physical, but to moral and social science, and is the object of what is called Political Economy.

The production of wealth, the extraction of the instruments of human subsistence and enjoyment from the materials of the globe, is evidently not an arbitrary thing. It has its necessary conditions. Of these, some are physical, depending on the properties of matter, and on the amount of those properties possessed at the particular place and time. These Political Economy does not investigate, but assumes, referring for the grounds to physical science or common experience. Combining with these facts of outward nature other truths relating to human nature, it attempts to trace the secondary or derivative laws, by which the production of wealth is determined; in which must lie the explanation of the diversities of riches and poverty in the present and past, and the ground of whatever increase in wealth is reserved for the future.

Unlike the laws of Production, those of Distribution are partly of human institution; since the manner in which wealth is distributed in any given society, depends on the statutes or usages therein obtaining. The conditions on which the power they possess over the distribution of wealth is dependent, and the manner in which the distribution is effected by the various modes of conduct which society may think fit to adopt, are as much a subject for scientific enquiry as any of the physical laws of nature.[37]

The stage is thus set for the larger text to follow, beginning with the study of production. These chapters are not, however, part of the text-within-the text section. As the Preface has prepared us, they take us through a consideration of such matters as the various roles that labor can play in the creation of wealth, such as, producing goods or services; descriptions of aspects of capital, for instance its source in saving or its division between fixed and circulating kinds; to a consideration of the constraints on output that stem from the limited availability and diminishing marginal fertility of land.

Much of this is interesting, none is worth our consideration here. One point, however, deserves note, if only because it indicates the breadth of Mill's interests. In Chapter IX of Book I he speaks of the advantages that may stem from organization as a joint-stock (corporate) entity and calls attention to the economies of large-scale over small-scale production. More significant, he notes that there exists, as a consequence of these advantages, "a tendency to substitute more and more, in one branch of industry after another, large establishments for small ones." Mill is thus the first economist to foresee the concentration of business that will become a major focus of economic and political attention in the century ahead.

These preliminaries concluded, we turn to Book II on distribution. Here is Mill at his best, expounding in detail the difference between production and distribution. The long, often prescient, chapter merits our full attention:

---

[37] The excerpts to come are taken from the authoritative *Collected Works of John Stuart Mill*, vols. IV and V, University of Toronto Press, 1965. As before, additional headings and paragraphing have been added, for ease of reading. Books II through V of the *Principles*, to which our attention will be mainly directed, are also available in a World's Classics paperback, Oxford University Press, 1994.

Chapter I

Of Property

[*Introductory remarks*] The principles which have been set forth in the first part of this Treatise, are, in certain respects, strongly distinguished from those, on the consideration of which we are now about to enter. The laws and conditions of the production of wealth partake of the character of physical truths. There is nothing optional or arbitrary in them. Whatever mankind produce, must be produced in the modes, and under the conditions, imposed by the constitution of external things, and by the inherent properties of their own bodily and mental structure. Whether they like it or not, their productions will be limited by the amount of their previous accumulation, and, that being given, it will be proportional to their energy, their skill, the perfection of their machinery, and their judicious use of the advantages of combined labour. Whether they like it or not, a double quantity of labour will not raise, on the same land, a double quantity of food, unless some improvement takes place in the processes of cultivation. Whether they like it or not, the unproductive expenditure of individuals will *pro tanto* tend to impoverish the community, and only their productive expenditure will enrich it. The opinions, or the wishes, which may exist on these different matters, do not control the things themselves. We cannot, indeed, foresee to what extent the modes of production may be altered, or the productiveness of labour increased, by future extensions of our knowledge of the laws of nature, suggesting new processes of industry of which we have at present no conception. But howsoever we may succeed in making for ourselves more space within the limits set by the constitution of things, we know that there must be limits. We cannot alter the ultimate properties either of matter or mind, but can only employ those properties more or less successfully, to bring about the events in which we are interested.

It is not so with the Distribution of Wealth. That is a matter of human institution solely. The things once there, mankind, individually or collectively, can do with them as they like. They can place them at the disposal of whomsoever they please, and on whatever terms. Further, in the social state, in every state except total solitude, any disposal whatever of them can only take place by the consent of society, or rather of those who dispose of its active force. Even what a person has produced by his individual toil, unaided by any one, he cannot keep, unless by the permission of society. Not only can society take it from him, but individuals could and would take it from him, if society only remained passive; if it did not either interfere *en masse*, or employ and pay people for the purpose of preventing him from being disturbed in the possession. The distribution of wealth, therefore, depends on the laws and customs of society. The rules by which it is determined, are what the opinions and feelings of the ruling portion of the community make them, and are very different in different ages and countries; and might be still more different, if mankind so chose.

The opinions and feelings of mankind, doubtless, are not a matter of chance. They are consequences of the fundamental laws of human nature, combined with the existing state of knowledge and experience, and the existing condition of social institutions and intellectual and moral culture. But the laws of the generation of human opinions are not within our present subject. They are part of the general theory of human progress, a far larger and more difficult subject of inquiry than political economy. We have here to consider, not the causes, but the consequences, of the rules according to which wealth may be distributed. Those, at least, are as little arbitrary, and have as much the character of physical laws, as the laws of production. Human beings can control their own acts, but not the consequences of their acts either to themselves or to others. Society can subject the distribution of wealth to whatever rules it thinks best: but what practical results will flow from the operation of those rules, must be discovered, like any other physical or mental truths, by observation and reasoning.

We proceed, then, to the consideration of the different modes of distributing the produce of land and labour, which have been adopted in practice, or may be conceived in theory. Among these, our attention is first claimed by that primary and funda-mental institution, on which, unless in some exceptional and very limited cases, the economical arrangements of society have always rested, though in its secondary features it has varied, and is liable to vary, I mean, of course, the institution of individual property.

On Property

... If private property were adopted, we must presume that it would be accompanied by none of the initial inequalities and injustices which obstruct the beneficial operation of the principle in old societies. Every full grown man or woman, we must sup-pose, would be secured in the unfettered use and disposal of his or her bodily and mental faculties; and the instruments of production, the land and tools, would be divided fairly among them, so that all might start, in respect to outward appliances, on equal terms. It is possible also to conceive that in this original apportionment, compensation might be made for the injuries of nature, and the balance redressed by assigning to the less robust members of the community advantages in the distribution, suf-ficient to put them on a par with the rest.

But the division, once made, would not again be interfered with; individuals would be left to their own exertions and to the ordinary chances, for making an advantageous use of what was assigned to them. If individual property, on the con-trary, were excluded, the plan which must be adopted would be to hold the land and all instruments of production as the joint property of the community, and to carry on the operations of industry on the common account. The direction of the labour of the community would devolve upon a magistrate or magistrates, whom we may suppose elected by the suffrages of the commu-nity, and whom we must assume to be voluntarily obeyed by them. The division of the produce would in like manner be a public act. The principle might either be that of complete equal-ity, or of apportionment to the necessities or deserts of individu-als, in whatever manner might be conformable to the ideas of justice or policy prevailing in the community.

Examples of such associations, on a small scale, are the monastic orders, the Moravians, the followers of Rapp, and others: and from the hopes which they hold out of relief from the miseries and iniquities of a state of much inequality of wealth, schemes for a larger application of the same idea have reappeared and become popular at all periods of active speculation on the first principles of society.

Examination of Communism*

Whatever may be the merits or defects of these various schemes, they cannot be truly said to be impracticable. No reasonable person can doubt that a village community, composed of a few thousand inhabitants cultivating in joint ownership the same extent of land which at present feeds that number of people, and producing by combined labour and the most improved processes the manufactured articles which they required, could raise an amount of productions sufficient to maintain them in comfort; and would find the means of obtaining, and if need be, exacting, the quantity of labour necessary for this purpose, from every member of the association who was capable of work. . . .

A more real difficulty is that of fairly apportioning the labour of the community among its members. There are many kinds of work, and by what standard are they to be measured one against another? Who is to judge how much cotton spinning, or distributing goods from the stores, or bricklaying, or chimney sweeping, is equivalent to so much ploughing? The difficulty of making the adjustment between different qualities of labour is so strongly felt by Communist writers, that they have usually thought it necessary to provide that all should work by turns at every description of useful labour: an arrangement which, by putting an end to the division of employments, would sacrifice so much of the advantage of co-operative production as greatly to diminish the productiveness of labour. Besides, even in the

*Mill does not, of course, refer to the communism of our century, surely an abomination to the author of *On Liberty*. In his day the word referred to vague egalitarian schemes, then in vogue among Utopian reformers.

same kind of work, nominal equality of labour would be so great a real inequality, that the feeling of justice would revolt against its being enforced. All persons are not equally fit for all labour; and the same quantity of labour is an unequal burthen on the weak and the strong, the hardy and the delicate, the quick and the slow, the dull and the intelligent.

But these difficulties, though real, are not necessarily insuperable. The apportionment of work to the strength and capacities of individuals, the mitigation of a general rule to provide for cases in which it would operate harshly, are not problems to which human intelligence, guided by a sense of justice, would be inadequate. And the worst and most unjust arrangement which could be made of these points, under a system aiming at equality, would be so far short of the inequality and injustice with which labour (not to speak of remuneration) is now apportioned, as to be scarcely worth counting in the comparison. We must remember too, that Communism, as a system of society, exists only in idea; that its difficulties, at present, are much better understood than its resources; and that the intellect of mankind is only beginning to contrive the means of organizing it in detail, so as to overcome the one and derive the greatest advantage from the other.

Communism vs. Present State of Society

If, therefore, the choice were to be made between Communism with all its chances, and the present state of society with all its sufferings and injustices; if the institution of private property necessarily carried with it as a consequence, that the produce of labour should be apportioned as we now see it, almost in an inverse ratio to the labour—the largest portions to those who have never worked at all, the next largest to those whose work is almost nominal, and so in a descending scale, the remuneration dwindling as the work grows harder and more disagreeable, until the most fatiguing and exhausting bodily labour cannot count with certainty on being able to earn even the necessaries of life; if this or Communism were the alternative, all the difficulties, great or small, of Communism would be but as dust in the balance.

But to make the comparison applicable, we must compare Communism at its best, with the régime of individual property, not as it is, but as it might be made. The principle of private property has never yet had a fair trial in any country; and less so, perhaps, in this country than in some others. The social arrangements of modern Europe commenced from a distribution of property which was the result, not of just partition, or acquisition by industry, but of conquest and violence: and notwithstanding what industry has been doing for many centuries to modify the work of force, the system still retains many and large traces of its origin. The laws of property have never yet conformed to the principles on which the justification of private property rests. They have made property of things which never ought to be property, and absolute property where only a qualified property ought to exist. They have not held the balance fairly between human beings, but have heaped impediments upon some, to give advantage to others; they have purposely fostered inequalities, and prevented all from starting fair in the race. That all should indeed start on perfectly equal terms, is inconsistent with any law of private property: but if as much pains as has been taken to aggravate the inequality of chances arising from the natural working of the principle, had been taken to temper that inequality by every means not subversive of the principle itself; if the tendency of legislation had been to favour the diffusion, instead of the concentration of wealth—to encourage the subdivision of the large masses, instead of striving to keep them together; the principle of individual property would have been found to have no necessary connexion with the physical and social evils which almost all Socialist writers assume to be inseparable from it.

Private property, in every defence made of it, is supposed to mean the guarantee to individuals of the fruits of their own labour and abstinence. The guarantee to them of the fruits of the labour and abstinence of others, transmitted to them without any merit or exertion of their own, is not of the essence of the institution, but a mere incidental consequence, which, when it reaches a certain height, does not promote, but conflicts with, the ends which render private property legitimate. To judge of the final destination of the institution of property, we must suppose everything rectified, which causes the institution to work in a manner opposed to that equitable principle, of proportion between remuneration and exertion, on which in every vindication of it that will bear the light, it is assumed to be grounded.

We must also suppose two conditions realized, without which neither Communism nor any other laws or institutions could make the condition of the mass of mankind other than degraded and miserable. One of these conditions is, universal education; the other, a due limitation of the numbers of the community. With these, there could be no poverty, even under the present social institutions: and these being supposed, the question of Socialism is not, as generally stated by Socialists, a question of flying to the sole refuge against the evils which now bear down humanity; but a mere question of comparative advantages, which futurity must determine. We are too ignorant either of what individual agency in its best form, or Socialism in its best form, can accomplish, to be qualified to decide which of the two will be the ultimate form of human society.

Crucial Role of Liberty

If a conjecture may be hazarded, the decision will probably depend mainly on one consideration, viz. which of the two systems is consistent with the greatest amount of human liberty and spontaneity. After the means of subsistence are assured, the next in strength of the personal wants of human beings is liberty; and (unlike the physical wants, which as civilization advances become more moderate and more amenable to control) it increases instead of diminishing in intensity, as the intelligence and the moral faculties are more developed. The perfection both of social arrangements and of practical morality would be, to secure to all persons complete independence and freedom of action, subject to no restriction but that of not doing injury to others: and the education which taught or the social institutions which required them to exchange the control of their own actions for any amount of comfort or affluence, or to renounce liberty for the sake of equality, would deprive them of one of the most elevated characteristics of human nature.

It remains to be discovered how far the preservation of this characteristic would be found compatible with the Communistic organization of society.* No doubt, this, like all the other objections to the Socialist schemes, is vastly exaggerated. The members of the association need not be required to live together more than they do now, nor need they be controlled in the disposal of their individual share of the produce, and of the probably large amount of leisure which, if they limited their production to things really worth producing, they would possess. Individuals need not be chained to an occupation, or to a particular locality. The restraints of Communism would be freedom in comparison with the present condition of the majority of the human race. The generality of labourers in this and most other countries, have as little choice of occupation or freedom of locomotion, are practically as dependent on fixed rules and on the will of others, as they could be on any system short of actual slavery; to say nothing of the entire domestic subjection of one half the species, to which it is the signal honour of Owenism and most other forms of Socialism that they assign equal rights, in all respects, with those of the hitherto dominant sex.

But it is not by comparison with the present bad state of society that the claims of Communism can be estimated; nor is it sufficient that it should promise greater personal and mental freedom than is now enjoyed by those who have not enough of either to deserve the name. The question is, whether there would be any asylum left for individuality of character; whether public opinion would not be a tyrannical yoke; whether the absolute dependence of each on all, and surveillance of each by all, would not grind all down into a tame uniformity of thoughts, feelings, and actions. This is already one of the glaring evils of the existing state of society, notwithstanding a much greater diversity of education and pursuits, and a much less absolute dependence of the individual on the mass, than would exist in the Communistic

*I remind the reader that Mill is writing in the 1840s, and that Communism refers to various Utopian blueprints for society that were beginning to appear.

régime. No society in which eccentricity is a matter of reproach, can be in a wholesome state. It is yet to be ascertained whether the Communistic scheme would be consistent with that multiform development of human nature, those manifold unlikenesses, that diversity of tastes and talents, and variety of intellectual points of view, which not only form a great part of the interest of human life, but by bringing intellects into stimulating collision, and by presenting to each innumerable notions that he would not have conceived of himself, are the mainspring of mental and moral progression.

The whole chapter evokes Mill's personality—moral intensity balanced by scrupulous fairness, utopian yearnings side by side with a recognition of practical difficulties. The final passage, in its denunciation of the intellectual and political intolerance that might accompany socialism bespeaks a disturbing historical prevision, although I should add that Mill never heard of Marx, much less Marxism.

What we have here, however, is not an attempt to anticipate history, but the foundation of the text-within-a-text on which I wish to concentrate attention. The larger, encompassing text consists of the systematic enunciation of the "principles" of political economy, rather in the manner of a textbook. The text within is a scenario of socioeconomic evolution, comparable to that of Smith or Ricardo, but with a difference. The difference is that the scenario unfolds not merely as the consequence of the operation of impersonal forces, but because these forces make possible the intervention of conscious human intent into historical evolution. This intent utilizes the favorable outcome of historical forces to create a society that conjoins private property with a high degree of socioeconomic equality. This will be Mill's unique design for a worker-run, competitive, libertarian society.

To reach that scenario we must read through, or pass by, many chapters of the "textbook"—chapters on slavery, peasants, cottage industry; wages, rents and profits; value and money; international trade, and a great deal more—some 600 pages in all—until we reach Book IV, Chapter II: "The Influence of the Progress of Industry and Population on Rents, Profits and Wages." Here Mill examines different "models"—to use a modern term—to deduce what happens when population, capital, and technology change their relative positions vis-a-vis one another, and finally settles on what he considers the most likely case, population and the quantity of capital both growing, and the level of technology improving.

This has results that look at first much like the Ricardian scenario: (1) the rise in population forces less fertile lands into use, raising the price of food, and therefore the wages needed to procure the worker's subsistence as well as the rents that accrue to superior lands as a consequence of pushing lands of lesser fertility into cultivation; (2) the rise in wages and rents squeezes capitalist profits; (3) improvements in agricultural machinery serve temporarily to mitigate the squeeze; but (4) in the end, the steady increase of population benefits the landlord and hurts the capitalist. Like Ricardo, it is a vision of an approaching stationary state, perhaps held in abeyance by "commercial revulsions," or unexpected new technologies, or the import of cheap machines, but in the end suffering the inescapable fate of a capitalist system that cannot generate enough profits to grow.

What, then is the difference from Ricardo? Mill sees in the attainment of such a state not an end, but a beginning. It will and it can be the launching platform for the worker's cooperatives that he envisions as the possible outcome of the system's dynamics. Here we can do no better than to reproduce much of Mill's own chapter on the subject:

Chapter VI

Of the Stationary State

[*Stationary state of wealth and population is dreaded and deprecated by writers*] The preceding chapters comprise the general theory of the economical progress of society, in the sense in which those terms are commonly understood; the progress of capital, of population, and of the productive arts. But in contemplating any progressive movement, not in its nature unlimited, the mind is not satisfied with merely tracing the laws of the movement; it cannot but ask the further question, to what goal? Towards what ultimate point is society tending by its industrial progress? When the progress ceases, in what condition are we to expect that it will leave mankind?

It must always have been seen, more or less distinctly, by political economists, that the increase of wealth is not boundless: that at the end of what they term the progressive state lies the stationary state, that all progress in wealth is but a postponement of this, and that each step in advance is an approach to it. We have now been led to recognise that this ultimate goal is at all times near enough to be fully in view; that we are always on the verge of it, and that if we have not reached it long ago, it is because the goal itself flies before us. The richest and most prosperous countries would very soon attain the stationary state, if no further improvements were made in the productive arts, and if there were a suspension of the overflow of capital from those countries into the uncultivated or ill-cultivated regions of the earth.

This impossibility of ultimately avoiding the stationary state— this irresistible necessity that the stream of human industry should finally spread itself out into an apparently stagnant sea— must have been, to the political economists of the last two generations, an unpleasing and discouraging prospect; for the tone and tendency of their speculations goes completely to identify all that is economically desirable with the progressive state, and ... with that alone. Adam Smith always assumes that the condition of the mass of the people, though it may not be positively distressed, must be pinched and stinted in a stationary condition of wealth, and can only be satisfactory in a progressive state. The doctrine that, to however distant a time incessant struggling may put off our doom, the progress of society must "end in shallows and in miseries," far from being, as many people still believe, a wicked invention of Mr. Malthus, was either expressly or tacitly affirmed by his most distinguished predecessors, and can only be successfully combated on his principles. Before attention had been directed to the principle of population as the active force in determining the remuneration of labour, of population as the active force in determining the remuneration of labour, the increase of mankind was virtually treated as a constant quantity; it was, at all events, assumed that in the natural and normal state of human affairs population must constantly increase, from which it followed that a constant increase of the means of support was essential to the physical comfort of the mass of mankind. The publication of Mr. Malthus' Essay is the era from which better views of this subject must be dated; and notwithstanding the acknowledged errors of his first edition, few writers have done more than himself, in the subsequent editions, to promote these juster and more hopeful anticipations. . . .

[But the Stationary State is Not in Itself Undesirable]

I cannot, therefore, regard the stationary state of capital and wealth with the unaffected aversion so generally manifested towards it by political economists of the old school. I am inclined to believe that it would be, on the whole, a very considerable improvement on our present condition. I confess I am not charmed with the ideal of life held out by those who think that the normal state of human beings is that of struggling to get on; that the trampling, crushing, elbowing, and treading on each other's heels, which form the existing type of social life, are the most desirable lot of human kind, or anything but the disagreeable symptoms of one of the phases of industrial progress. . . .

That the energies of mankind should be kept in employment by the struggle for riches, as they were formerly by the struggle of war, until the better minds succeed in educating the others into better things, is undoubtedly more desirable than that they should rust and stagnate. While minds are coarse they require coarse stimuli, and let them have them. In the meantime, those who do not accept the present very early stage of human improvement as its ultimate type, may be excused for being comparatively indifferent to the kind of economical progress which excites the congratulations of ordinary politicians; the mere increase of production and accumulation. For the safety of national independence it is essential that a country should not fall much behind its neighbours in these things. But in themselves they are of little importance, so long as either the increase of population or anything else prevents the mass of the people from reaping any part of the benefit of them. I know not why it should be matter of congratulation that persons who are already richer than any one needs to be, should have doubled their means of consuming things which give little or no pleasure except as representative of wealth; or that numbers of individuals should pass over, every year, from the middle classes into a richer class, or from the class of the occupied rich to that of the unoccupied. It is only in the backward countries of the world that increased production is still an important object: in those most advanced, what is economically needed is a better distribution, of which one indispensable means is a stricter restraint on population. Levelling institutions, either of a just or of an unjust kind, cannot alone accomplish it; they may lower the heights of society, but they cannot, of themselves, permanently raise the depths.

On the other hand, we may suppose this better distribution of property attained, by the joint effect of the prudence and frugality of individuals, and of a system of legislation favouring equality of fortunes, so far as is consistent with the just claim of the individual to the fruits, whether great or small, of his or her own industry. We may suppose, for instance . . . , a limitation of the sum which any one person may acquire by gift or inheritance, to the amount sufficient to constitute a moderate independence. Under this two-fold influence, society would exhibit these leading features: a well-paid and affluent body of labourers; no enormous fortunes, except what were earned and accumulated during a single lifetime; but a much larger body of persons than at present, not only exempt from the coarser toils, but with sufficient leisure, both physical and mental, from mechanical details, to cultivate freely the graces of life, and afford examples of them to the classes less favourably circumstanced for their growth. This condition of society, so greatly preferable to the present, is not only perfectly compatible with the stationary state, but, it would seem, more naturally allied with that state than with any other.

It is scarcely necessary to remark that a stationary condition of capital and population implies no stationary state of human improvement. There would be as much scope as ever for all kinds of mental culture, and moral and social progress; as much room for improving the Art of Living, and much more likelihood of its being improved, when minds ceased to be engrossed by the art of getting on. Even the industrial arts might be as earnestly and as successfully cultivated, with this sole difference, that instead of serving no purpose but the increase of wealth, industrial improvements would produce their legitimate effect, that of abridging labor. Hitherto it is questionable if all the mechanical inventions yet made have lightened the day's toil of any human being. They have enabled a greater population to live the same life of drudgery and imprisonment, and an increased number of manufacturers and others to make fortunes. They have increased the comforts of the middle classes. But they have not yet begun to effect those great changes in human destiny, which it is in their nature and in their futurity to accomplish. Only when, in addition to just institutions, the increase of mankind shall be under the deliberate guidance of judicious foresight, can the conquests made from the powers of nature by the intellect and energy of scientific discoverers, become the common property of the species, and the means of improving and elevating the universal lot.

———————

Thus the lengthy consideration of the stationary state, with its mixture of a buoyant spirit and a saving realism ("while men's minds are coarse they require coarse stimuli, and let them have them"), brings us to the threshold of social change announced in the title of the next chapter: "On the Probable Futurity of the Labouring Class." It is not, let us make clear at the outset, a leap into socialism. The "probable futurity" of the working class is better seen as a series of gradual assertions of its potential for social management—a futurity that has been opened up precisely because the stationary state has taken away the ongoing expansion that was the ultimate raison d'être of the system.

This forward-looking sketch begins with a brief statement of how things now stand:

Chapter VII

On the Probable Futurity of the Laboring Classes

Considered in its moral and social aspect, the state of the labouring people has latterly been a subject of much more speculation and discussion than formerly; and the opinion that it is not now what it ought to be, has become very general. The suggestions which have been promulgated, and the controversies which have been excited, on detached points rather than on the foundations of the subject, have put in evidence the existence of two conflicting theories, respecting the social position desirable for manual labourers. The one may be called the theory of dependence and protection, the other that of self-dependence.

According to the former theory, the lot of the poor, in all things which affect them collectively, should be regulated *for* them, not *by* them. They should not be required or encouraged to think for themselves, or give to their own reflection or forecast an influential voice in the determination of their destiny. It is supposed to be the duty of the higher classes to think for them, and to take the responsibility of their lot, as the commander and officers of an army take that of the soldiers composing it. This function, it is contended, the higher classes should prepare themselves to perform conscientiously, and their whole demeanour should impress the poor with a reliance on it, in order that, while yielding passive and active obedience to the rules prescribed for them, they may resign themselves in all other respects to a trustful *insouciance*, and repose under the shadow of their protectors. The relation between rich and poor, according to this theory (a theory also applied to the relation between men and women) should be only partly authoritative; it should be amiable, moral, and sentimental: affectionate tutelage on the one side, respectful and grateful deference on the other. The rich should be *in loco parentis* to the poor, guiding and restraining them like children.

Of spontaneous action on their part there should be no need. They should be called on for nothing but to do their day's work, and to be moral and religious. Their morality and religion should be provided for them by their superiors, who should see them properly taught it, and should do all that is necessary to ensure their being, in return for labour and attachment, properly fed, clothed, housed, spiritually edified, and innocently amused.

This state of affairs, Mill notes, is designed for a period in which "lawless violence and insecurity" might be prevalent, and would no longer be needed when the working class felt more secure and gained some foothold in society, not least that of literacy. He goes on to say that:

the relation of masters and workpeople will be gradually super- seded by partnership, in one of two forms: in some cases, associ- ation of the laborers with the capitalist; in others, and perhaps finally in all, association of laborers among themselves.

The first of these forms of association has long been practised, not indeed as a rule, but as an exception. In several departments of industry there are already cases in which everyone who con- tributes to the work, either by labor or by pecuniary resources, has a partner's interest in it, proportional to the value of his con- tribution. It is already a common practice to remunerate those in whom peculiar trust is reposed, by means of a percentage on the profits: and cases exist in which the principle is, with excellent success, carried down to the class of mere manual laborers.

The form of association, however, which if mankind continue to improve, must be expected in the end to predominate, is not that which can exist between a capitalist as chief, and workpeo- ple without a voice in the management, but the association of the laborers themselves on terms of equality, collectively owning the capital with which they carry on their operations, and work- ing under managers elected and removable by themselves. . . . So long as this idea remained in a state of theory, from the pro- gressive advance of the co-operative movement, a great increase may be looked for even in the aggregate productiveness of industry. The sources of the increase are two-fold. In the first place, the class of mere distributors, who are not producers but auxiliaries of production, and whose inordinate numbers, far more than the gains of capitalists, are the cause why so great a portion of the wealth produced does not reach the producers—will be reduced to more modest dimensions. . . .

The other mode in which co-operation tends, still more efficaciously, to increase the productiveness of labor, consists in the vast stimulus given to productive energies, by placing the laborers, as a mass, in a relation to their work which would make it their principle and their interest—at present it is neither—to do the utmost instead of the least possible in exchange for their remuneration. It is scarcely possible to rate too highly this material benefit, which yet is as nothing compared with the moral revolution in society that would accompany it: the healing of the standing feud between capital and labor; the transformation of human life, from a conflict of classes struggling for opposite interests, to a friendly rivalry in the pursuit of a good common to all; the elevation of the dignity of labor, a new sense of security and independence in the laboring class, and the conversion of each human being's daily occupation into a school of the social sympathies and the practical intelligence. . . .

When, however, co-operative societies shall have sufficiently multiplied, it is not probable that any but the least valuable workpeople will any longer consent to work all their lives for wages merely: and both private capitalists and associations will gradually find it necessary to make the entire body of laborers participants in profits. Eventually, and in perhaps a less remote future than may be supposed, we may, through the co-operative principle, see our way to a change in society, which would combine the freedom and independence of the individual, with the moral, intellectual, and economical advantages of aggregate production; and which, without violence or spoliation, or even any sudden disturbance of existing habits and expectations, would realize, at least in the industrial department, the best aspirations of the democratic spirit, by putting an end to the division of society into the industrious and the idle, and effacing all social distinctions but those fairly earned by personal services and exertions.

As this change proceeded, owners of capital would gradually find it to their advantage, instead of maintaining the struggle of the old system with work-people of only the worst description, to lend their capital to the associations; to do this at a diminishing rate of interest, and at last, perhaps, even to exchange their capital for terminable annuities. In this or some such mode, the existing accumulations of capital might honestly, and by a kind of spontaneous process, become in the end the joint property of all who participate in their productive employment: a transformation which, thus effected (and assuming of course that both sexes participate equally in the rights and in the government of the association) would be the nearest approach to social justice, and the most beneficial ordering of industrial affairs for the universal good, which it is possible at present to foresee.

What we have then is a sketch of a gradual restructuring of society from one of forelock-tugging underlings to an association of social equals. Such a transformation must today seem hopelessly unrealistic. Yet, it is worth bearing in mind that for a time, in the post-World War II era, some such cooperatization of Swedish industry seemed within reach. Perhaps, if conditions change, the scenario may reappear, in at least some countries. Here one last remark seems necessary. Realistic or not, what Mill has given us is a remarkable exercise in social imagination. For the transformation itself ultimately depends on the advent of the stationary state where profits would be under heavy pressure. Otherwise why would employers be tempted to sell out to their workers, no matter how generous their annuities? Thus Mill has changed the stationary state from a feared terminus of social dynamics to a possible staging area for social advance. Unlike Marx, to whose work we will turn next, radical social change is envisioned as a peaceful process.

There remains only one important element to add to the text-within-a-text. The advent of workers' cooperatives will be a slow and long drawn out process. Meanwhile, something like the current state of capitalism is likely to continue, the pressure on profits being relieved, from time to time, by "convulsions in trade," imports of cheaper machines, and the advent of new agricultural machinery.

In this period of slowly maturing capitalism—and indeed, afterward, in the emerging society of workers' cooperatives—what is to be the role of government? In particular, what is to be its reach into the private sector, its legitimate use of regulatory or other means of influencing the direction of socioeconomic affairs?

Here we find Mill addressing directly a question that is very much at the heart of contemporary affairs, which workers' cooperatives are not. So we turn to the final chapter of the *Principles:*

Chapter XI

Of the Grounds and Limits of the Laissez-Faire or Non-interference Principle

We must set out by distinguishing between two kinds of intervention by the government, which, though they may relate to the same subjects, differ widely in their nature and effects, and require for their justification, motives of a very different degree of urgency. The intervention may extend to controlling the free agency of individuals. Government may interdict all persons from doing certain things; or from doing them without its authorization; or may prescribe to them certain things to be done, or a certain manner of doing things which it is left optional with them to do or to abstain from. This is the *authoritative* interference of government. There is another kind of intervention which is not authoritative: when a government, instead of issuing a command and enforcing it by penalties, adopts the course so seldom resorted to by governments, and of which such important use might be made, that of giving advice, and promulgating information; or when, leaving individuals free to use their own means of pursuing any object of general interest, the government, not meddling with them, but not trusting the object solely to their care, establishes, side by side with their arrangements, an agency of its own for a like purpose. Thus, it is one thing to maintain a Church Establishment, and another to refuse toleration to other religions, or to persons professing no religion. It is one thing to provide schools or colleges, and another to require that no person shall act as an instructor of youth without a government license. There might be a national bank, or a government manufactory, without any monopoly against private banks and manufactories. There might be a post office, without penalties against the conveyance of letters by other means. There may be a corps of government engineers for civil purposes, while the profession of a civil engineer is free to be adopted by every one. There may be public hospitals, without any restriction upon private medical or surgical practice.

Whatever theory we adopt respecting the foundation of the social union, and under whatever political institutions we live, there is a circle around every individual human being, which no government, be it that of one, of a few, or of the many, ought to be permitted to overstep: there is a part of the life of every person who has come to years of discretion within which the individuality of that person ought to reign uncontrolled either by any other individual or by the public collectively. That there is, or ought to be, some space in human existence thus entrenched around, and sacred from authoritative intrusion, no one who professes the smallest regard to human freedom or dignity will call in question: the point to be determined is, where the limit should be placed; how large a province of human life this reserved territory should include. I apprehend that it ought to include all that part which concerns only the life, whether inward or outward, of the individual, and does not affect the interests of others, or affects them only through the moral influence of example. With respect to the domain of the inward consciousness, the thoughts and feelings, and as much of external conduct as is personal only, involving no consequences, none at least of a painful or injurious kind, to other people; I hold that it is allowable in all, and in the more thoughtful and cultivated often a duty, to assert and promulgate, with all the force they are capable of, their opinion of what is good or bad, admirable or contemptible, but not to compel others to conform to that opinion; whether the force used is that of extra-legal coercion, or exerts itself by means of the law.

Even in those portions of conduct which do affect the interest of others, the onus of making out a case always lies on the defenders of legal prohibitions. It is not a merely constructive or presumptive injury to others, which will justify the interference of law with individual freedom. To be prevented from doing what one is inclined to, or from acting according to one's own judgment of what is desirable, is not only always irksome, but always tends, *pro tanto*, to starve the development of some portion of the bodily or mental faculties, either sensitive or active; and unless the conscience of the individual goes freely with the legal restraint, it partakes, either in a great or in a small degree, of the degradation of slavery. Scarcely any degree of utility, short of absolute necessity, will justify a prohibitory regulation, unless it can also be made to recommend itself to the general conscience; unless persons of ordinary good intentions either believe already, or can be induced to believe, that the thing prohibited is a thing which they ought not to wish to do.

It is otherwise with governmental interferences which do not restrain individual free agency. When a government provides means for fulfilling a certain end, leaving individuals free to avail themselves of different means if in their opinion preferable, there is no infringement of liberty, no irksome or degrading restraint. One of the principal objections to government interference is then absent. There is, however, in almost all forms of government agency, one thing which is compulsory; the provision of the pecuniary means. These are derived from taxation; or, if existing in the form of an endowment derived from public property, they are still the cause of as much compulsory taxation as the sale of the annual proceeds of the property would enable to be dispensed with. And the objection necessarily attaching to compulsory contributions, is almost always greatly aggravated by the expensive precautions and onerous restrictions, which are indispensable to prevent evasion of a compulsory tax.

It is, we can see, a restatement of the principles of liberty from which we began our study of Mill, and it is therefore not surprising that the chapter leads, after some consideration of special cases, to the conclusion that "*Laissez-faire* . . . should be the general practice; every departure from it, unless required by some great good, is a certain evil." We have but to turn a few pages of the chapter, however, to discover exceptions to this "general practice. There are, in fact, sixteen of them, the first few innocuous, the last two certainly not. Let us look at both ends of the spectrum.

1. Cases in which the consumer is an incompetent judge of the commodity: The case in question takes us by surprise—it is not "the material objects produced for his use." Of these, says Mill, "he is generally the best judge," although he adds "even this is not true universally." It is "things which are chiefly useful as tending to raise the character of human beings," of which, in turn, the chief example is *education*. Thus, Mill concludes:

> I hold it therefore the duty of government to [give] pecuniary support to elementary schools, such as to render them accessible to the poor, either freely, or for a payment too inconssiderable to be sensibly felt.

2. Cases of persons exercising power over others. Here the issue is the protection of children—and animals:

> To take an example from the peculiar province of political economy; it is right that children, and young persons not yet arrived at maturity, should be protected, so far as the eye and hand of the state can reach, from being over-worked. Laboring for too many hours in the day, or on work beyond their strength, should not be permitted to them, for if permitted it may always be compelled. Freedom of contract, in the case of children, is but another word for freedom of coercion. Education also, the best which circumstances admit of their receiving, is not a thing which parents or relatives, from indifference, jealousy, or avarice, should have it in their power to withhold.

> The reasons for legal intervention in favor of children, apply not less strongly to the case of those unfortunate slaves and vic-

tims of the most brutal part of mankind, the lower animals. It is by the grossest misunderstanding of the principles of liberty, that the infliction of exemplary punishment or ruffianism practised towards these defenceless creatures, has been treated as a meddling by government with things beyond its province; an interference with domestic life. The domestic life of domestic tyrants is one of the things which it is the most imperative on the law to interfere with; and it is to be regretted that metaphysical scruples respecting the nature and source of the authority of government, should induce many warm supporters of laws against cruelty to animals, to seek for a justification of such laws in the incidental consequences of the indulgence of ferocious habits, to the interests of human beings, rather than in the intrinsic merits of the case itself.

But now we come to the end of the list. The exceptions still begin harmlessly enough with colonization. Too much in the spirit of his time, Mill holds that government must play a tutelary role for peoples who have not developed our skills and knowledge; and from this he moves on, more unexceptionably, to support for "voyages of geographic or scientific exploration." Then, suddenly, we reach an astonishing change. The libertarian who begins with the principle that "every departure from the principle of laissez-faire is a certain evil" ends with a bold vision of government that in many ways embraces the tenets of the modern welfare state.

Here we must read the words themselves:

It may be said generally, that anything which it is desirable should be done for the general interests of mankind or of future generations, or for the present interests of those members of the community who require external aid, but which is not of a nature to remunerate individuals or associations for undertaking it, is in itself a suitable thing to be undertaken by government: though, before making the work their own, governments ought always to consider if there be any rational probability of its being done on what is called the voluntary principle, and if so, whether it is likely to be done in a better or more effectual manner by government agency, than by the zeal and liberality of individuals.

And this is not yet the finale. In case #16, he examines instances in which "private agency" is lacking, and therefore government must undertake the effort.

The business of society can be best performed by private and voluntary agency. It is, however, necessary to add, that the intervention of government cannot always practically stop short at the limit which defines the cases intrinsically suitable for it. In the particular circumstances of a given age or nation, there is scarcely anything, really important to the general interest, which it may not be desirable, or even necessary, that the government should take upon itself, not because private individuals cannot effectually perform it, but because they will not. At some times and places there will be no roads, docks, harbors, canals, works of irrigation, hospitals, schools, colleges, printing presses, unless the government establishes them; the public being either too poor to command the necessary resources, or too little advanced in intelligence to appreciate the ends, or not sufficiently practised in joint action to be capable of the means. This is true, more or less, of all countries inured to despotism, and particularly of those in which there is a very wide distance in civilization between the people and the government: as in those which have been conquered and are retained in subjection by a more energetic and more cultivated people.

In many parts of the world, the people can do nothing for themselves which requires large means and combined action; all such things are left undone, unless done by the state. In these cases, the mode in which the government can most surely demonstrate the sincerity with which it intends the greatest good of its subjects, is by doing the things which are made incumbent on it by the helplessness of the public, in such a manner as shall tend not to increase and perpetuate but to correct that helplessness. A good government will give all its aid in such a shape, as to encourage and nurture any rudiments it may find of a spirit of individual exertion. It will be assiduous in removing obstacles and discouragements to voluntary enterprise, and in giving whatever facilities and whatever direction and guidance may be necessary: its pecuniary means will be applied, when practicable, in aid of private efforts rather than in supersession of them, and it will call into play its machinery of rewards and honors to elicit such efforts. Government aid, when given merely in default of private enterprise, should be so given as to be as far as possible a course of education for the people in the art of accomplishing great objects by individual energy and voluntary co-operation.

I have not thought it necessary here to insist on that part of the functions of government which all admit to be indispensable, the function of prohibiting and punishing such conduct on the part of individuals in the exercise of their freedom, as is clearly injurious to other persons, whether the case be one of force, fraud, or negligence. Even in the best state which society has yet reached, it is lamentable to think how great a proportion of all the efforts and talents in the world are employed in merely neutralizing one another. It is the proper end of government to reduce this wretched waste to the smallest possible amount, by taking such measures as shall cause the energies now spent by mankind in injuring one another, or in protecting themselves against injury, to be turned to the legitimate employment of the human faculties, that of compelling the powers of nature to be more and more subservient to physical and moral good.

Is there a need to give some summative judgment to this extraordinary attempt to combine moral judgment and economic analysis? I think not. Mill's voice is not one that speaks to today's world, so much the worse for us, but it is a voice one hopes will find resonance some time in the future.

IV

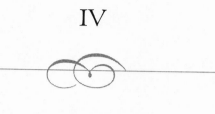

KARL

MARX

KARL MARX

(1818–1883)

The collected works of Karl Marx and his lifelong friend and collaborator Friedrich Engels comprise forty volumes, each 700 to 1,000 pages in length. I have room for no more than one-tenth of one percent of those pages here, a daunting state of affairs, to which I shall respond as follows. First, there will be no room for many documents of great historical importance, such as the wonderful historical essays on *The Class Struggles in France* or *The Eighteenth Brumaire of Louis Bonaparte,* as well as many philosophical pieces. All these are indispensable for the study of Marx, but not for an appreciation of his economics. For that we must turn to *Capital,* by general agreement his masterwork. Its three main volumes fill over 2,500 pages, not counting the three supplementary volumes of *Theories of Surplus Value.*[38]

In the circumstances, my starting point is pre-ordained: it must be the first chapter—or rather, portions of this lengthy, often difficult, but always remarkable chapter—of *Capital.*

---

[38] Karl Marx, *Capital: A Critique of Political Economy*, New York: Random House, Vintage Books, 1977. I have omitted the numerous, often long and interesting footnotes, and added breaks, as before. For easy reference see also *The Marx-Engels Reader*, 2d ed. Robert Tucker, ed. New York: W. W. Norton, 1978, pp. 302 ff.

Chapter I

Commodities

The wealth of those societies in which the capitalist mode of production prevails, presents itself as "an immense accumulation of commodities," its unit being a single commodity. Our investigation must therefore begin with the analysis of a commodity.

A commodity is, in the first place, an object outside us, a thing that by its properties satisfies human wants of some sort or another. The nature of such wants, whether, for instance, they spring from the stomach or from fancy, makes no difference. Neither are we here concerned to know how the object satisfies these wants, whether directly as means of subsistence, or indirectly as means of production.

Every useful thing, as iron, paper, &c., may be looked at from the two points of view of quality and quantity. It is an assemblage of many properties, and may therefore be of use in various ways. To discover the various uses of things is the work of history. So also is the establishment of socially-recognised standards of measure for the quantities of these useful objects. The diversity of these measures has its origin partly in the diverse nature of the objects to be measured, partly in convention.

The utility of a thing makes it a use-value. But this utility is not a thing of air. Being limited by the physical properties of the commodity, it has no existence apart from that commodity. A commodity, such as iron, corn, or a diamond, is therefore, so far as it is a material thing, a use-value, something useful. This property of a commodity is independent of the amount of labour required to appropriate its useful qualities. When treating of use-value, we always assume to be dealing with definite quantities, such as dozens of watches, yards of linen, or tons of iron. The use-values of commodities furnish the material for a special study, that of the commercial knowledge of commodities. Use-values become a reality only by use or consumption: they also constitute the substance of all wealth, whatever may be the social form of that wealth. In the form of society we are about to consider, they are, in addition, the material depositories of exchange-value.

Exchange-value, at first sight, presents itself as a quantitative relation, as the proportion in which values in use of one sort are exchanged for those of another sort, a relation constantly changing with time and place. Hence exchange-value appears to be something accidental and purely relative, and consequently an intrinsic value, *i.e.*, an exchange-value that is inseparably connected with, inherent in commodities, seems a contradiction in terms. Let us consider the matter a little more closely. . . .

Let us take two commodities, *e.g.*, corn and iron. The proportions in which they are exchangeable, whatever those proportions may be, can always be represented by an equation in which a given quantity of corn is equated to some quantity of iron: *e.g.*, 1 quarter corn = x cwt. iron. What does this equation tell us? It tells us that in two different things—in 1 quarter of corn and x cwt. of iron, there exists in equal quantities something common to both. The two things must therefore be equal to a third, which in itself is neither the one nor the other. Each of them, so far as it is exchange-value, must therefore be reducible to this third.

This common "something" cannot be a geometrical, physical, chemical or other natural property of commodities. Such properties come into consideration only to the extent that they make the commodities useful, *i.e.* turn them into use-values. But clearly, the exchange relation of commodities is characterized precisely by its abstraction from their use-values,

––––––––––

Quoting from the seventeenth century pamphleteer Nicholas Barbon, Marx writes: "One hundred pounds worth of lead or iron is of as great a value as one hundred pounds worth of silver or gold."[39] What, then, is the ultimate thing to which exchange values will have to be reduced? We are not surprised to discover that it is labor; Smith already believed that labor was the sole source of value in the early stages of human society, before land came to be privately owned and capital first appeared. Ricardo went Smith

[39] Op. cit., p. 127–28.

one better by removing land from consideration because, as we have seen, it was only a claimant on value, not a source of it. Ricardo similarly downgraded the contribution of capital to "6 or 7 percent," which he believed to be the minimum profit rate that capital required, causing the late Nobelist George Stigler to call Ricardo's formulation "the 93 percent labor theory of value."[40] But Marx goes all the way:

If then we leave out of consideration the use-value of commodities, they have only one common property left, that of being products of labour. But even the product of labour itself has undergone a change in our hands. If we make abstraction from its use-value, we make abstraction at the same time from the material elements and shapes that make the product a use-value; we see in it no longer a table, a house, yarn, or any other useful thing. Its existence as a material thing is put out of sight. Neither can it any longer be regarded as the product of the labour of the joiner, the mason, the spinner, or of any other definite kind of productive labour. Along with the useful qualities of the products themselves, we put out of sight both the useful character of the various kinds of labour embodied in them, and the concrete forms of that labour; there is nothing left but what is common to them all; all are reduced to one and the same sort of labour, human labour in the abstract.

It is these last words—"in the abstract"—that decisively separate Marx from Ricardo, or from his more distant predecessors such as Aristotle, who, we remember, also identified labor as the great common denominator of exchange. For the "abstract" aspect of labor on which Marx lays such special emphasis allows him to see that labor in exchange is different from living labor. The difference is that abstract labor becomes a commodity called *labor-power;* and a commodity, as we shall next see, is a very peculiar thing. Indeed, in the case of the commodity called labor-power, it creates a strange misperception that Marx calls "fetishism":

[40] George J. Stigler, *Essays in the History of Economics,* Chicago: University of Chicago Press, 1965, Ch. 6.

The Fetishism of Commodities and the Secret Thereof

A commodity appears, at first sight, a very trivial thing, and easily understood. Its analysis shows that it is, in reality, a very queer thing, abounding in metaphysical subtleties and theological niceties. So far as it is a value in use, there is nothing mysterious about it, whether we consider it from the point of view that by its properties it is capable of satisfying human wants, or from the point that those properties are the product of human labour. It is as clear as noon-day, that man, by his industry, changes the forms of the materials furnished by Nature, in such a way as to make them useful to him. The form of wood, for instance, is altered, by making a table out of it. Yet, for all that, the table continues to be that common, every-day thing, wood. But, so soon as it steps forth as a commodity, it is changed into something transcendent. It not only stands with its feet on the ground, but, in relation to all other commodities, it stands on its head, and evolves out of its wooden brain grotesque ideas, far more wonderful than "table-turning" ever was.

The mystical character of commodities does not originate, therefore, in their use-value. Just as little does it proceed from the nature of the determining factors of value. For, in the first place, however varied the useful kinds of labour, or productive activities, may be, it is a physiological fact, that they are functions of the human organism, and that each such function, whatever may be its nature or form, is essentially the expenditure of human brain, nerves, muscles, &c. Secondly, with regard to that which forms the groundwork for the quantitative determination of value, namely, the duration of that expenditure, or the quantity of labour, it is quite clear that there is a palpable difference between its quantity and quality. In all states of society, the labour-time that it costs to produce the means of subsistence, must necessarily be an object of interest to mankind, though not of equal interest in different stages of development. And lastly, from the moment that men in any way work for one another, their labour assumes a social form.

Whence, then, arises the enigmatical character of the product of labour, so soon as it assumes the form of commodities? Clearly from this form itself. The equality of all sorts of human labour is expressed objectively by their products all being equally values; the measure of the expenditure of labour-power by the duration of that expenditure, takes the form of the quantity of value of the products of labour; and finally, the mutual relations of the producers, within which the social character of their labour affirms itself, take the form of a social relation between the products. . . .

A commodity is therefore a mysterious thing, simply because in it the social character of men's labour appears to them as an objective character stamped upon the product of that labour; because the relation of the producers to the sum total of their own labour is presented to them as a social relation, existing not between themselves, but between the products of their labour. This is the reason why the products of labour become commodities, social things whose qualities are at the same time perceptible and imperceptible by the senses. In the same way the light from an object is perceived by us not as the subjective excitation of our optic nerve, but as the objective form of something outside the eye itself. But, in the act of seeing, there is at all events, an actual passage of light from one thing to another, from the external object to the eye. There is a physical relation between physical things.

But it is different with commodities. There, the existence of the things *quâ* commodities, and the value-relation between the products of labour which stamps them as commodities, have absolutely no connexion with their physical properties and with the material relations arising therefrom. There it is a definite social relation between men, that assumes, in their eyes, the fantastic form of a relation between things. In order, therefore, to find an analogy, we must have recourse to the mist-enveloped regions of the religious world. In that world the productions of the human brain appear as independent beings endowed with life, and entering into relation both with one another and the human race. So it is in the world of commodities with the products of men's hands. This I call the Fetishism which attaches itself to the products of labour, so soon as they are produced as commodities, and which is therefore inseparable from the production of commodities.

Having identified the curious tendency to perceive the exchange values of commodities—including that key commodity, labor power—as embodying forces above and beyond mere human determination, Marx turns his attention to an even more mystifying aspect of the social order he was examining. This is the element of capital, so important that the social order takes on its very name. Capital to Marx is not just a thing, like machines or even sums of money. Capital is a *process,* or more accurately, a stopping point, a "moment" in an ongoing process in which the value of capital seeks to expand. Here is truly the "secret" of capitalism, which we now examine:

The General Formula for Capital

The circulation of commodities is the starting-point of capital. The production of commodities, their circulation, and that more developed form of their circulation called commerce, these form the historical ground-work from which it rises. The modern history of capital dates from the creation in the 16th century of a world-embracing commerce and a world-embracing market.

If we abstract from the material substance of the circulation of commodities, that is, from the exchange of the various use-values, and consider only the economic forms produced by this process of circulation, we find its final result to be money: this final product of the circulation of commodities is the first form in which capital appears.

As a matter of history, capital, as opposed to landed property, invariably takes the form at first of money; it appears as moneyed wealth, as the capital of the merchant and of the usurer. But we have no need to refer to the origin of capital in order to discover that the first form of appearance of capital is money. We can see it daily under our very eyes. All new capital, to commence with, comes on the stage, that is, on the market, whether of commodities, labour, or money, even in our days, in the shape of money that by a definite process has to be transformed into capital.

The first distinction we notice between money that is money only, and money that is capital, is nothing more than a difference in their form of circulation.

The simplest form of the circulation of commodities is C—M—C, the transformation of commodities into money, and the change of the money back again into commodities; or selling in order to buy. But alongside of this form we find another specifically different form: M—C—M, the transformation of money into commodities, and the change of commodities back again into money; or buying in order to sell. Money that circulates in the latter manner is thereby transformed into, becomes capital, and is already potentially capital. . . . The simple circulation of commodities—selling in order to buy—is a means of carrying out a purpose unconnected with circulation, namely, the appropriation of use-values, the satisfaction of wants. The circulation of money as capital is, on the contrary, an end in itself, for the expansion of value takes place only within this constantly renewed movement. The circulation of capital has therefore no limits. . . .

As the conscious representative of this movement, the possessor of money becomes a capitalist. His person, or rather his pocket, is the point from which the money starts and to which it returns. The expansion of value, which is the objective basis or main-spring of the circulation M—C—M, becomes his subjective aim, and it is only in so far as the appropriation of ever more and more wealth in the abstract becomes the sole motive of his operations, that he functions as a capitalist, that is, as capital personified and endowed with consciousness and a will. Use-values must therefore never be looked upon as the real aim of the capitalist; neither must the profit on any single transaction. The restless never-ending process of profit-making alone is what he aims at. This boundless greed after riches, this passionate chase after exchange-value, is common to the capitalist and the miser; but while the miser is merely a capitalist gone mad, the capitalist is a rational miser. The never-ending augmentation of exchange-value, which the miser strives after, by seeking to save his money from circulation, is attained by the more acute capitalist, by constantly throwing it afresh into circulation.

Value therefore now becomes value in process, money in process, and, as such, capital. It comes out of circulation, enters into it again, preserves and multiplies itself within its circuit, comes back out of it with expanded bulk, and begins the same round ever afresh. M—M', money which begets money, such is the description of Capital from the mouths of its first interpreters, the Mercantilists.

Buying in order to sell, or, more accurately, buying in order to sell dearer, M—C—M', appears certainly to be a form peculiar to one kind of capital alone, namely, merchants' capital. But industrial capital too is money, that is changed into commodities, and by the sale of these commodities, is re-converted into more money. The events that take place outside the sphere of circulation, in the interval between the buying and selling, do not affect the form of this movement. Lastly, in the case of interest-bearing capital, the circulation M—C—M' appears abridged. We have its result without the intermediate stage, in the form M—M', "en style lapidaire" so to say, money that is worth more money, value that is greater than itself.

M—C—M' is therefore in reality the general formula of capital as it appears prima facie within the sphere of circulation.

Marx has now laid out a description of a system in a state of constant pent-up energy, as each possessor of M seeks to buy a C which, upon sale, will yield a larger M'. But if this description lays out a strategy, it also presents an immense obstacle. For Marx now points out that M cannot, by itself, become M': "as hard cash, it is value petrified, never varying." "Just as little," he goes on to say, "can it originate in the second act of circulation, the re-sale of the commodity, which does no more than transform the article from its bodily form back into its money form."

Marx does not mean, of course, that we cannot make fortuitous purchases and sell them for a profit. But our profit is then some-one's loss. That which we must demonstrate is that there the sys-tem as a whole can yield profits to those who begin the process of M—C—M'—that is, to its capitalists. How can this take place? Let us see what Marx has to say about the matter in the impassioned Chapter VI—easy to read, and of absolutely central importance.

The Buying and Selling of Labour Power

The change must, therefore, take place in the commodity bought by the first act, M—C, but not in its value, for equivalents are exchanged, and the commodity is paid for at its full value. We are, therefore, forced to the conclusion that the change originates in the use-value, as such, of the commodity, *i.e.*, in its consump-tion. In order to be able to extract value from the consumption of a commodity, our friend, Moneybags, must be so lucky as to find, within the sphere of circulation, in the market, a commod-ity, whose use-value possesses the peculiar property of being a source of value, whose actual consumption, therefore, is itself an embodiment of labour, and, consequently, a creation of value. The possessor of money does find on the market such a special commodity in capacity for labour or labour-power.

By labour-power or capacity for labour is to be understood the aggregate of those mental and physical capabilities existing in a human being, which he exercises whenever he produces a use-value of any description.

But in order that our owner of money may be able to find labour-power offered for sale as a commodity, various condi-tions must first be fulfilled. The exchange of commodities of itself implies no other relations of dependence than those which result from its own nature. On this assumption, labour-power can appear upon the market as a commodity, only if, and so far as, its possessor, the individual whose labour-power it is, offers it for sale, or sells it, as a commodity. In order that he may be able to do this, he must have it at his disposal, must be the untram-melled owner of his capacity for labour, *i.e.*, of his person. He and the owner of money meet in the market, and deal with each other as on the basis of equal rights, with this difference alone, that one is buyer, the other seller; both, therefore, equal in the eyes of the law. The continuance of this relation demands that the owner of the labour-power should sell it only for a definite period, for if he were to sell it rump and stump, once for all, he would be selling himself, converting himself from a free man into a slave, from an owner of a commodity into a commodity. He must constantly look upon his labour-power as his own property, his own commodity, and this he can only do by placing it at the disposal of the buyer temporarily, for a definite period of time. By this means alone can he avoid renouncing his rights of ownership over it.

The second essential condition to the owner of money finding labour-power in the market as a commodity is this—that the labourer instead of being in the position to sell commodities in which his labour is incorporated, must be obliged to offer for sale as a commodity that very labour-power, which exists only in his living self.

For the conversion of his money into capital, therefore, the owner of money must meet in the market with the free labourer, free in the double sense, that as a free man he can dispose of his labour-power as his own commodity, and that on the other hand he has no other commodity for sale, is short of everything necessary for the realisation of his labour-power.

The question why this free labourer confronts him in the market, has no interest for the owner of money, who regards the labour-market as a branch of the general market for commodities. And for the present it interests us just as little. We cling to the fact theoretically, as he does practically. One thing, however, is clear—Nature does not produce on the one side owners of money or commodities, and on the other men possessing nothing but their own labour-power. This relation has no natural basis, neither is its social basis one that is common to all historical periods. It is clearly the result of a past historical development, the product of many economic revolutions, of the

extinction of a whole series of older forms of social production.
. . . Capital, therefore, announces from its first appearance a new
epoch in the process of social production.

We must now examine more closely this peculiar commodity,
labour-power. Like all others it has a value. How is that value
determined?

The value of labour-power is determined, as in the case of
every other commodity, by the labour-time necessary for the
production, and consequently also the reproduction, of this special article. So far as it has value, it represents no more than a
definite quantity of the average labour of society incorporated in
it. Labour-power exists only as a capacity, or power of the living
individual. Its production consequently pre-supposes his existence. Given the individual, the production of labour-power consists in his reproduction of himself or his maintenance. For his
maintenance he requires a given quantity of the means of subsistence. Therefore the labour-time requisite for the production of
labour-power reduces itself to that necessary for the production
of those means of subsistence; in other words, the value of
labour-power is the value of the means of subsistence necessary
for the maintenance of the labourer.

Labour-power, however, becomes a reality only by its exercise;
it sets itself in action only by working. But thereby a definite
quantity of human muscle, nerve, brain, &c., is wasted, and these
require to be restored.

We now know how the value paid by the purchaser to the
possessor of this peculiar commodity, labour-power, is determined. The use-value which the former gets in exchange, mani-
fests itself only in the actual usufruct, in the consumption of the
labour-power. The money-owner buys everything necessary for
this purpose, such as raw material, in the market, and pays for it
at its full value. The consumption of labour-power is at one and
the same time the production of commodities and of surplus-
value. The consumption of labour-power is completed, as in the
case of every other commodity, outside the limits of the market
or of the sphere of circulation. Accompanied by Mr. Moneybags

and by the possessor of labour-power, we therefore take leave for a time of this noisy sphere, where everything takes place on the surface and in view of all men, and follow them both into the hidden abode of production, on whose threshold there stares us in the face "No admittance except on business." Here we shall see, not only how capital produces, but how capital is produced. We shall at last force the secret of profit making.

This sphere that we are deserting, within whose boundaries the sale and purchase of labour-power goes on, is in fact a very Eden of the innate rights of man. There alone rule Freedom, Equality, Property and Bentham.* Freedom, because both buyer and seller of a commodity, say of labour-power, are constrained only by their own free will. They contract as free agents, and the agreement they come to, is but the form in which they give legal expression to their common will. Equality, because each enters into relation with the other, as with a simple owner of commodities, and they exchange equivalent for equivalent. Property, because each disposes only of what is his own. And Bentham, because each looks only to himself. The only force that brings them together and puts them in relation with each other, is the selfishness, the gain and the private interests of each. Each looks to himself only, and no one troubles himself about the rest, and just because they do so, do they all, in accordance with the pre-established harmony of things, or under the auspices of an all-shrewd providence, work together to their mutual advantage, for the common weal and in the interest of all.

That Marx can write with bitterness and fury is amply demon-strated in the last paragraphs above. But Marx's greatness as a worldly philosopher—and he is assuredly in the Pantheon, along with philosophers of quite different political values—does not lie in his capacity for invective, but in his extraordinary analytical penetration. We see that capability at its best in the excerpt from the famous Chapter VII to follow. Here Marx demonstrates that the process of capital expansion has a simple explanation, once

---

*We will look into Bentham in our next reading.

one has looked further into the peculiar nature of that all-important entity, labor power.

_____

On the Production of Surplus Value

The capitalist buys labour-power in order to use it; and labour-power in use is labour itself. The purchaser of labour-power consumes it by setting the seller of it to work. By working, the latter becomes actually, what before he only was potentially, labour-power in action, a labourer. In order that his labour may re-appear in a commodity, he must, before all things, expend it on something useful, on something capable of satisfying a want of some sort. Hence, what the capitalist sets the labourer to produce, is a particular use-value, a specified article. The fact that the production of use-values, or goods, is carried on under the control of a capitalist and on his behalf, does not alter the general character of that production. We shall, therefore, in the first place, have to consider the labour-process independently of the particular form it assumes under given social conditions.

Labour is, in the first place, a process in which both man and Nature participate, and in which man of his own accord starts, regulates, and controls the material re-actions between himself and Nature. He opposes himself to Nature as one of her own forces, setting in motion arms and legs, head and hands, the natural forces of his body, in order to appropriate Nature's productions in a form adapted to his own wants. By thus acting on the external world and changing it, he at the same time changes his own nature. He develops his slumbering powers and compels them to act in obedience to his sway. We are not now dealing with those primitive instinctive forms of labour that remind us of the mere animal. An immeasurable interval of time separates the state of things in which a man brings his labour-power to market for sale as a commodity, from that state in which human labour was still in its first instinctive stage. We pre-suppose labour in a form that stamps it as exclusively human. A spider conducts operations that resemble those of a weaver, and a bee puts to shame many an architect in the construction of her cells.

But what distinguishes the worst architect from the best of bees is this, that the architect raises his structure in imagination before he erects it in reality. At the end of every labour-process, we get a result that already existed in the imagination of the labourer at its commencement. He not only effects a change of form in the material on which he works, but he also realises a purpose of his own that gives the law to his modus operandi, and to which he must subordinate his will. And this subordination is no mere momentary act. Besides the exertion of the bodily organs, the process demands that, during the whole operation, the work-man's will be steadily in consonance with his purpose. This means close attention. The less he is attracted by the nature of the work, and the mode in which it is carried on, and the less, therefore, he enjoys it as something which gives play to his bodily and mental powers, the more close his attention is forced to be. . . .

Let us now return to our would-be capitalist. We left him just after he had purchased, in the open market, all the necessary factors of the labour-process; its objective factors, the means of production, as well as its subjective factor, labour-power. With the keen eye of an expert, he has selected the means of production and the kind of labour-power best adapted to his particular trade, be it spinning, bootmaking, or any other kind. He then proceeds to consume the commodity, the labour-power that he has just bought, by causing the labourer, the impersonation of that labour-power, to consume the means of production by his labour. The general character of the labour-process is evidently not changed by the fact, that the labourer works for the capitalist instead of for himself; moreover, the particular methods and operations employed in bootmaking or spinning are not immediately changed by the intervention of the capitalist. He must begin by taking the labour-power as he finds it in the market, and consequently be satisfied with labour of such a kind as would be found in the period immediately preceding the rise of capitalists. Changes in the methods of production by the subordination of labour to capital, can take place only at a later period, and therefore will have to be treated of in a later chapter.

The labour-process, turned into the process by which the capitalist consumes labour-power, exhibits two characteristic phenomena. First, the labourer works under the control of the capitalist to whom his labour belongs; the capitalist taking good care that the work is done in a proper manner, and that the means of production are used with intelligence, so that there is no unnecessary waste of raw material, and no wear and tear of the implements beyond what is necessarily caused by the work.

Secondly, the product is the property of the capitalist and not that of the labourer, its immediate producer. Suppose that a capitalist pays for a day's labour-power at its value; then the right to use that power for a day belongs to him, just as much as the right to use any other commodity, such as a horse that he has hired for the day. To the purchaser of a commodity belongs its use, and the seller of labour-power, by giving his labour, does no more, in reality, than part with the use-value that he has sold. From the instant he steps into the workshop, the use-value of his labour-power, and therefore also its use, which is labour, belongs to the capitalist. By the purchase of labour-power, the capitalist incorporates labour, as a living ferment, with the lifeless constituents of the product. From his point of view, the labour-process is nothing more than the consumption of the commodity purchased, i.e., of labour-power; but this consumption cannot be effected except by supplying the labour-power with the means of production. The labour-process is a process between things that the capitalist has purchased, things that have become his property. The product of this process belongs, therefore, to him, just as much as does the wine which is the product of a process of fermentation completed in his cellar.

––––––––––

At this point we reach the crucial moment in the M—C—M' process—the moment in which profit is born. As we already know, profit lies in the capitalist's appropriation of a quantum of value that inheres in labor power—a quantum for which he has not been forced to pay. That unpaid labor, now vested in a product or service which will be sold for a price that includes its value, is the source—indeed, the very embodiment—of profit.

How can this come about? Marx's answer is that the *exchange value* of a day's labor power is the value of the commodities needed to "reproduce" the laborer's working capacity—his living wage, as it is often called—whereas the *use-value* of that same quantum of labor is the selling price of the commodities in which that labor is embodied. Thus if a capitalist can buy a day's labor for less money than he can realize from putting that labor to work, there will be a source of profit in the unpaid labor in the transaction. This is what Marx calls the *surplus value* that inheres in the institution of wage labor.

We can understand surplus value better when we recall that Smith said the master needed the labor of his workman as much as the workman needed the wage of his master, but that the need was not so immediate. (See page 91 above). So, too, in Marx's analysis. It may take only four hours of work to create the value needed to pay the worker's wage, but the worker signs on for more—perhaps much more—than those four hours, because he has no choice if he needs a job. Marx puts it in these words:

The fact that half a day's labour is necessary to keep the labourer alive during 24 hours, does not in any way prevent him from working a whole day. Therefore, the value of labour-power, and the value which that labour-power creates in the labour-process, are two entirely different magnitudes; and this difference of the two values was what the capitalist had in view, when he was purchasing the labour-power. The useful qualities that labour-power possesses, and by virtue of which it makes yarn or boots, were to him nothing more than a conditio sine qua non; for in order to create value, labour must be expended in a useful manner. What really influenced him was the specific use-value which this commodity possesses of being *a source not only of value, but of more value than it has itself.* This is the special service that the capitalist expects from labour-power, and in this transaction he acts in accordance with the "eternal laws" of the exchange of commodities. The seller of labour-power, like the seller of any other commodity, realises its exchange-value, and parts with its use-value. He cannot take the one without giving the other. The use-value of labour-power, or in other words, labour, belongs just as little to its seller, as the use-value of oil after it has been sold belongs to the dealer who has sold it. The owner of the money has paid the value of a day's labour-power; his, therefore, is the use of it for a day; a day's labour belongs to him. The circumstance, that on the one hand the daily sustenance of labour-power costs only half a day's labour, while on the other hand the very same labour-power can work during a whole day, that consequently the value which its use during one day creates, is double what he pays for that use, this circumstance is, without doubt, a piece of good luck for the buyer, but by no means an injury to the seller.

———————————

Thus the necessary condition for surplus value is clear: the price one must pay for an hour of labor must be less than the value the same hour will create when put to work. In Marx's world that difference is explained as a consequence of the fact that the cost of a worker's subsistence will cost less than the sales value of his output. This depends crucially, of course, on a presupposition that the worker will not be in a position to bargain on equal terms with the capitalist. In turn, this presupposition rested, as Marx was fully aware, on the disparities in the respective abilities of the parties to wait for their payments. Workers were assumed to have little reserves, in terms of cash on hand or the offer of higher-paid jobs elsewhere, that would enable them to hold out for a wage equal to the value of what they produced, not merely one sufficient for them to subsist. The capitalist, on the contrary, was supposed to have reserves sufficient to allow him to wait for a considerable time before signing a wage contract that threatened to eat too far into the value of the workers' output.

Put in these everyday terms, the theory of surplus value seems realistic enough, even if we assume the working force is organized. And of course the case for the theory is considerably strengthened if we look at the conditions of the British working class in Marx's time.

In the early 1840s, Friedrich Engels, a young German idealist, had been packed off to Manchester by his father, a Rhineland

manufacturer, to learn the economic facts of life. Engels faithfully
applied himself to his duties, as a consequence of which he performed very well for his father; but on the side he wrote a scathing
book, *The Condition of the Working Class in England in 1844.*
Thereafter he soon met young Marx, the idealist editor of a moderately liberal newspaper, not yet so radical-minded as Engels, and
the two quickly became intimate friends: when Marx and his wife
sought refuge abroad in 1849, Engels, by then a successful businessman in England, provided for their lifelong support. In addition, the two were close collaborators. Some of Marx's most
famous writings, including the *Communist Manifesto,* published
in 1848, were joint products with Engels, and Marx wrote little
that did not pass his friend's critical appraisal.

Engel's report on the British working class finds its echo and a
good deal of its material, in Chapter X of *Capital,* "The Working
Day." A few pages will convey the tone of the chapter as a whole,
which lends powerful support to the generalized argument of the
preceding pages on the existence and importance of surplus
value:

The Factory Act of 1850 now in force [1867] allows for the
average working-day 10 hours, *i.e.,* for the first 5 days 12 hours
from 6 a. m. to 6 p. m., including ½ an hour for breakfast, and
an hour for dinner, and thus leaving 10½ working-hours, and 8
hours for Saturday, from 6 a. m. to 2 p. m., of which ½ an hour
is subtracted for breakfast. 60 working-hours are left, 10½ for
each of the first 5 days, 7½ for the last. Certain guardians of these
laws are appointed, Factory Inspectors, directly under the Home
Secretary, whose reports are published half-yearly, by order of
Parliament. They give regular and official statistics of the capitalistic greed for surplus-labour.

Let us listen, for a moment, to the Factory Inspectors. "The
fraudulent mill-owner begins work a quarter of an hour (sometimes more, sometimes less) before 6 a. m., and leaves off a quarter of an hour (sometimes more, sometimes less) after 6 p. m. He
takes 5 minutes from the beginning and from the end of the half
hour nominally allowed for breakfast, and 10 minutes at the

beginning and end of the hour nominally allowed for dinner. He works for a quarter of an hour (sometimes more, sometimes less) after 2 p. m. on Saturday. Thus his gain is—

Before 6 a. m., ...	15 minutes.
After 6 p. m., ...	15 "
At breakfast time, ...	10 "
At dinner time, ...	20 "
Five days—300 minutes,	60 "
On Saturday before 6 a. m., ...	15 minutes.
At breakfast time, ...	10 "
After 2 p. m., ...	15 "
	40 minutes.
Total weekly, ...	340 minutes.

. . . From the report of the Commissioners in 1863, the following: Dr. J. T. Arledge, senior physician of the North Staffordshire Infirmary, says: "The potters as a class, both men and women, represent a degenerated population, both physically and morally. They are, as a rule, stunted in growth, ill-shaped, and frequently ill-formed in the chest; they become prematurely old, and are certainly short-lived; they are phlegmatic and bloodless, and exhibit their debility of constitution by obstinate attacks of dyspepsia, and disorders of the liver and kidneys, and by rheumatism. But of all diseases they are especially prone to chest-disease, to pneumonia, phthisis, bronchitis, and asthma. One form would appear peculiar to them, and is known as potter's asthma, or potter's consumption. Scrofula attacking the glands, or bones, or other parts of the body, is a disease of two-thirds or more of the potters. . . . That the 'degenerescence' of the population of this district is not even greater than it is, is due to the constant recruiting from the adjacent country, and intermarriages with more healthy races."

Mr. Charles Parsons, late house surgeon of the same institution, writes in a letter to Commissioner Longe, amongst other things: "I can only speak from personal observation and not from statistical data, but I do not hesitate to assert that my indignation has been aroused again and again at the sight of poor children whose health has been sacrificed to gratify the avarice of either parents or employers." He enumerates the causes of the diseases of the potters, and sums them up in the phrase, "long hours." The report of the Commission trusts that "a manufacture which has assumed so prominent a place in the whole world, will not long be subject to the remark that its great success is accompanied with the physical deterioration, widespread bodily suffering, and early death of the workpeople ... by whose labour and skill such great results have been achieved." And all that holds of the potteries in England is true of those in Scotland.

Quoting the anonymous author of a pamphlet "An Essay on Trade and Commerce," (1770), Marx, gives us these words:

If the making of every seventh day a holiday is supposed to be of divine institution, as it implies the appropriating the other six days to labour" (he means capital as we shall soon see) "surely it will not be thought cruel to enforce it. . . . That mankind in general, are naturally inclined to ease and indolence, we fatally experience to be true, from the conduct of our manufacturing populace, who do not labour, upon an average, above four days in a week, unless provisions happen to be very dear. . . . Put all the necessaries of the poor under one denomination; for instance, call them all wheat, or suppose that . . . the bushel of wheat shall cost five shillings and that he (a manufacturer) earns a shilling by his labour he then would be obliged to work five days only in a week. If the bushel of wheat should cost but four shillings, he would be obliged to work but four days; but as wages in this kingdom are much higher in proportion to the price of necessaries . . . the manufacturer, who labours four days, has a surplus of money to live idle with the rest of the week. . . . I hope I have said enough to make it appear that the moderate labour of six days in a week is no slavery. Our labouring people do this, and to all appearance are the happiest of all our labouring poor, but the Dutch do this in manufactures, and appear to be a very happy people. The French do so, when holidays do not intervene. But our populace have adopted a notion, that as Englishmen they enjoy a birthright privilege of being more free and independent than in any country in Europe. Now this idea, as far as it may affect the bravery of our troops, may be of some use; but the less the manufacturing poor have of it, certainly the better for themselves and for the State. The labouring people should never think themselves independent of their superiors. . . . It is extremely dangerous to encourage mobs in a commercial state like ours, where, perhaps, seven parts out of eight of the whole, are people with little or no property. The cure will not be perfect, till our manufacturing poor are contented to labour six days for the same sum which they now earn in four days.

———————

There are about 60 pages of such testimony, not to mention the much larger number devoted to the condition of the working force in manufacturing industry and mining. The testimony with respect to the overworking and brutalizing of the work force in Marx's day takes away some of the feeling of overkill we feel at the commencement of the chapter on the Working Day when we read "Capital is dead labour that, vampire-like, only lives by sucking living labour, and lives the more, the more labour it sucks."

These instances may, however, strike us as referring to a time long past. No one denies that brutally abused labor exists as a commodity in most of the backward areas of the world, but to attribute the profits of today's frontline industry mainly to "surplus value" no longer seems an unchallengeable contention.

This is particularly the case in one respect. In Marx's day, interfirm competition took on a different form from that of the present. Big business was then more the exception than the rule, and advertising and product differentiation—the main competitive strategies of big business—had not yet become the principal means by which competition was waged. In today's advanced economies, therefore, it is less easy to claim the persisting importance of overworked and underpaid labor as the chief origin of profits, rather than superior product design or more seductive advertising.

This does not rule out exploitation as a source of profit: what, after all, does capital—not management—contribute to exchange value, over and above the labor embodied in it? But today's exploitation seems more likely to wrest profit from the consumer than from the worker, or from both. Thus if surplus value in its most nakedly visible form is surely less than in Karl Marx's day, this does not deny that workers are still the underdogs in wage negotiations, as Adam Smith pointed out, and thereby the recipients of less value than they produce.

But we have yet to reach the heart of *Capital*—its scenario for the self-inflicted undoing of capitalism. Curiously, in contrast to the extraordinary detail that surrounds the theory and "practice" of surplus value, the exposition of this terminus of Marx's theory does not receive systematic examination. Although the particulars of the problem lie scattered through the text, its climactic moment is disposed of in a few pages of vivid, but hardly closely reasoned prose. As we shall see, moreover, the pages begin with a variant of Smith's emphasis on the division of labor. Chapters XIII through XXII of *Capital* describe the changes in the deployment of the labor force in terms that have a different ring, but not a different conclusion from that of Smith's work:

Chapter XIII

Co-operation

Capitalist production only then really begins, as we have already seen, when each individual capital employs simultaneously a comparatively large number of labourers; when consequently the labour-process is carried on on an extensive scale and yields, relatively, large quantities of products. A greater number of labourers working together, at the same time, in one place (or, if you will, in the same field of labour), in order to produce the same sort of commodity under the mastership of one capitalist, constitutes, both historically and logically, the starting-point of capitalist production. With regard to the mode of production itself, manufacture, in its strict meaning, is hardly to be distinguished, in its earliest stages, from the handicraft trades of the guilds, otherwise than by the greater number of workmen simultaneously employed by one and the same individual capital. The workshop of the mediæval master handicraftsman is simply enlarged.

At first, therefore, the difference is purely quantitative. We have shown that the surplus-value produced by a given capital is equal to the surplus-value produced by each workman multiplied by the number of workmen simultaneously employed. The number of workmen in itself does nor affect, either the rate of surplus-value, or the degree of exploitation of labour-power. If a working-day of 12 hours be embodied in six shillings, 1,200 such days will be embodied in 1,200 times 6 shillings. In one case $12 \times 1,200$ working-hours, and in the other 12 such hours are incorporated in the product. In the production of value a number of workmen rank merely as so many individual workmen; and it therefore makes no difference in the value produced whether the 1,200 men work separately, or united under the control of one capitalist.

Nevertheless, within certain limits, a modification takes place. The labour realised in value, is labour of an average social quality; is consequently the expenditure of average labour-power. . . . Thus the laws of the production of value are only fully realized for the individual producer, when he produces as a capitalist, and employs a number of workmen together, whose labour, by its collective nature, is at once stamped as average social labour.

Even without an alteration in the system of working, the simultaneous employment of a large number of labourers effects a revolution in the material conditions of the labour-process. The buildings in which they work, the store-houses for the raw material, the implements and utensils used simultaneously or in turns by the workmen; in short, a portion of the means of production, are now consumed in common. . . . On the other hand, they are used in common, and therefore on a larger scale than before. A room where twenty weavers work at twenty looms must be larger than the room of a single weaver with two assistants. But it costs less labour to build one workshop for twenty persons than to build ten to accommodate two weavers each; thus the value of the means of production that are concentrated for use in common on a large scale does not increase in direct proportion to the expansion and to the increased useful effect of those means. . . . The effect is the same as if the means of production had cost less.

Now comes an important difference between Smith and Marx. Both are interested in the deleterious effect on the worker's well-being of factory production, with its division of labor. Both also recognize the huge leverage imparted to the worker's productivity by the use of machinery. But Marx now pays heed to an effect of mechanization of which Smith is unaware—rendering redundant the worker himself. In Chapter XV, "Machinery and Large-Scale Industry," Marx writes:

The instrument of labour, when it takes the form of a machine, immediately becomes a competitor of the workman himself. The self-expansion of capital by means of machinery is thenceforward directly proportional to the number of the workpeople, whose means of livelihood have been destroyed by that machinery. The whole system of capitalist production is based on the fact that the workman sells his labour-power as a commodity. Division of labour specialises this labour-power, by reducing it to skill in handling a particular tool. So soon as the handling of this tool becomes the work of a machine, then, with the use-value, the exchange-value too, of the workman's labour-power vanishes; the workman becomes unsaleable, like paper money thrown out of currency by legal enactment. That portion of the working-class, thus by machinery rendered superfluous, *i.e.*, no longer immediately necessary for the self-expansion of capital, either goes to the wall in the unequal contest of the old handicrafts and manufactures with machinery, or else floods all the more easily accessible branches of industry, swamps the labour-market, and sinks the price of labour-power below its value. It is impressed upon the workpeople, as a great consolation, first, that their sufferings are only temporary ("a temporary inconvenience"), secondly, that machinery acquires the mastery over the whole of a given field of production, only by degrees, so that the extent and intensity of its destructive effect is diminished. The first consolation neutralises the second. When machinery seizes on an industry by degrees, it produces chronic misery among the operatives who compete with it.

. . . A couple of examples from the Reports of the Inspectors of Factories will suffice on this point. A Manchester manufacturer states: "We formerly had 75 carding engines, now we have 12, doing the same quantity of work. . . . We are doing with fewer hands by 14, at a saving in wages of £10 a-week. Our estimated saving in waste is about 10% in the quantity of cotton consumed." "In another fine-spinning mill in Manchester, I was informed that through increased speed and the adoption of some self-acting processes, a reduction had been made, in number, of a fourth in one department, and of above half in another, and that the introduction of the combing machine in place of the second carding, had considerably reduced the number of hands formerly employed in the carding-room." Another spinning-mill is estimated to effect a saving of labour of 10%. The Messrs. Gilmour, spinners at Manchester, state: "In our blowing-room department we consider our expense with new machinery is fully one-third less in wages and hands . . . in the jack-frame and drawing-frame room, about one-third less in expense, and likewise one-third less in hands; in the spinning-room about one-third less in expenses. . . .

The labouring population therefore produces, along with the accumulation of capital produced by it, the means by which it itself is made relatively superfluous, is turned into a relative surplus-population; and it does this to an always increasing extent. This is a law of population peculiar to the capitalist mode of production. . . .

But if a surplus labouring population is a necessary product of accumulation or of the development of wealth on a capitalist basis, this surplus-population becomes, conversely, the lever of capitalistic accumulation, nay, a condition of existence of the capitalist mode of production. It forms a disposable industrial reserve army, that belongs to capital quite as absolutely as if the latter had bred it at its own cost. Independently of the limits of the actual increase of population, it creates, for the changing needs of the self-expansion of capital, a mass of human material always ready for exploitation. . . .

————————

At this point, the pace quickens. The race for market share begins, with capitals competing for labor power in brisk times, and constricting their work forces in slumps. Note that the scenario, unmistakeably different from that of any of the previous economists, takes on a dramatic—even a melodramatic—character, at the expense of the painstaking analysis that has marked what has gone before. It is as if Marx, sensing the approach of the goal, shifts into high gear, assuming that his readers will themselves supply the not always explicit internal linkages.* At any rate, the prelude to Armageddon must be read:

————————

The mass of social wealth, overflowing with the advance of accumulation, and transformable into additional capital, thrusts itself frantically into old branches of production, whose market suddenly expands, or into newly formed branches, such as railways, &c., the need for which grows out of the development of the old ones. In all such cases, there must be the possibility of throwing great masses of men suddenly on the decisive points without injury to the scale of production in other spheres. Overpopulation supplies these masses. The course characteristic of modern industry, viz., a decennial cycle (interrupted by smaller oscillations), of periods of average activity, production at high pressure, crisis and stagnation, depends on the constant formation, the greater or less absorption, and the re-formation of the industrial reserve army or surplus-population. In their turn, the varying phases of the industrial cycle recruit the surplus-population, and become one of the most energetic agents of its reproduction. . . .

The impulse that additional capital, seeking an outlet, would otherwise have given to the general demand for labour, is there-

————————

*In the interests of clarifying this argument, I have switched the positions of Marx's paragraphs in the following excerpt.

fore in every case neutralised to the extent of the labourers thrown out of employment by the machine. That is to say, the mechanism of capitalistic production so manages matters that the absolute increase of capital is accompanied by no corresponding rise in the general demand for labour. And this the apologist calls a compensation for the misery, the sufferings, the possible death of the displaced labourers during the transition period that banishes them into the industrial reserve army!

The greater the social wealth, the functioning capital, the extent and energy of its growth, and, therefore, also the absolute mass of the proletariat and the productiveness of its labour, the greater is the industrial reserve army. The same causes which develop the expansive power of capital, develop also the labour-power at its disposal. The relative mass of the industrial reserve army increases therefore with the potential energy of wealth. But the greater this reserve army in proportion to the active labour-army, the greater is the mass of a consolidated surplus-population, whose misery is in inverse ratio to its torment of labour. The more extensive, finally, the lazarus-layers of the working-class, and the industrial reserve army, the greater is official pauperism. *This is the absolute general law of capitalist accumulation.*

What remains is dénouement. Here, in its entirety, is the famous Chapter XXXII of *Capital:*

Chapter XXXII

Historical Tendency of Capitalist Accumulation

What does the primitive accumulation of capital, *i.e.*, its historical genesis, resolve itself into? In so far as it is not immediate transformation of slaves and serfs into wage-labourers, and therefore a mere change of form, it only means the expropriation of the immediate producers, *i.e.*, the dissolution of private property based on the labour of its owner. Private property, as the antithesis to social, collective property, exists only where the means of labour and the external conditions of labour belong to private individuals. But according as these private individuals are labourers or not labourers, private property has a different character. The numberless shades, that it at first sight presents, correspond to the intermediate stages lying between these two extremes. The private property of the labourer in his means of production is the foundation of petty industry, whether agricultural, manufacturing, or both; petty industry, again, is an essential condition for the development of social production and of the free individuality of the labourer himself. Of course, this petty mode of production exists also under slavery, serfdom, and other states of dependence. But it flourishes, it lets loose its whole energy, it attains its adequate classical form, only where the labourer is the private owner of his own means of labour set in action by himself: the peasant of the land which he cultivates, the artisan of the tool which he handles as a virtuoso. This mode of production pre-supposes parcelling of the soil, and scattering of the other means of production. As it excludes the concentration of these means of production, so also it excludes co-operation, division of labour within each separate process of production, the control over, and the productive application of the forces of Nature by society, and the free development of the social productive powers. It is compatible only with a system of production, and a society, moving within narrow and more or less primitive bounds. To perpetuate it would be, as Pecqueur rightly says, "to decree universal mediocrity." At a certain stage of development it brings forth the material agencies for its own dissolution.

From that moment new forces and new passions spring up in the bosom of society; but the old social organisation fetters them and keeps them down. It must be annihilated; it is annihilated. Its annihilation, the transformation of the individualised and scattered means of production into socially concentrated ones, of the pigmy property of the many into the huge property of the few, the expropriation of the great mass of the people from the soil, from the means of subsistence, and from the means of labour, this fearful and painful expropriation of the mass of the people forms the prelude to the history of capital. It comprises a series of forcible methods, of which we have passed in review only those that have been epoch-making as methods of the primitive accumulation of capital. The expropriation of the immediate producers was accomplished with merciless Vandalism, and under the stimulus of passions the most infamous, the most sordid, the pettiest, the most meanly odious. Self-earned private property, that is based, so to say, on the fusing together of the isolated, independent labouring-individual with the conditions of his labour, is supplanted by capitalistic private property, which rests on exploitation of the nominally free labour of others, *i.e.*, on wage-labour.

As soon as this process of transformation has sufficiently decomposed the old society from top to bottom, as soon as the labourers are turned into proletarians, their means of labour into capital, as soon as the capitalist mode of production stands on its own feet, then the further socialisation of labour and further transformation of the land and other means of production into socially exploited and, therefore, common means of production, as well as the further expropriation of private proprietors, takes a new form. That which is now to be expropriated is no longer the labourer working for himself, but the capitalist exploiting many labourers. This expropriation is accomplished by the action of the immanent laws of capitalistic production itself, by the centralisation of capital. One capitalist always kills many. Hand in hand with this centralisation, or this expropriation of many capitalists by few, develop, on an ever-extending scale, the co-operative form of the labour-process, the conscious technical application of science, the methodical cultivation of the soil, the transformation of the instruments of labour into instruments of labour only usable in common, the economising of all means of production by their use as the means of production of combined, socialised labour, the entanglement of all peoples in the net of the world-market, and with this, the international character of the capitalistic régime. Along with the constantly diminishing number of the magnates of capital, who usurp and monopolise all advantages of this process of transformation, grows the mass of misery, oppression, slavery, degradation, exploitation; but with this too grows the revolt of the working-class, a class always increasing in numbers, and disciplined, united, organised by the very mechanism of the process of capitalist production itself. The monopoly of capital becomes a fetter upon the mode of production, which has sprung up and flourished along with, and under it. Centralisation of the means of production and socialisation of labour at last reach a point where they become incompatible with their capitalist integument. Thus integument is burst asunder. The knell of capitalist private property sounds. The expropriators are expropriated.

The capitalist mode of appropriation, the result of the capitalist mode of production, produces capitalist private property. This is the first negation of individual private property, as founded on the labour of the proprietor. But capitalist production begets, with the inexorability of a law of Nature, its own negation. It is the negation of negation. This does not re-establish private property for the producer, but gives him individual property based on the acquisitions of the capitalist era: *i.e.*, on co-operation and the possession in common of the land and of the means of production.

The transformation of scattered private property, arising from individual labour, into capitalist private property is, naturally, a process, incomparably more protracted, violent, and difficult, than the transformation of capitalistic private property, already practically resting on socialised production, into socialised property. In the former case, we had the expropriation of the mass of the people by a few usurpers; in the latter, we have the expropriation of a few usurpers by the mass of the people.

It is not, however, the end of Marx's worldly philosophy, or for that matter of *Capital*, which goes on for two more volumes to delve into various largely technical matters—"circuits" of different kinds of capital, turnover times of different capitals, aspects of the falling rate of profit, considerations of money and rent, to name but a sample; followed by three remarkable volumes, *Theories of*

Surplus Value, in which virtually all economic thinkers preceding Marx are subjected to his often stinging, always penetrative analysis. I shall leave these questions unexamined here, for there remains a last aspect of Marx's larger scenario that requires our attention: Marx's and Engel's thoughts on the possibilities for socialism and of the course of history itself.

And where does one find such a summation? In the *Communist Manifesto,* of course.[41] Written in 1848, long before *Capital,* and therefore in no possible way a deliberate conclusion of that immense work, the *Manifesto* seems, for all its hopelessly unrealistic expectations and exhortations, to capture the basic view of history that permeates *Capital.* Here, then, are relevant portions of that pronunciamento—the outline of a vision waiting for the formal analysis that would not follow for twenty years.

Manifesto of the Communist Party

The bourgeoisie, during its rule of scarce one hundred years, has created more massive and more colossal productive forces than have all preceding generations together. Subjection of Nature's forces to man, machinery, application of chemistry to industry and agriculture, steam-navigation, railways, electric telegraphs, clearing of whole continents for cultivation, canalisation of rivers, whole populations conjured out of the ground—what earlier century had even a presentiment that such productive forces slumbered in the lap of social labour?

We see then: the means of production and of exchange, on whose foundation the bourgeoisie built itself up, were generated in feudal society. At a certain stage in the development of these means of production and of exchange, the conditions under which feudal society produced and exchanged, the feudal organisation of agriculture and manufacturing industry, in one word, the feudal relations of property became no longer compatible with the already developed productive forces; they became so many fetters. They had to be burst asunder; they were burst asunder.

[41] From the *Marx-Engels Reader,* supra cit., p. 469 f.

Into their place stepped free competition, accompanied by a social and political constitution adapted to it, and by the economical and political sway of the bourgeois class.

A similar movement is going on before our own eyes. Modern bourgeois society with its relations of production, of exchange and of property, a society that has conjured up such gigantic means of production and of exchange, is like the sorcerer, who is no longer able to control the powers of the nether world whom he has called up by his spells. For many a decade past the history of industry and commerce is but the history of the revolt of modern productive forces against modern conditions of production, against the property relations that are the conditions for the existence of the bourgeoisie and of its rule. It is enough to mention the commercial crises that by their periodical return put on its trial, each time more threateningly, the existence of the entire bourgeois society. In these crises a great part not only of the existing products, but also of the previously created productive forces, are periodically destroyed. In these crises there breaks out an epidemic that, in all earlier epochs, would have seemed an absurdity—the epidemic of over-production. Society suddenly finds itself put back into a state of momentary barbarism; it appears as if a famine, a universal war of devastation had cut off the supply of every means of subsistence; industry and commerce seem to be destroyed; and why? Because there is too much civilisation, too much means of subsistence, too much industry, too much commerce. The productive forces at the disposal of society no longer tend to further the development of the conditions of bourgeois property; on the contrary, they have become too powerful for these conditions, by which they are fettered, and so soon as they overcome these fetters, they bring disorder into the whole of bourgeois society, endanger the existence of bourgeois property. The conditions of bourgeois society are too narrow to comprise the wealth created by them. And how does the bourgeoisie get over these crises? On the one hand by enforced destruction of a mass of productive forces; on the other, by the conquest of new markets, and by the more thorough exploitation of the old ones. That is to say, by paving the way for more extensive and more destructive crises, and by diminishing the means whereby crises are prevented.

The weapons with which the bourgeoisie felled feudalism to the ground are now turned against the bourgeoisie itself.

But not only has the bourgeoisie forged the weapons that bring death to itself; it has also called into existence the men who are to wield those weapons—the modern working class—the proletarians.

In proportion as the bourgeoisie, *i.e.*, capital, is developed, in the same proportion is the proletariat, the modern working class, developed—a class of labourers, who live only so long as they find work, and who find work only so long as their labour increases capital. These labourers, who must sell themselves piece-meal, are a commodity, like every other article of commerce, and are consequently exposed to all the vicissitudes of competition, to all the fluctuations of the market.

Owing to the extensive use of machinery and to division of labour, the work of the proletarians has lost all individual character, and consequently, all charm for the workman. He becomes an appendage of the machine, and it is only the most simple, most monotonous, and most easily acquired knack, that is required of him. Hence, the cost of production of a workman is restricted, almost entirely, to the means of subsistence that he requires for his maintenance, and for the propagation of his race. But the price of a commodity, and therefore also of labour, is equal to its cost of production. In proportion, therefore, as the repulsiveness of the work increases, the wage decreases. Nay more, in proportion as the use of machinery and division of labour increases, in the same proportion the burden of toil also increases, whether by prolongation of the working hours, by increase of the work exacted in a given time or by increased speed of the machinery, etc.

Modern industry has converted the little workshop of the patriarchal master into the great factory of the industrial capitalist. Masses of labourers, crowded into the factory, are organised like soldiers. As privates of the industrial army they are placed under the command of a perfect hierarchy of officers and sergeants. Not only are they slaves of the bourgeois class, and of the bourgeois State; they are daily and hourly enslaved by the machine, by the over-looker, and, above all, by the individual bourgeois manufacturer himself. The more openly this despotism proclaims gain to be its end and aim, the more petty, the more hateful and the more embittering it is. . . .

The essential condition for the existence, and for the sway of the bourgeois class, is the formation and augmentation of capital; the condition for capital is wage-labour. Wage-labour rests exclusively on competition between the labourers. The advance of industry, whose involuntary promoter is the bourgeoisie, replaces the isolation of the labourers, due to competition, by their revolutionary combination, due to association. The development of Modern Industry, therefore, cuts from under its feet the very foundation on which the bourgeoisie produces and appropriates products. What the bourgeoisie, therefore, produces, above all, is its own grave-diggers. Its fall and the victory of the proletariat are equally inevitable. . . .

What last word can one append to a declaration of faith that for more than a century moved millions, and is today relegated to the Museum of Failed Hopes? Perhaps it is the recognition, never stronger than in our time, that the engines of history do not draw all their energies from economic drives and institutions. If socialism failed, it was for political, more than economic reasons; and if capitalism is to succeed it will be because it finds the political will and means to tame its economic forces.

V

THE
MARGINALISTS

JEREMY BENTHAM

⌒

(1748–1832)

Marginalism begins with utility, and utility begins with Jeremy Bentham. That is what leads to my placement of Bentham, whose influential *Introduction to the Principles of Morals and Legislation* was composed in the 1780s, into the company of the marginalists, whose work first appears almost a century later.

The cause of that influence is not altogether easy to trace. At a superficial level it expresses a growing eagerness among up-and-coming thinkers to break out from the benign, but ultimately wearisome omnipresence of John Stuart Mill. At a deeper level I suspect it reflected a growing disquiet with the framework of classical Political Economy itself, above all with the openly acknowledged class basis from which its analysis proceeded and to to which it was directed. The building blocks of land, labor, and capital were not merely categories of production and distribution for the classics, but representations of a stratified order that Smith, Ricardo, Malthus, and even Mill accepted as an historical given—and to which all, save Mill and, of course, Marx, foresaw no real alternative.

Such a view could be unembarrassedly expressed in the late eighteenth and early nineteenth century, But a half century later changes in the political climate, perhaps also in the underlying cultural view, made such a social philosophy unwelcome. It is at this point that marginalism entered, shifting the emphasis away from land, labor, and capital, with their class implications, to the calculations of the classless and apolitical individual, with a capital I. Paralleling this was a second reason for the change—the growing prestige and importance of science, with which economists wished more and more could be identified.

At the very conclusion of our book we will reflect again on this sea-change in the orientation of economic thought. But first we need to familiarize ourselves with the change itself. Here is where Bentham enters. For his *Principles* seemed to offer a new angle of entry into economic investigation by subjecting to a numerical calculus the very act that, more than any other, expressed the focal point of individual economic activity—the act of exchange.

As its title announces, *The Principles of Morals and Legislation* is addressed to the establishment of a new approach to determining Right and Wrong, and a new means of embodying this determination in legislation.[42] We will not be concerned at all with the latter objective, but the first will assuredly give us something to think about. Its famous first paragraph announces with a flourish the conceptual basis from which the new approach proceeds, and its succeeding numbered sections bring us quickly to its striking summation. I should remind the reader that a much more sophisticated version of the pleasure and pain calculus appeared in 1863 in Mill's *Utilitarianism,* an exposition that elevated Bentham's often risible calculus into a philosophical system that still attracts.

Let us start, then, with the general statement of the argument for utility as the touchstone for human moral guidance. For all its verbosity, Bentham's exposition below bears perusal, especially section 14; its ten points will test anyone's critical faculties:

---

[42] Jeremy Bentham, *The Principles of Morals and Legislation*, Hafner Library of Classics, 1948, original sidenotes omitted.

THE PRINCIPLES OF MORALS AND LEGISLATION

Chapter I

Of the Principle of Utility

1. Nature has placed mankind under the governance of two sovereign masters, *pain* and *pleasure*. It is for them alone to point out what we ought to do, as well as to determine what we shall do. On the one hand the standard of right and wrong, on the other the chain of causes and effects, are fastened to their throne. They govern us in all we do, in all we say, in all we think: every effort we can make to throw off our subjection, will serve but to demonstrate and confirm it. In words a man may pretend to abjure their empire: but in reality he will remain subject to it all the while. The *principle of utility* recognises this subjection, and assumes it for the foundation of that system, the object of which is to rear the fabric of felicity by the hands of reason and of law. Systems which attempt to question it, deal in sounds instead of sense, in caprice instead of reason, in darkness instead of light.

But enough of metaphor and declamation: it is not by such means that moral science is to be improved.

2. The principle of utility is the foundation of the present work: it will be proper therefore at the outset to give an explicit and determinate account of what is meant by it. By the principle of utility is meant that principle which approves or disapproves of every action whatsoever, according to the tendency which it appears to have to augment or diminish the happiness of the party whose interest is in question: or, what is the same thing in other words, to promote or to oppose that happiness. I say of every action whatsoever; and therefore not only of every action of a private individual, but of every measure of government.

3. By utility is meant that property in any object, whereby it tends to produce benefit, advantage, pleasure, good, or happiness, (all this in the present case comes to the same thing) or (what comes again to the same thing) to prevent the happening of mischief, pain, evil, or unhappiness to the party whose interest is considered: if that party be the community in general, then the

happiness of the community: if a particular individual, then the happiness of that individual.

4. The interest of the community is one of the most general expressions that can occur in the phraseology of morals: no wonder that the meaning of it is often lost. When it has a meaning, it is this. . . . The interest of the community is the sum of the interests of the several members who compose it.

5. It is in vain to talk of the interest of the community, without understanding what is the interest of the individual. A thing is said to promote the interest, or to be *for* the interest, of an individual, when it tends to add to the sum total of his pleasures: or, what comes to the same thing, to diminish the sum total of his pains.

6. An action then may be said to be conformable to the principle of utility, or, for shortness sake, to utility, (meaning with respect to the community at large) when the tendency it has to augment the happiness of the community is greater than any it has to diminish it.

7. A measure of government (which is but a particular kind of action, performed by a particular person or persons) may be said to be conformable to or dictated by the principle of utility, when in like manner the tendency which it has to augment the happiness of the community is greater than any which it has to diminish it.

I will spare the reader number 8 and number 9, but urge that numbers 10 to 13 bear scrutiny.

---

10. Of an action that is conformable to the principle of utility, one may always say either that it is one that ought to be done, or at least that it is not one that ought not to be done. One may say also, that it is right it should be done; at least that it is not wrong it should be done: that it is a right action; at least that it is not a wrong action. When thus interpreted, the words *ought*, and *right* and *wrong*, and others of that stamp, have a meaning: when otherwise, they have none.

11. Has the rectitude of this principle been ever formally con-

tested? Is it susceptible of any direct proof? . . . it should seem not: for that which is used to prove every thing else, cannot itself be proved: a chain of proofs must have their commencement somewhere. To give such proof is as impossible as it is needless.

12. Not that there is or ever has been that human creature breathing, however stupid or perverse, who has not on many, perhaps on most occasions of his life, deferred to it. By the natural constitution of the human frame, on most occasions of their lives men in general embrace this principle, without thinking of it: if not for the ordering of their own actions, yet for the trying of their own actions, as well as of those of other men. . . .

13. When a man attempts to combat the principle of utility, it is with reasons drawn, without his being aware of it, from that very principle itself. His arguments, if they prove any thing, prove not that the principle is *wrong,* but that, according to the applications he supposes to be made of it, it is *misapplied.* Is it possible for a man to move the earth? Yes; but he must first find out another earth to stand upon.

Now number 14 comes, to be read carefully.

---

14. To disprove the propriety of it by arguments is impossible; but, from the causes that have been mentioned, or from some confused or partial view of it, a man may happen to be disposed not to relish it. Where this is the case, if he thinks the settling of his opinions on such a subject worth the trouble, let him take the following steps, and at length, perhaps, he may come to reconcile himself to it.

(1) Let him settle with himself, whether he would wish to discard this principle altogether; if so, let him consider what it is that all his reasonings (in matters of politics especially) can amount to?

(2) If he would, let him settle with himself, whether he would judge and act without any principle, or whether there is any other he would judge and act by?

(3) If there be, let him examine and satisfy himself whether the

principle he thinks he has found is really any separate intelligible principle; or whether it be not a mere principle in words, a kind of phrase, which at bottom expresses neither more nor less than the mere averment of his own unfounded sentiments; that is, what in another person he might be apt to call caprice?

(4) If he is inclined to think that his own approbation or disapprobation, annexed to the idea of an act, without any regard to its consequences, is a sufficient foundation for him to judge and act upon, let him ask himself whether his sentiment is to be a standard of right and wrong, with respect to every other man, or whether every man's sentiment has the same privilege of being a standard to itself?

(5) In the first case, let him ask himself whether his principle is not despotical, and hostile to all the rest of human race?

(6) In the second case, whether it is not anarchical, and whether at this rate there are not as many different standards of right and wrong as there are men? and whether even to the same man, the same thing, which is right today, may not (without the least change in its nature) be wrong to-morrow? and whether the same thing is not right and wrong in the same place at the same time? and in either case, whether all argument is not at an end? and whether, when two men have said, 'I like this', and 'I don't like it', they can (upon such a principle) have any thing more to say?

(7) If he should have said to himself, No: for that the sentiment which he proposes as a standard must be grounded on reflection, let him say on what particulars the reflection is to turn? if on particulars having relation to the utility of the act, then let him say whether this is not deserting his own principle, and borrowing assistance from that very one in opposition to which he sets it up: or if not on those particulars, on what other particulars?

(8) If he should be for compounding the matter, and adopting his own principle in part, and the principle of utility in part, let him say how far he will adopt it?

(9) When he has settled with himself where he will stop, then

let him ask himself how he justifies to himself the adopting it so far? and why he will not adopt it any farther?

(10) Admitting any other principle than the principle of utility to be a right principle, a principle that it is right for a man to pursue; admitting (what is not true) that the word *right* can have a meaning without reference to utility, let him say whether there is any such thing as a *motive* that a man can have to pursue the dictates of it: if there is, let him say what that motive is, and how it is to be distinguished from those which enforce the dictates of utility: if not, then lastly let him say what it is this other principle can be good for?

We move now to Chapter IV where the calculus of utility begins to emerge, both in its labyrinthine Benthamite formulation, and less distinctly in its yet-to-be-realized economic expression. I should add that the chapter deserves a glance to appreciate its flavor, but not a close reading.

Chapter IV

Value of a Lot of Pleasure or Pain, How to be Measured

1. Pleasures then, and the avoidance of pains, are the *ends* which the legislator has in view: it behoves him therefore to understand their *value*. Pleasures and pains are the *instruments* he has to work with: it behoves him therefore to understand their force, which is again, in another point of view, their value.

2. To a person considered *by himself*, the value of a pleasure or pain considered *by itself*, will be greater or less, according to the four following circumstances:

    1. Its *intensity*.
    2. Its *duration*.
    3. Its *certainty* or *uncertainty*.
    4. Its *propinquity* or *remoteness*.

3. These are the circumstances which are to be considered in esti-mating a pleasure or a pain considered each of them by itself. But when the value of any pleasure or pain is considered for

the purpose of estimating the tendency of any *act* by which it is produced, there are two other circumstances to be taken into the account; these are,

Its *fecundity*, or the chance it has of being followed by sensations of the *same* kind: that is, pleasures, if it be a pleasure: pains, if it be a pain.

Its *purity*, or the chance it has of *not* being followed by sensations of the *opposite* kind: that is, pains, if it be a pleasure: pleasures, if it be a pain.

These two last, however, are in strictness scarcely to be deemed properties of the pleasure or the pain itself; they are not, therefore, in strictness to be taken into the account of the value of that pleasure or that pain. They are in strictness to be deemed properties only of the act, or other event, by which such pleasure or pain has been produced; and accordingly are only to be taken into the account of the tendency of such act or such event.

4. To a *number* of persons, with reference to each of whom the value of a pleasure or a pain is considered, it will be greater or less, according to seven circumstances: to wit, the six preceding ones; viz.

1. Its *intensity*.
2. Its *duration*.
3. Its *certainty* or *uncertainty*.
4. Its *propinquity* or *remoteness*.
5. Its *fecundity*.
6. Its *purity*.

And one other; to wit:

7. Its *extent*; that is, the number of persons to whom it *extends*; or (in other words) who are affected by it. . . .

———————

Chapter IV is now followed by nine more like it, all tedious and logic-chopping, until we reach this provocative conclusion to Chapter XIV.

———————

There are some, perhaps, who, at first sight, may look upon the nicety employed in the adjustment of such rules, as so much labour lost: for gross ignorance, they will say, never troubles itself about laws, and passion does not calculate. But the evil of ignorance admits of cure: and as to the proposition that passion does not calculate, this like most of these very general and oracular propositions, is not true. When matters of such importance as pain and pleasure are at stake, and these in the highest degree (the only matters, in short, that can be of importance) who is there that does not calculate? Men calculate, some with less exactness, indeed, some with more: but all men calculate. I would not say, that even a madman does not calculate. Passion calculates, more or less, in every man: in different men, according to the warmth or coolness of their dispositions: according to the firmness or irritability of their minds: according to the nature of the motives by which they are acted upon. Happily, of all passions, that is the most given to calculation, from the excesses of which, by reason of its strength, constancy, and universality, society has most to apprehend: I mean that which corresponds to the motive of pecuniary interest: so that these niceties, if such they are to be called, have the best chance of being efficacious, where efficacy is of the most importance.

Is the argument as conclusive as Bentham believes? Utilitarianism—certainly in the form of a naive calculus—has long since lost its cogency. It is, after all, easily reduced to a mere tautology in which whatever course one pursues is "explained" as maximizing one's pleasures, or is reduced to a balance sheet for which there is absolutely no basis to guide the hand of the accountant. Nonetheless, the influence of Bentham lingers on, for the very reasons he himself offers at the end: one may not like the Pleasure Principle as the foundation for a system of morality, but his ghost mocks us with its empty grin: "What, then do you propose to set in its place?"* There are assuredly answers to this question, but none as simple, or as seemingly irrefutable, as Bentham's.

*Under the terms of his will, his preserved body, seated with hat between his feet, was on display in a glass case in Union College, London.

WILLIAM STANLEY JEVONS

⌒

(1835–1882)

Perhaps the assiduous reader will recall that Jevons's name has already appeared in this book, when he mentions in passing the thousand works he had perused in the course of placing Cantillon high among the gallery of the early economists. The mention will suffice to establish Jevons as a formidable scholar, the publication of whose *Theory of Political Economy* in 1871, was assuredly one of the major pronouncements of the new turn of economic thought.[43]

We should also bear in mind that Jevons was among the first of the marginalists, not the last; and that his degree of mathematization is simple compared with what will come. But it must also be plain that two things are about to be accomplished: (1) the "magnificent dynamics" of the classical school will disappear, to make way for an analytic task almost entirely directed to the investigation of the individual weighing how much to buy at varying prices; and (2) the "scientificity" of economics will achieve a prominence—indeed, a centrality—quite unknown before.

Last, what was Jevons's connection with the work of Bentham? I

---

[43] W. S. Jevons, *The Theory of Political Economy*, Penguin Classics, 1970, pp. 77–78.

can do no better than cite the words of R. D. Collison Black, a leading scholar of Jevons's work:

> [The economic] task which Bentham never undertook was the one which Jevons set himself. When this point is borne in mind, the layout of the *Theory of Political Economy* can be seen as clear and logical. Having discussed method in his Introduction, Jevons goes on to set out the basic Theory of Pleasure and Pain. Then comes the Theory of Utility, which explains how pleasure is derived from the consumption of commodities. This brings us to the centre-piece of the work, the Theory of Exchange, with its demonstration of how utility is increased by exchange, and how the parties to exchange can maximize utility. The Theory of Labour is then seen as the correlative of the Theory of Utility: 'Labour is the painful exertion which we undergo to ward off pains of a greater amount, or to procure pleasures which leave a balance in our favour. What this chapter affords is not theory of wages but a theory of the cost of production in terms of disutility.[44]

The excerpts that follow make explicit the framework that Black has described:

THEORY OF POLITICAL ECONOMY

Introduction

The science of Political Economy rests upon a few notions of an apparently simple character. Utility, wealth, value, commodity, labour, land, capital, are the elements of the subject; and whoever has a thorough comprehension of their nature must possess or be soon able to acquire a knowledge of the whole science. . . . Accordingly, I have devoted the following pages to an investigation of the conditions and relations of the above-named notions.

Repeated reflection and inquiry have led me to the somewhat

[44] Jevons, op. cit., Introduction, pp. 18–19.

novel opinion, that *value depends entirely upon utility*. Prevailing opinions make labour rather than utility the origin of value; and there are even those who distinctly assert that labour is the *cause* of value. I show, on the contrary, that we have only to trace out carefully the natural laws of the variation of utility, as depending upon the quantity of commodity in our possession, in order to arrive at a satisfactory theory of exchange, of which the ordinary laws of supply and demand are a necessary consequence. This theory is in harmony with facts; and, whenever there is any apparent reason for the belief that labour is the cause of value, we obtain an explanation of the reason. Labour is found often to determine value, but only in an indirect manner, by varying the degree of utility of the commodity through an increase or limitation of the supply. . . .

It is clear that Economics, if it is to be a science at all, must be a mathematical science. There exists much prejudice against attempts to introduce the methods and language of mathematics into any branch of the moral sciences. Many persons seem to think that the physical sciences form the proper sphere of mathematical method, and that the moral sciences demand some other method—I know not what. My theory of Economics, however, is purely mathematical in character. Nay, believing that the quantities with which we deal must be subject to continuous variation, I do not hesitate to use the appropriate branch of mathematical science, involving though it does the fearless consideration of infinitely small quantities. The theory consists in applying the differential calculus to the familiar notions of wealth, utility, value, demand, supply, capital, interest, labour, and all the other quantitative notions belonging to the daily operations of industry. . . .

To me it seems that our science must be mathematical, simply because it deals with quantities. Wherever things treated are capable of being *greater or less*, there the laws and relations must be mathematical in nature. The ordinary laws of supply and demand treat entirely of quantities of commodities demanded or supplied, and express the manner in which the quantities vary

in connexion with the price. In consequence of this fact the laws
are mathematical. . . .

Jevons has made his intention clear—the problem is how to realize it. His solution marks an important change in the presentation
of economic arguments, namely, a resort to diagrams. We have
previously seen their persuasive appeal in the work of the Physiocrats, where they depicted the circulation of goods throughout the
economy. Jevons uses diagrams for another purpose—to present,
in "scientific" form, the relation between increments of consumption of a good and the pleasures derived therefrom. The two-
dimensional diagram below will become, in time, the "demand
curve" that we find in every economic textbook today.

Chapter III

The Theory of Utility

My principal work now lies in tracing out the exact nature and
conditions of utility. It seems strange indeed that economists
have not bestowed more minute attention on a subject which
doubtless furnishes the true key to the problem of Economics.

In the first place, utility, though a quality of things, is no *inherent quality*. It is better described as *a circumstance of things arising
out of their relation to man's requirements*. . . .

Let us now investigate this subject a little more closely. Utility
must be considered as measured by, or even as actually identical
with, the addition made to a person's happiness. It is a convenient name for the aggregate of the favorable balance of feeling
produced,—the sum of the pleasure created and the pain prevented. We must now carefully discriminate between the *total
utility* arising from any commodity and the utility attaching to
any particular portion of it. Thus the total utility of the food we
eat consists in maintaining life, and may be considered as infinitely great; but if we were to subtract a tenth part from what we
eat daily, our loss would be but slight. We should certainly not

lose a tenth part of the whole utility of food to us. It might be doubtful whether we should suffer any harm at all.

Let us imagine the whole quantity of food which a person consumes on an average during twenty-four hours to be divided into ten equal parts. If his food be reduced by the last part, he will suffer but little; if a second tenth part be deficient, he will feel the want distinctly; the subtraction of the third tenth part will be decidedly injurious; with every subsequent subtraction of a tenth part his sufferings will be more and more serious, until at length he will be upon the verge of starvation. Now, if we call each of the tenth parts *an increment*, the meaning of these facts is, that each increment of food is less necessary, or possesses less utility, than the previous one. To explain this variation of utility we may make use of space representations, which I have found convenient in illustrating the laws of economics in my college lectures during fifteen years past.

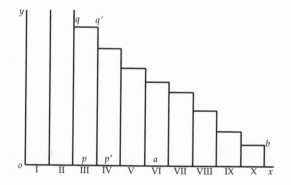

Let the line *ox* be used as a measure of the quantity of food, and let it be divided into ten equal parts to correspond to the ten portions of food mentioned above. Upon these equal lines are constructed rectangles and the area of each rectangle may be assumed to represent the utility of the increment of food corresponding to its base. Thus the utility of the last increment is small, being proportional to the small rectangle on X. As we approach towards *o*, each increment bears a larger rectangle, that standing upon III being the largest complete rectangle. The utility of the next increment, II, is undefined, as also that of I, since these portions of food would be indispensable to life, and their utility, therefore, infinitely great.

But the division of the food into ten equal parts is an arbitrary supposition. If we had taken twenty or a hundred or more equal parts, the same general principle would hold true, namely, that each small portion would be less useful and necessary than the last. The law may be considered to hold true theoretically, however small the increments are made; and in this way we shall at last reach a figure which is undistinguishable from a continuous curve. The notion of infinitely small quantities of food may seem absurd as regards the consumption of one individual; but when we consider the consumption of a nation as a whole, the consumption may well be conceived to increase or diminish by quantities which are, practically speaking, infinitely small compared with the whole consumption. The laws which we are about to trace out are to be conceived as theoretically true of the individual; they can only be practically verified as regards the aggregate transactions, productions, and consumptions of a large body of people. But the laws of the aggregate depend of course upon the laws applying to individual cases. . . .

We shall seldom need to consider the degree of utility except as regards the last increment which has been consumed, or, which comes to the same thing, the next increment which is about to be consumed. I shall therefore commonly use the expression *final degree of utility*, as meaning the degree of utility of the last addition, or the next possible addition of a very small, or infinitely small, quantity to the existing stock. In ordinary circumstances, too, the final degree of utility will not be great compared with what it might be. Only in famine or other extreme circumstances do we approach the higher degrees of utility.

The Final Degree of Utility

The final degree of utility is that function upon which the theory of economics will be found to turn. Economists, generally speaking, have failed to discriminate between this function and the total utility, and from this confusion has arisen much perplexity. Many commodities which are most useful to us are esteemed and desired but little. We cannot live without water, and yet in ordinary circumstances we set no value on it. Why is this? Simply because we usually have so much of it that its final degree of utility is reduced nearly to zero. We enjoy every day the almost infinite utility of water, but then we do not need to consume more than we have. Let the supply run short by drought, and we begin to feel the higher degrees of utility, of which we think but little at other times.

The variation of the function expressing the final degree of utility is the all-important point in economic problems. We may state, as a general law, that *the degree of utility varies with the quantity of commodity, and ultimately decreases as that quantity increases.* No commodity can be named which we continue to desire with the same force, whatever be the quantity already in use or possession. All our appetites are capable of *satisfaction* or *satiety* sooner or later, in fact, both these words mean, etymologically, that we have had *enough,* so that more is of no use to us. It does not follow, indeed, that the degree of utility will always sink to zero. This may be the case with some things, especially the simple animal requirements, such as food, water, air, etc. But the more refined and intellectual our needs become, the less are they capable of satiety. To the desire for articles of taste, science, or curiosity, when once excited, there is hardly a limit. . . .

However abbreviated our presentation, it must be clear that we are moving toward a depiction of the crucial act of exchange in a *mathematical* manner. And that is indeed the destination to which we quickly arrive, once the crucial importance of the final degree of utility has been established. To repeat the admonition with which I began, what is important for our purposes is not so much to follow the precise calculations below, but to appreciate the extraordinary change that has come over economics. That is a subject to which we will return many times. But first, the crucial act of exchange must be witnessed.

The Act of Exchange, in Mathematics

The keystone of the whole Theory of Exchange, and of the principal problems of Economics, lies in this proposition—*The ratio of exchange of any two commodities will be the reciprocal of the ratio of the final degrees of utility of the quantities of commodity available for consumption after the exchange is completed.* When the reader has reflected a little upon the meaning of this proposition, he will see, I think, that it is necessarily true, if the principles of human nature have been correctly represented in previous pages.

Imagine that there is one trading body possessing only corn, and another possessing only beef. It is certain that, under these circumstances, a portion of the corn may be given in exchange for a portion of the beef with a considerable increase of utility. How are we to determine at what point the exchange will cease to be beneficial? This question must involve both the ratio of exchange and the degrees of utility. Suppose, for a moment, that the ratio of exchange is approximately that of ten pounds of corn for one pound of beef: then if, to the trading body which possesses corn, ten pounds of corn are less useful than one of beef, that body will desire to carry the exchange further. Should the other body possessing beef find one pound less useful than ten pounds of corn, this body will also be desirous to continue the exchange. Exchange will thus go on until each party has obtained all the benefit that is possible, and loss of utility would result if more were exchanged. Both parties, then, rest in satisfaction and equilibrium, and the degrees of utility have come to their level, as it were.

This point of equilibrium will be known by the criterion, that an infinitely small amount of commodity exchanged in addition, at the same rate, will bring neither gain nor loss of utility. In other words, if increments of commodities be exchanged at the established ratio, their utilities will be equal for both parties. Thus, if ten pounds of corn were of exactly the same utility as one pound of beef, there would be neither harm nor good in further exchange at this ratio. . . .

To represent this process of reasoning in symbols, let Δx

denote a small increment of corn, and Δy a small increment of beef exchanged for it. Now our Law of Indifference comes into play. As both the corn and the beef are homogeneous commodities, no parts can be exchanged at a different ratio from other parts in the same market: hence, if x be the whole quantity of corn given for y the whole quantity of beef received, Δy must have the same ratio to Δx as y to x; we have then,

$$\frac{\Delta y}{\Delta x} = \frac{y}{x}, \quad \text{or} \quad \Delta y = \frac{y}{x} \Delta x.$$

In a state of equilibrium, the utilities of these increments must be equal in the case of each party, in order that neither more nor less exchange would be desirable. Now the increment of beef, Δy, is y/x times as great as the increment of corn, Δx, so that, in order that their utilities shall be equal, the degree of utility of beef must be x/y times as great as the degree of utility of corn. Thus we arrive at the principle that *the degrees of utility of commodities exchanged will be in the inverse proportion of the magnitudes of the increments exchanged.*

Let us now suppose that the first body, A, originally possessed the quantity a of corn, and that the second body, B, possessed the quantity b of beef. As the exchange consists in giving x of corn for y of beef, the state of things after exchange will be as follows:—

A holds $a - x$ of corn, and y of beef,
B holds x of corn, and $b - y$ of beef.

Let $\phi_1(a - x)$ denote the final degree of utility of corn to A, and $\phi_2 x$ the corresponding function for B. Also let $\psi_1 y$ denote A's final degree of utility for beef, and $\psi_2(b - y)$ B's similar function. Then, as explained previously A will not be satisfied unless the following equation holds true:—

$$\phi_1(a - x) \cdot dx = \psi_1 y \cdot dy;$$
$$\text{or} \quad \frac{\phi_1(a - x)}{\psi_1 y} = \frac{dy}{dx}.$$

Hence, substituting for the second member by the equation given previously, we have

$$\frac{\phi_1(a-x)}{\psi_1 y} = \frac{y}{x}.$$

What holds true of A will also hold true of B, *mutatis mutandis*. He must also derive exactly equal utility from the final increments, otherwise it will be for his interest to exchange either more or less, and he will disturb the conditions of exchange. Accordingly [substituting as before] the following final equation must hold true. . . :

$$\frac{\phi_2 x}{\psi_2(b-y)} = \frac{y}{x}.$$

We arrive, then at the conclusion that whenever two commodities are exchanged for each other, and *more or less can be given or received in infinitely small quantities,* the quantities exchanged satisfy two equations, which may be stated thus in a concise form

$$\frac{\phi_1(a-x)}{\psi_1 y} = \frac{y}{x} = \frac{\phi_2 x}{\psi_2(b-y)}.$$

It should be noted that Jevons also wrote about matters of social concern, including *A Serious Fall in the Value of Gold* (1864) in which he was perhaps the first observer to suggest that the cause of the ten-year "cycle" of business might be related to a shifting direction of investment between long-term and short-term projects, or *The Coal Question* (1865) a remarkably pessimistic analysis of what appeared to be England's prospective exhaustion of its coal resources.

Nonetheless, in keeping with his marginalist approach, Jevons shied away from large-scale dynamics because they seemed beyond the reach of scientific analysis. Thus at the end of his *Theory of Political Economy* he formulates "the problem of economics" in italics as follows:

Given a certain population, with various needs and powers of production, in possession of certain lands and other sources of material: required, the mode of employing their labour which will maximize the utility of the product.[45]

Despite the title of his book, it is a very far cry from *Political Economy.*

[45] Jevons, op. cit., p. 254.

LÉON WALRAS

(1834–1910)

Jevons was perhaps the most important marginalist in England, although Francis Ysidro Edgeworth left his mark in the "indifference curves" and "box diagrams" known to all students of modern microeconomics; while in Austria, Carl Menger steered economics in a marginalist direction without mathematics or Benthamite utilitarianism. Oddly enough, however, the single most influential member of the marginalist school was none of the above, but an obscure professor at the University of Lausanne, Switzerland, Marie Esprit Léon Walras.

Unknown for many years, Walras's work is today possibly the most frequently cited of all the marginalists. What seems at first curious about his rise to fame is that, while marginalism is generally associated with a conservative approach to economic policy, Walras was himself something of an agrarian socialist, advocating the nationalization of land. Even in this advocacy, however, he revealed a characteristically conservative marginalist viewpoint, in that he urged nationalization not so much to improve the socioeconomic condition of farm laborers, as to enhance their mobility, thereby hastening the attainment of the "general equilibrium of exchange" he considered necessary for maximum social well-being.

Walras is a mathematical economist par excellence, which severely limits the use that can be made of his work in a book of this kind, especially with regard to the nature of general equilibrium itself, the key contribution of Walrasian economics. Before launching into an examination of his work, we ought, therefore to say a word about his method.

Can economics be a "mathematical" science? The unequivocal answer must be yes and no. Yes, because economics involves quantities, and quantities are, by definition, capable of mathematical exploration and manipulation. No, because economics seeks not only to measure but to clarify, and many of its most important quantities, such as "labor" or "gross domestic product" can be understood, and therefore clarified, in more than one way. To put it differently, "pure"—that is, highly abstract—economics is unequivocally mathematical in character; but "applied"—real-world—economics will mislead anyone who reads equations and forgets about the very different ways in which the "real" world can be translated into abstract representations.

Walras was himself acutely aware of these difficulties, and indeed pursued his explorations in pure theory in order to provide the strongest possible foundation for—not representation of—real world tendencies. In this regard, he was not the first to see mathematics (or diagrams) as a means of penetrating the confusion of daily life in order to perceive relationships that would otherwise elude us. Pure analysis had already been explored to some extent by the Physiocrats (we recall Quesnay's diagrams) and by Ricardo, as well as other less well-known investigators. Hence Walras was not inventing a new mode of analysis so much as perfecting it, in a very self-conscious way. In particular, he sought to set forth in the form of equations the exact relations that would have to prevail if a state of affairs called general equilibrium were to be attained.

Can such an analysis lead to practical results? That is a difficult question to answer. As many modern economists would point out, we cannot assume, as Ricardo did, that because free trade was optimal in theory it would therefore best serve our specific national interests. But not to have Ricardo's theoretical insight involves us in perhaps an even greater problem, namely having no guidance with respect to the *direction* in which we wish to move in order to reach the best possible state of affairs.

That is not a problem we can explore deeply in this book. We are only going to catch a glimpse of Walras's analysis, first looking into his article "Geometrical Determination of Prices" published in 1892, which sets out in a very accessible manner how using algebra and calculus can help us understand "the nature of things." Thereafter we take a look into the famous book *Elements of Pure Economics,* published two years later, catching at least a flavor of his analytical style and larger theoretical vision.

GEOMETRICAL THEORY OF THE DETERMINATION OF PRICES

[Some critics] . . . laugh at the number of pages I use in demonstrating that we may arrive at a current price by raising in case of an excess of the demand over the supply, and lowering in case of an excess of the supply over the demand. "And you," I said once to one of them, "how do you demonstrate it?" "Well," he answered me, a little surprised and embarrassed, "is there any need of demonstrating it? It seems to me self-evident." "There is nothing evident except axioms, and this is not an axiom. But one naturally follows the mode of reasoning which Jevons has formulated so clearly in his little treatise on *Political Economy,* that a rise, making necessarily a diminution of the demand and an augmentation of the supply, causes equality in case of a surplus of the one over the other." "Precisely." "But there is an error there. A rise necessarily diminishes the demand; but it does not necessarily augment the supply. If you are a supplier of wine, it may well be that you supply less at a million, than at a thousand francs, less at a billion than at a million, simply because you prefer to drink your wine yourself, rather than use the surplus which you could procure by selling it beyond a certain limit. The same is true of labor. We easily conceive that a man, who supplies ten hours a day of his time at the price of one franc an hour, would not supply more than four at the price of 10 francs, or than one at 100 francs. We see, every day, in the large towns, that the laborers, when they earn 20 or 25 francs a day, do not work more than three or four days a week." "But if that is so, how is raising it a means of reaching the current price?" "It is this that the theory explains. Two individuals, who have separated, may meet again, either by moving each, in an opposite direction to the other, or by one going faster than the other. Supply and demand equalize themselves, sometimes in one way, sometimes in another."

Is it not worth while to demonstrate rigorously the fundamental laws of a science? We count to-day I do not know how many schools of political economy. . . . For me, I recognize but two: the school of those who do not demonstrate, and the school, which I hope to see founded, of those who do demonstrate their conclusions. It is in demonstrating rigorously the elementary theorems of geometry and algebra, then the theorems of the calculus and mechanics which result from them, in order to apply them to experimental ideas, that we realize the marvels of modern industry. Let us proceed in the same way in political economy, and we shall, without doubt, succeed in dealing with the nature of things in the economic and social order, as they are dealt with in the physical and industrial order.[46]

This does not mean that we have no control over prices. Because gravity is a natural phenomenon and obeys natural laws, it does not follow that all we can do is to watch it operate. We can either resist it or give it free rein, whichever we please, but we cannot change its essence or its laws. It is said we cannot command nature except by obeying her. This applies also to value. In the case of wheat, for example, we could either raise its price by destroying part of its supply, or lower the price by eating rice or potatoes or some other foodstuff in place of wheat. We could even fix the price of wheat by decree at 20 francs instead of 24 francs a hectolitre. In the first instance, we should be acting upon the causes of the phenomenon of value in such a

[46]Taken from *Source Readings in Economic Thought*. Phillip C. Newman, Arthus D. Gayer, and Milton H. Spencer, eds. W. W. Norton & Co., 1954, pp. 466–67.

way as to substitute one natural value for another natural value. In the second instance, we should be acting directly upon the phenomenon itself, substituting an artificial value for a natural one. It would even be possible, in an extreme case, to abolish value altogether by abolishing exchange. If, however, exchanges do take place, we cannot prevent them from giving rise to or tending to give rise to certain exchange values, naturally under given conditions of supply and demand, in short, of scarcity.

Wheat is worth 24 francs a hectolitre. We observe, now, that this phenomenon is *mathematical* in character as well. The value of wheat in terms of money, or the price of wheat, was 22 or 23 francs yesterday. A short while before it was 23 francs 50 centimes or 23 francs 75 centimes. Soon it will be 24 francs 25 centimes or 24 francs 50 centimes. Tomorrow it will be 25 or 26 francs. But at this present moment, today, it is 24 francs, *neither more nor less.* This phenomenon is so clearly mathematical in character that I shall proceed immediately to state it in terms of an equation and thereby give it its true expression.

The hectolitre being taken as the quantitative unit of measure for wheat, and the gramme as the quantitative unit of measure for silver, we can say with utmost precision that, if 5 hectolitres of wheat are exchanged for 600 grammes of silver, it means that "5 hectolitres of wheat *have the same value* as 600 grammes of silver", or that "the *value in exchange* of 5 hectolitres of wheat *equals* the *value in exchange* of 600 grammes of silver", or finally, that "5 times the value in exchange of 1 hectolitre of wheat equals 600 times the value in exchange of 1 gramme of silver".

Accordingly, let v_b be the value in exchange of 1 hectolitre of wheat and let v_a be the value in exchange of 1 gramme of silver 0·900 fine. Using ordinary mathematical notations, we obtain the equation:

$$5v_b = 600v_a,$$

and, if we divide both sides of the equation by 5, we obtain

$$v_b = 120v_a. \tag{1}$$

If we agree to conform to the practice of this hypothetical market selected for our example, and choose as the unit of measure of value, not the value in exchange of 1 gramme of silver, but the value in exchange of 5 grammes of silver 0·900 fine, called a franc, that is to say, if we postulate that

$$5v_a = 1 \text{ franc,}$$

it follows that

$$v_b = 24 \text{ francs.} \qquad (2)$$

In form (1), precisely as in form (2), the equation is an exact translation of the following phrase, or, as I should prefer to put it, the scientific representation of the following fact: "Wheat is worth 24 francs a hectolitre."

Value in exchange is thus a magnitude, which, as we now see, is measurable. If the object of mathematics in general is to study magnitudes of this kind, the theory of value in exchange is really a branch of mathematics which mathematicians have hitherto neglected and left undeveloped.

It must be evident to the reader from the previous discussion that I do not claim that this science constitutes the whole of economics. Force and velocity are also measurable magnitudes, but the mathematical theory of force and velocity is not the whole of mechanics. Nevertheless, pure mechanics surely ought to precede applied mechanics. Similarly, given the *pure theory of economics,* it must precede *applied economics;* and this pure theory of economics is a science which resembles the physico-mathematical sciences in every respect. This assertion is new and will seem strange; but I have just proved it to be true, and I shall elaborate the proof in what follows.

If the pure theory of economics or the theory of exchange and value in exchange, that is, the theory of social wealth considered by itself, is a physico-mathematical science like mechanics or hydrodynamics, then economists should not be afraid to use the methods and language of mathematics.

The mathematical method is not an *experimental* method; it is a *rational* method. Are the sciences which are strictly speaking natural sciences restricted to a pure and simple description of

nature, or do they transcend the bounds of experience? I leave it
to the natural scientists to answer this question. This much is
certain, however, that the physico-mathematical sciences, like
the mathematical sciences, in the narrow sense, do go beyond
experience as soon as they have drawn their type concepts from
it. From real-type concepts, these sciences abstract ideal-type
concepts which they define, and then on the basis of these definitions they construct *a priori* the whole framework of their theorems and proofs. After that they go back to experience not to
confirm but to apply their conclusions. Everyone who has studied any geometry at all knows perfectly well that only in an
abstract, ideal circumference are the radii all equal to each other
and that only in an abstract, ideal triangle is the sum of the
angles equal to the sum of two right angles. Reality confirms
these definitions and demonstrations only approximately, and
yet reality admits of a very wide and fruitful application of these
propositions. Following this same procedure, the pure theory of
economics ought to take over from experience certain type concepts, like those of exchange, supply, demand, market, capital,
income, productive services and products. From these real-type
concepts the pure science of economics should then abstract and
define ideal-type concepts in terms of which it carries on its reasoning. The return to reality should not take place until the science is completed and then only with a view to practical
applications. Thus in an ideal market we have ideal prices which
stand in an exact relation to an ideal demand and supply. And
so on. Do these pure truths find frequent application? To be sure,
the scholar has a right to pursue science for its own sake, just as
the geometer has the right (which, in fact, he exercises every day)
to study the most singular properties of geometric figures, however fantastic, if he finds that they excite his curiosity. We shall
see, however, that the truths of pure economics yield solutions
of very important problems of applied economics and social economics, which are highly controversial and very little understood.

As to mathematical language, why should we persist in using
everyday language to explain things in the most cumbrous and

incorrect way, as Ricardo has often done and as John Stuart Mill does repeatedly in his *Principles of Political Economy*, when these same things can be stated far more succinctly, precisely and clearly in the language of mathematics?

———————————

Now is the time to meet Walras's most important and enduring contribution—his theory of General Equilibrium. The key word here is the adjective *general*. We are already familiar with Adam Smith's conception of a "natural" price, to which market prices would gravitate as the consequence of competition among buyers and sellers. This natural price resembled an equilibrium price, but it was not a *general* equilibrium price in that it referred only to the state of affairs for a single commodity—what would come to be called a state of "partial" equilibrium. The Walrasian contribution is to demonstrate the possibility of an equilibrium that prevails simultaneously in all markets. Here the difficulties are immediately apparent. A change in any one market will almost certainly absorb purchasing power from other markets or expel it into them. Thus if the amount of spending on wine rises, it must come from somewhere else; and if it falls, it must find some other outlet, or be held as cash, changing the condition of the financial markets.

To calculate the adjustments needed to achieve a simultaneous equilibrium in all markets is therefore an extraordinarily complex matter. The difficulty arises because adjustment is not a one-time change, but a *process* in which changing demands and supplies exert repercussions that spread across the system, altering everything at the same time.

Walras did not, in fact, completely resolve the problem. But in the course of his heroic attempt to do so, he devised a mode of exposition that is of some interest. It involves the idea of an auction, in which prices, presumably for all goods, are announced by an "auctioneer." To these announcements all buyers and sellers submit "pledges"—that is, binding bids and offers at the announced price for the good. The auctioneer now compares these bids and offers to see if they match in all markets. If not, he announces other prices, more likely to bring about a match between all bids and offers. Walras calls this process of successive approximations *"tâtonnement"*—groping—and finds in it the route to a simultaneous resolution of all partial equilibria into the overall "fit" of a general equilibrium.

It goes without saying that the process of groping is wildly unrealistic. Then why bother to describe it? The reason begins with partial equilibrium as a state that maximizes the utilities of the buyers and sellers in one distinct market. From this starting point, it follows that a configuration in which mutually compatible partial equilibria were everywhere attained would represent a *summum bonum* for society as a whole.

The theoretical feasibility of such a grand maximization of utility is a challenge that must attract any marginalist-minded theorist. Walras's attempt, flawed and imperfect though it is, provided the stimulus, and often the entry point for many previously unexplored lines of inquiry into aspects of "real life economics," ranging from the stability of the very idea of general equilibrium itself, to analyses of entrepreneurship or the structures of firms, or even of production itself.

We shall return at the end of our survey to the tension between theorizing at a very high level of abstraction and the need to adapt economic inquiry to the down-to-earth needs of social problems. But the obvious fact that such a tension must exist serves to introduce our next economic thinker as someone in whom this very conflict plays an important role in shaping his overall vision of economics itself.

ALFRED MARSHALL

(1842–1924)

Alfred Marshall dominates economics from 1890, when his
magisterial *Principles of Economics* appears, until the eve of
World War I when his most gifted pupil, John Maynard Keynes,
begins to outshine his master. Indeed, in 1938, when I took my
first serious course in economics at Harvard, the textbook we used
was Marshall.

That which makes Marshall of special interest for a study of the
evolution of economic thought is not, however, just his extraordinary stature. Marshall gives voice simultaneously to two
approaches to economics. One of them is unquestionably that of
marginalism, to which he made contributions of great importance.
The second is a very un-, even anti-marginalist conception of economics as intrinsically sociological, or, to say the dreaded word,
moral. Throughout the text the two approaches intertwine, not
always for the best from the viewpoint of logical clarity, but unfail-
ingly to the interest of those who see in the economy a subject
that may have law-like "natural" attributes, but which also possesses a core for which there is no counterpart in the worlds to
which science directs its gaze.

We see this moral emphasis in the very first page of the *Principles*:[47]

Chapter I

Introduction

§ 1. POLITICAL ECONOMY or ECONOMICS is a study of mankind in the ordinary business of life; it examines that part of individual and social action which is most closely connected with the attainment and with the use of the material requisites of wellbeing.

Thus it is on the one side a study of wealth; and on the other, and more important side, a part of the study of man. For man's character has been moulded by his every-day work, and the material resources which he thereby procures, more than by any other influence unless it be that of his religious ideals; and the two great forming agencies of the world's history have been the religious and the economic. Here and there the ardour of the military or the artistic spirit has been for a while predominant: but religious and economic influences have nowhere been displaced from the front rank even for a time; and they have nearly always been more important than all others put together. Religious motives are more intense than economic, but their direct action seldom extends over so large a part of life. For the business by which a person earns his livelihood generally fills his thoughts during by far the greater part of those hours in which his mind is at its best; during them his character is being formed by the way in which he uses his faculties in his work, by the thoughts and the feelings which it suggests, and by his relations to his associates in work, his employers or his employees.

(sidehead) Economics is a study of wealth and a part of the study of man.

(sidehead) Man's character formed by his daily work.

Note the disarmingly simple style in which Marshall presents his argument. That style is no accident: the *Principles* was originally directed as much to leaders in the business world as it was to students. Moreover, the charm of his low-keyed discourse

[47] Alfred Marshall, *Principles of Economics*, 8th ed., New York: Macmillan, 1948. The sideheads retain some of the flavor of the original edition.

enables Marshall to get around many problems that are, in fact, more obdurate than he reveals. Here he is, a few pages after his introduction, turning to the vexing question of whether one can compare the utility of goods or money among individuals. Let us savor Marshall's answer before we look more deeply into it:

The same price measures different satisfactions even to persons with equal incomes;

A shilling may measure a greater pleasure (or other satisfaction) at one time than at another even for the same person; because money may be more plentiful with him, or because his sensibility may vary. And persons whose antecedents are similar, and who are outwardly like one another, are often affected in very different ways by similar events. When, for instance, a band of city school children are sent out for a day's holiday in the country, it is probable that no two of them derive from it enjoyment exactly the same in kind, or equal in intensity. The same surgical operation causes different amounts of pain to different people. Of two parents who are, so far as we can tell, equally affectionate, one will suffer much more than the other from the loss of a favourite son. Some who are not very sensitive generally are yet specially susceptible to particular kinds of pleasure and pain; while differences in nature and education make one man's total capacity for pleasure or pain much greater than another's.

It would therefore not be safe to say that any two men with the same income derive equal benefit from its use; or that they would suffer equal pain from the same diminution of it. Although when a tax of £1 is taken from each of two persons having an income of £300 a-year, each will give up that £1 worth of pleasure (or other satisfaction) which he can most easily part with, i.e. each will give up what is measured to him by just £1; yet the intensities of the satisfaction given up may not be nearly equal.

but these differences may generally be neglected when we consider the average of large numbers of people.

Nevertheless, if we take averages sufficiently broad to cause the personal peculiarities of individuals to counterbalance one another, the money which people of equal incomes will give to obtain a benefit or avoid an injury is a good measure of the benefit or injury. If there are a thousand persons living in Sheffield, and another thousand in Leeds, each with about £100 a-year, and a tax of £1 is levied on all of them; we may be sure that the loss of pleasure or other injury which the tax will cause in Sheffield is of about equal importance with that which it will cause in Leeds: and anything that increased all the incomes by £1 would give command over equivalent pleasures and other benefits in the two towns. This probability becomes greater still if all of them are adult males engaged in the same trade; and therefore presumably somewhat similar in sensibility and temperament, in taste and education. Nor is the probability much diminished, if we take the family as our unit, and compare the loss of pleasure that results from diminishing by £1 the income of each of a thousand families with incomes of £100 a-year in the two places.

Next we must take account of the fact that a stronger incentive will be required to induce a person to pay a given price for anything if he is poor than if he is rich. A shilling is the measure of less pleasure, or satisfaction of any kind, to a rich man than to a poor one. A rich man in doubt whether to spend a shilling on a single cigar, is weighing against one another smaller pleasures than a poor man, who is doubting whether to spend a shilling on a supply of tobacco that will last him for a month. The clerk with £100 a-year will walk to business in a much heavier rain than the clerk with £300 a-year; for the cost of a ride by tram or omnibus measures a greater benefit to the poorer man than to the richer. If the poorer man spends the money, he will suffer more from the want of it afterwards than the richer would. The benefit that is measured in the poorer man's mind by the cost is greater than that measured by it in the richer man's mind.

The significance of a given price is greater for the poor than the rich.

But this source of error also is lessened when we are able to consider the actions and the motives of large groups of people. If we know, for instance, that a bank failure has taken £200,000 from the people of Leeds and £100,000 from those of Sheffield, we may fairly assume that the suffering caused in Leeds has been about twice as great as in Sheffield; unless indeed we have some special reason for believing that the shareholders of the bank in the one town were a richer class than those in the other; or that the loss of employment caused by it pressed in uneven proportions on the working classes in the two towns.

But this is not important in comparing two groups composed of rich and poor in like proportions.

Increase of material means sometimes a fair measure of real progress.

By far the greater number of the events with which economics deals affect in about equal proportions all the different classes of society; so that if the money measures of the happiness caused by two events are equal, it is reasonable and in accordance with common usage to regard the amounts of the happiness in the two cases as equivalent. And, further, as money is likely to be turned to the higher uses of life in about equal proportions, by any two large groups of people taken without special bias from any two parts of the western world, there is even some *primâ facie* probability that equal additions to their material resources will make about equal additions to the fulness of life, and the true progress of the human race.

It is impossible not to enjoy the behaviors of the clerks with £100 and with £200 a year, but Marshall's earnestness and genuine concern allows him to end his exposition with a very dubious generalization. Is it really the case that "by far the greater number of events with which economics deals affect in about equal proportions all the different classes of society?" Ricardo would certainly not have thought so: as we have seen, he was acutely aware of the different effects exerted by population growth on the fortunes of landlords and capitalists, and Smith was equally aware that the introduction of machinery, while certainly redounding to the benefit of the capitalist class was injurious to the intelligence (and, Ricardo would have added, the prospects for employment) of the laboring class.

Was Marshall aware that his own values found expression in what purported to be objective argument? I suspect not—ideology is much more a matter of unconscious deception of self than of conscious deception of others. But the intermeshing of argument and belief is nonetheless an aspect of Marshall's work to which we must pay heed, even if he did not.

Let us first, however, pay proper respect to the subtlety of Marshall as economic analyst. Take, for instance, this elegant exposition of the question of the "laws" that "regulate" economic activities such as supply and demand. Are they to be compared with the laws of nature?

Every cause has a tendency to produce some definite result if nothing occurs to hinder it. Thus gravitation tends to make things fall to the ground: but when a balloon is full of gas lighter than air, the pressure of the air will make it rise in spite of the tendency of gravitation to make it fall. The law of gravitation states how any two things attract one another; how they tend to move towards one another, and will move towards one another if nothing interferes to prevent them. The law of gravitation is therefore a statement of tendencies.

Nearly all laws of science are statements of tendencies.

It is a very exact statement—so exact that mathematicians can calculate a Nautical Almanac, which will show the moments at which each satellite of Jupiter will hide itself behind Jupiter. They make this calculation for many years beforehand; and navigators take it to sea, and use it in finding out where they are. Now there are no economic tendencies which act as steadily and can be measured as exactly as gravitation can: and consequently there are no laws of economics which can be compared for precision with the law of gravitation.

The exact laws of simple sciences.

But let us look at a science less exact than astronomy. The science of the tides explains how the tide rises and falls twice a day under the action of the sun and the moon: how there are strong tides at new and full moon, and weak tides at the moon's first and third quarter; and how the tide running up into a closed channel, like that of the Severn, will be very high; and so on. Thus, having studied the lie of the land and the water all round the British isles, people can calculate beforehand when the tide will *probably* be at its highest on any day at London Bridge or at Gloucester; and how high it will be there. They have to use the word *probably*, which the astronomers do not need to use when talking about the eclipses of Jupiter's satellites. For, though many forces act upon Jupiter and his satellites, each one of them acts in a definite manner which can be predicted beforehand: but no one knows enough about the weather to be able to say beforehand how it will act. A heavy downpour of rain in the upper Thames valley, or a strong north-east wind in the German Ocean, may make the tides at London Bridge differ a good deal from what had been expected.

The inexact laws of complex sciences.

The science of man is complex and its laws are inexact.

The laws of economics are to be compared with the laws of the tides, rather than with the simple and exact law of gravitation. For the actions of men are so various and uncertain, that the best statement of tendencies, which we can make in a science of human conduct, must needs be inexact and faulty. This might be urged as a reason against making any statements at all on the subject; but that would be almost to abandon life. Life is human conduct, and the thoughts and emotions that grow up around it. By the fundamental impulses of our nature we all—high and low, learned and unlearned—are in our several degrees constantly striving to understand the courses of human action, and to shape them for our purposes, whether selfish or unselfish, whether noble or ignoble. And since we *must* form to ourselves some notions of the tendencies of human action, our choice is between forming those notions carelessly and forming them carefully. The harder the task, the greater the need for steady patient inquiry; for turning to account the experience, that has been reaped by the more advanced physical sciences; and for framing as best we can well thought-out estimates, or provisional laws, of the tendencies of human action.

The term "law" means then nothing more than a general proposition or statement of tendencies, more or less certain, more or less definite. Many such statements are made in every science: but we do not, indeed we cannot, give to all of them a formal character and name them as laws. We must select; and the selection is directed less by purely scientific considerations than by practical convenience. If there is any general statement which we want to bring to bear so often, that the trouble of quoting it at length, when needed, is greater than that of burdening the discussion with an additional formal statement and an additional technical name, then it receives a special name, otherwise not.

Definition of law social, and economic

Thus a law of social science, or a *Social Law,* is a statement of social tendencies; that is, a statement that a certain course of action may be expected under certain conditions from the members of a social group.

Economic laws, or statements of economic tendencies, are those social laws which relate to branches of conduct in which the

strength of the motives chiefly concerned can be measured by a
money price.

There is thus no hard and sharp line of division between those
social laws which are, and those which are not, to be regarded
also as economic laws. For there is a continuous gradation from
social laws concerned almost exclusively with motives that can
be measured by price, to social laws in which such motives have
little place; and which are therefore generally as much less precise and exact than economic laws, as those are than the laws of
the more exact physical sciences.[48]

It is again Marshall's unmistakeable voice—reassuring, earnest,
common-sensical, but this time, I think, used for a good purpose—to argue that economics is distinguised from its sister disci-
plines precisely because a greater degree of reliability attaches to
the activities it observes than is true of the activities to which students of sociology or politics turn their attention.

Marshall's contributions to these law-like aspects of economics
concern a number of different problems of great interest to economic theorists, somewhat less to readers who seek only an overview of economic thought. One of these accomplishments is said
to have caused Marshall, who was sunning himself in a tin bath
on a rooftop in Palermo, to leap into the air, crying "Eureka!". The
lightning bolt was the possibility of systematically describing, and
accounting for, differences in the manner in which our demands
for goods (or our willingness to supply them) varied as their prices
changed. For some goods a small percentage change in price
would result in a large proportional change in the quantity
demanded or supplied; for others, only a small change. Marshall
coined the term *elasticity* to describe this relationship, and enumerated the conditions, such as the good's applicability to many
or few uses, that determined whether its response would be elastic
(proportionally great), as in the case when the good had many
uses, or ineleastic (relatively unchanged), as when it had but few.

Perhaps of greater significance was Marshall's clarification of

---

[48] Op. cit., Book I, Chap. 3, pp. 31–33.

the relative importance of supply and demand in determining price. As the first sentence of the extract below tells us, both supply and demand are always involved, but considerations of utility, which affect demand, play a larger role in the short run, whereas problems affecting cost of production increase in importance as the time period lengthens:

We might as reasonably dispute whether it is the upper or the under blade of a pair of scissors that cuts a piece of paper, as whether value is governed by utility or cost of production. It is true that when one blade is held still, and the cutting is effected by moving the other, we may say with careless brevity that the cutting is done by the second; but the statement is not strictly accurate, and is to be excused only so long as it claims to be merely a popular and not a strictly scientific account of what happens.

The former preponderates in market values:

In the same way, when a thing already made has to be sold, the price which people will be willing to pay for it will be governed by their desire to have it, together with the amount they can afford to spend on it. Their desire to have it depends partly on the chance that, if they do not buy it, they will be able to get another thing like it at as low a price: this depends on the causes that govern the supply of it, and this again upon cost of production. But it may so happen that the stock to be sold is practically fixed. This, for instance, is the case with a fish market, in which the value of fish for the day is governed almost exclusively by the stock on the slabs in relation to the demand: and if a person chooses to take the stock for granted, and say that the price is governed by demand, his brevity may perhaps be excused so long as he does not claim strict accuracy. So again it may be pardonable, but it is not strictly accurate to say that the varying prices which the same rare book fetches, when sold and resold at Christie's auction room, are governed exclusively by demand.

the latter in normal values.

Taking a case at the opposite extreme, we find some commodities which conform pretty closely to the law of constant return; that is to say, their average cost of production will be very nearly the same whether they are produced in small quantities or in large. In such a case the normal level about which the market price fluctuates will be this definite and fixed (money) cost of production. If the demand happens to be great, the market price will rise for a time above the level; but as a result production will increase and the market price will fall: and conversely, if the demand falls for a time below its ordinary level.

In such a case, if a person chooses to neglect market fluctuations, and to take it for granted that there will anyhow be enough demand for the commodity to insure that some of it, more or less, will find purchasers at a price equal to this cost of production, then he may be excused for ignoring the influence of demand, and speaking of (normal) price as governed by cost of production—provided only he does not claim scientific accuracy for the wording of his doctrine, and explains the influence of demand in its right place.

Thus we may conclude that, *as a general rule,* the shorter the period which we are considering, the greater must be the share of our attention which is given to the influence of demand on value; and the longer the period, the more important will be the influence of cost of production on value. For the influence of changes in cost of production takes as a rule a longer time to work itself out than does the influences of changes in demand. The actual value at any time, the market value as it is often called, is often more influenced by passing events and by causes whose action is fitful and short lived, than by those which work persistently. But in long periods these fitful and irregular causes in large measure efface one another's influence; so that in the long run persistent causes dominate value completely. Even the most persistent causes are however liable to change. For the whole structure of production is modified, and the relative costs of production of different things are permanently altered, from one generation to another.[49]

Marshall is remembered as well for a number of other advances concerning the marginalist analytic approach. He invented the term *quasi-rent* to identify the higher-than-normal profits accruing to enterprises that enjoyed competitive advantages from special

[49] Marshall, Book V, Chap. III. pp. 348–50.

machinery or other sources during the period in which other firms had not yet caught up to their levels of efficiency; and identified a gain called *consumers' surplus* that represented the amount by which the total utility enjoyed by a consumer from the purchase of a commodity could exceed the loss of utility represented by their expenditure to acquire it.

Were these, and other refinements of lasting importance? Once again, yes and no. Marshall certainly made errors in his somewhat idealized depiction of a market, but in general, he was the first economist to make marginalist economics accessible to the educated public. All difficult matters, or diagrammatic clarifications were relegated to footnotes or appendices (with the result that Keynes remarked that these, not the main text, were all that warranted reading in the *Principles*); and the text itself, with its engaging style, demystified a subject that was beginning to appear arcane.

In one central area, however, Marshall's marginalist focus on price-determination may have set back the development of economic understanding. Already in Chapter II he notes the strategic importance of "social income," and he also shows that he understands the problems in calculating such an aggregate income:

Elements of social income that are in danger of being counted twice or of being omitted.

Social income may be estimated by adding together the incomes of the individuals in the society in question, whether it be a nation or any other group of persons. We must however not count the same thing twice. If we have counted a carpet at its full value, we have already counted the values of the yarn and the labour that were used in making it; and these must not be counted again. And further, if the carpet was made of wool that was in stock at the beginning of the year, the value of that wool must be deducted from the value of the carpet before the net income of the year is reached; while similar deduction must be made for the wear and tear of machinery and other plant used in making it. This is required by the general rule, with which we started, that true or net income is found by deducting from gross income the outgoings that belong to its production.

But if the carpet is cleaned by domestic servants or at steam scouring works, the value of the labour spent in cleaning it must be counted in separately; for otherwise the results of this labour would be altogether omitted from the inventory of those newly-produced commodities and conveniences which constitute the real income of the country. The work of domestic servants is always classed as "labour" in the technical sense; and since it can be assessed *en bloc* at the value of their remuneration in money and in kind without being enumerated in detail, its inclusion raises no great statistical difficulty. There is however some inconsistency in omitting the heavy domestic work which is done by women and other members of the household, where no servants are kept.

Again, suppose a landowner with an annual income of £10,000 hires a private secretary at a salary of £500, who hires a servant at wages of £50. It may seem that if the incomes of all these three persons are counted in as part of the net income of the country, some of it will be counted twice over, and some three times. But this is not the case. The landlord transfers to his secretary, in return for his assistance, part of the purchasing power derived from the produce of land; and the secretary again transfers part of this to his servant in return for his assistance. The farm produce the value of which goes as rent to the landlord, the assistance which the landlord derives from the work of the secretary, and that which the secretary derives from the work of the servant are independent parts of the real net income of the country; and therefore the £10,000 and the £500 and the £50 which are their money measures, must all be counted in when we are estimating the income of the country. But if the landlord makes an allowance of £500 a year to his son, that must not be counted as an independent income, because no services are rendered for it. And it would not be assessed to the Income tax. . . .

The money income, or inflow, of wealth gives a measure of a nation's prosperity, which, untrustworthy as it is, is yet in some respects better than that afforded by the money value of its stock of wealth.[50]

National income is a better measure of general economic prosperity than national wealth.

[50] Marshall, Book II, Chap. 2.

It would seem that Marshall is on the track of identifying the national income as an aspect of the economy to which close attention must be directed. In the next chapter he begins to examine the constitutive ways in which national income might be usefully classified and studied. From our own knowledge of the direction in which economics was about to turn, we might wonder whether Marshall was about to make the crucial distinction between the behavior of consumption and investment in determining the stability or the dynamic properties of the nation's aggregate expenditure. But the negative tone of Marshall's discussion of the differences between these categories—"vague and perhaps not of much practical use"[51]—rules that out. Nothing comes of the interest in social income.

We cannot explain with certainty why Marshall fails to see the possibilities that seem to us to lie within grasp. But one plausible explanation is that the only analytic question of importance from Marshall's perspective concerns the determination of prices; from such a perspective, there is no important difference between consumption and investment goods. Put differently, from the viewpoint of marginalism, key aspects of economic behavior are invisible, such as the role of expectations in the calculation of marginal utility or the presumption that instability, not stability, might be the necessary starting point of analysis. Or yet again, from the Marshallian viewpoint, the larger economy appears as a collection of supply-and-demand criss-crosses—not a view that suggests a coherent means of aggregation. More precisely, such a view blocks out any grasp of total economic production, or its counterpart, total income, as a *flow* determined by two conjoined and interacting streams, consumption and investment. Marshall has thus unwittingly ruled out the perspective needed to see problems that would become the principal focus of his irreverent but very talented pupil, Maynard Keynes.

A last important question again ties together the analytic with the sociological Marshall. That is the disturbing appearance, during Marshall's day, of the concentration of industry to which Marx called attention. Marshall has a remedy for the threat that would

[51] Ibid., p. 80.

never occur to Marx. We see it in Marshall's discussion of the struggle for business longevity:

But here we may read a lesson from the young trees of the forest as they struggle upwards through the benumbing shade of their older rivals. Many succumb on the way, and a few only survive; those few become stronger with every year, they get a larger share of light and air with every increase of their height, and at last in their turn they tower above their neighbours, and seem as though they would grow on for ever, and for ever become stronger as they grow. But they do not. One tree will last longer in full vigour and attain a greater size than another; but sooner or later age tells on them all. Though the taller ones have a better access to light and air than their rivals, they gradually lose vitality; and one after another they give place to others, which, though of less material strength, have on their side the vigour of youth.

And as with the growth of trees, so was it with the growth of businesses as a general rule before the great recent development of vast joint-stock companies, which often stagnate, but do not readily die. Now that rule is far from universal, but it still holds in many industries and trades. Nature still presses on the private business by limiting the length of the life of its original founders, and by limiting even more narrowly that part of their lives in which their faculties retain full vigour. And so, after a while, the guidance of the business falls into the hands of people with less energy and less creative genius, if not with less active interest in its prosperity. If it is turned into a joint-stock company, it may retain the advantages of division of labour, of specialized skill and machinery: it may even increase them by a further increase of its capital; and under favourable conditions it may secure a permanent and prominent place in the work of production. But it is likely to have lost so much of its elasticity and progressive force, that the advantages are no longer exclusively on its side in its competition with younger and smaller rivals.[52]

[52] Marshall, Book IV, Chap. XIII, pp. 315–16.

What Marshall depicts is a kind of a rags-to-riches-to-retirement social setting that rescues the system from the threat of frozen centralization by a self-generated process of renewal. In the preceding chapter he has, in fact, already told the story in more personal terms:

The son of a business man has a good start.

It is obvious that the son of a man already established in business starts with very great advantages over others. He has from his youth up special facilities for obtaining the knowledge and developing the faculties that are required in the management of his father's business: he learns quietly and almost unconsciously about men and manners in his father's trade and in those from which that trade buys and to which it sells; he gets to know the relative importance and the real significance of the various problems and anxieties which occupy his father's mind: and he acquires a technical knowledge of the processes and the machinery of the trade. Some of what he learns will be applicable only to his father's trade; but the greater part will be serviceable in any trade that is in any way allied with that, while those general faculties of judgment and resource, of enterprise and caution, of firmness and courtesy, which are trained by association with those who control the larger issues of any one trade, will go a long way towards fitting him for managing almost any other trade. Further, the sons of successful business men start with more material capital than almost anyone else except those who by nurture and education are likely to be disinclined for business and unfitted for it: and if they continue their fathers' work, they have also the vantage ground of established trade connections.

But business men do not form a caste, because their abilities and tastes are not always inherited;

It would therefore at first sight seem likely that business men should constitute a sort of caste; dividing out among their sons the chief posts of command, and founding hereditary dynasties, which should rule certain branches of trade for many generations together. But the actual state of things is very different. For when a man has got together a great business, his descendants often fail, in spite of their great advantages, to develop the high abilities and the special turn of mind and temperament required for carrying it on with equal success. He himself was probably

brought up by parents of strong earnest character; and was educated by their personal influence and by struggle with difficulties
in early life. But his children, at all events if they were born after
he became rich, and in any case his grandchildren, are perhaps
left a good deal to the care of domestic servants who are not of
the same strong fibre as the parents by whose influence he was
educated. And while his highest ambition was probably success
in business, they are likely to be at least equally anxious for social
or academic distinction.

For a time indeed all may go well. His sons find a firmly established trade connection, and what is perhaps even more
important, a well-chosen staff of subordinates with a generous
interest in the business. By mere assiduity and caution, availing
themselves of the traditions of the firm, they may hold together
for a long time. But when a full generation has passed, when the
old traditions are no longer a safe guide, and when the bonds
that held together the old staff have been dissolved, then the
business almost invariably falls to pieces unless it is practically
handed over to the management of new men who have meanwhile risen to partnership in the firm.

But in most cases his descendants arrive at this result by a
shorter route. They prefer an abundant income coming to them
without effort on their part, to one which though twice as large
could be earned only by incessant toil and anxiety; and they sell
the business to private persons or a joint-stock company; or they
become sleeping partners in it; that is sharing in its risks and in
its profits, but not taking part in its management: in either case
the active control over their capital falls chiefly into the hands of
new men.[53]

[margin note:] and after a time new blood must be brought in by some method.

It is but a short step (although many pages) to the conclusion of
the *Principles:*

Now, as always, noble and eager schemers for the reorganization of society have painted beautiful pictures of life, as it might
be under institutions which their imagination constructs easily.

[53] Op. cit., pp. 298–300.

But it is an irresponsible imagination, in that it proceeds on the suppressed assumption that human nature will, under the new institutions, quickly undergo changes such as cannot reasonably be expected in the course of a century, even under favorable conditions. If human nature could thus be ideally transformed, economic chivalry would dominate life even under the existing institutions of private property. And private property, the necessity for which doubtless reaches no deeper than the qualities of human nature, would become harmless at the same time that it became unnecessary.

There is then need to guard against the temptation to overstate the economic evils of our own age, and to ignore the existence of similar and worse evils in earlier ages; even though some exaggeration may for the time stimulate others, as well as ourselves, to a more intense resolve that the present evils shall no longer be allowed to exist. But it is not less wrong, and generally it is much more foolish, to palter with truth for a good than for a selfish cause. And the pessimistic descriptions of our own age, combined with romantic exaggerations of the happiness of past ages, must tend to the setting aside of methods of progress, the work of which if slow is yet solid; and to the hasty adoption of others of greater promise, but which resemble the potent medicines of a charlatan, and while quickly effecting a little good, sow the seeds of widespread and lasting decay. . . .[54]

Extended comment seems unnecessary. The two Marshalls have been laid out before our eyes—Marshall the keen, but narrowly focused analyst, and Marshall the socially concerned, but wishful moralist. What might perhaps be raised as a final question is which of these modes of inquiry is, in the end, more useful: analysis that leads to logically persuasive results based on ultimately sterile premises, or inquiry that leads to apologistic results that stem, nonetheless, from an awareness of the inexpungeably social nature of economic inquiry itself?

[54] Marshall, Book VI, Chap. XIII. pp. 721–22.

VI

TWENTIETH CENTURY ECONOMISTS

THORSTEIN VEBLEN

(1857–1929)

Veblen is a strange figure in the gallery of the great economists. He made no analytical improvements to the existing models of economics, and developed no grand scenarios comparable to those of the great economists. Worse, the closest he came to the latter was to speculate about a "soviet of technicians" which might one day take over the administration of the business system, but he took the edge off this heretical suggestion by ending the book in which it appeared with the words: "There is nothing in the situation that should reasonably flutter the sensibilities of the Guardians or of that massive body of well-to-do citizens who make up the rank and file of the absentee owners, just yet." Those last two words—reassuring, alarming, mocking—are the essence of Veblen.

His major contribution—Veblen would have smiled at the word—was therefore not to add to the growing corpus of economic thought, but to cut away at the increasing "scientificity" on which that throught rested. Here is an example, taken from an essay entitled "Why Is Economics Not an Evolutionary Science?":

The psychological and anthropological preconceptions of the economists have been those which were accepted by the psychological and social sciences some generations ago. The hedonistic conception of man is that of a lightning calculator of pleasures and pains, who oscillates like a homogenous globule of happiness under the impulse of stimuli that shift him about the area, but leave him intact. He has neither antecedent or consequent. He is an isolated, definitive human datum, in stable equilibrium except for the buffets of the impinging forces that displace him in one direction or another. Self-imposed in elemental space, he spins symmetrically about his own spiritual axis until the parallelogram of forces bears down on him, whereupon he follows the line of the resultant. When the force of the impact is spent, he comes to rest, a self-contained globule of desire as before. Spiritually, the hedonistic man is not a prime mover. He is not the seat of a process of living, except in the sense that he is subject to a series of permutations imposed upon him by circumstances external and alien to him.[55]

The criticism might not apply quite fairly to Marshall, who was always aware of the sociality of the beings whose behavior was depicted in supply and demand diagrams, but it was penetrating with respect to the more abstract-minded theorists of Veblen's day and, I regret to add, of our own.

It is not surprising that Veblen himself was given scant notice by the profession against which his barbs were directed. It is the fate of critics—above all, those who aim their critique at the preconceptions, rather than the conclusions, of a discipline—to suffer from its studied indifference. Hence, it is not surprising that no serious attention was paid to Veblen by the economists who were his target, or that his admirers, for whom he never lacked, were gathered from other fields, or from leaders in intellectual life in general. That remains true to this day. Save for a stalwart group of self-styled institutionalists, Veblen has been ignored within the profession at large. His most famous book, *The Theory of the Leisure Class,* devoted to revealing the primitive aspects of what Veblen called "the pecuniary culture," has never, to my knowledge, been

[55] From *The Portable Veblen*. Max Lerner, ed. New York: Viking Press, 1950, pp. 232–33.

examined by members of my profession as a "serious" book in our discipline, but has always been treated as an essay in sociology, anthropology, or even belles lettres.

The problem is how to include this iconoclast in a volume intended to explore the changing structure of the economic thought that has influenced the western world. I have decided to give the reader a slightly condensed chapter of Veblen's *The Engineers and the Price System,* published in 1921, near the end of his life.[56] It is perhaps as close as he ever came to formulating a view of how the economy worked and how it might work under different auspices: incidentally, the book's final chapter, which raises the spectre of a "soviet of technicians," ends with those mocking words that conclude the first paragraph of this introduction. I have often wondered what Marshall would have thought of this heavy-handed, ornate, and yet devastating analysis. He would have been shocked, of course. Nonetheless, fair-minded as he was, Marshall might have appreciated that here, at last, was an economist willing to look inside the abstraction of "the firm" to see how business actually worked: before Veblen, Marshall was the *only* economist who had done so.

At any rate, here is Veblen for better and worse. Is it economics or sociology? Whichever, Veblen is its master exponent. Until the end, therefore, I will hold my peace, and withold my pen.

THE ENGINEERS AND THE PRICE SYSTEM

Chapter III

The Captains of Finance and the Engineers

In more than one respect the industrial system of today is notably different from anything that has gone before. It is eminently a system, self-balanced and comprehensive; and it is a system of interlocking mechanical processes, rather than of skilful manipulation. It is mechanical rather than manual. It is an organization

---

[56] Thorstein Veblen, *The Engineers and the Price System,* New York: Harcourt Brace & Ward, 1963, Chap. III, abridged.

of mechanical powers and material resources, rather than of skilled craftsmen and tools; although the skilled workmen and tools are also an indispensable part of its comprehensive mechanism. It is of an impersonal nature, after the fashion of the material sciences, on which it constantly draws. It runs to "quantity production" of specialized and standardized goods and services. For all these reasons it lends itself to systematic control under the direction of industrial experts, skilled technologists, who may be called "production engineers," for want of a better term.

This industrial system runs on as an inclusive organization of many and diverse interlocking mechanical processes, interdependent and balanced among themselves in such a way that the due working of any part of it is conditioned on the due working of all the rest. Therefore it will work at its best only on condition that these industrial experts, production engineers, will work together on a common understanding; and more particularly on condition that they must not work at cross purposes. These technological specialists whose constant supervision is indispensable to the due working of the industrial system constitute the general staff of industry, whose work it is to control the strategy of production at large and to keep an oversight of the tactics of production in detail.

Such is the nature of this industrial system on whose due working depends the material welfare of all the civilized peoples. It is an inclusive system drawn on a plan of strict and comprehensive interdependence, such that, in point of material welfare, no nation and no community has anything to gain at the cost of any other nation or community. In point of material welfare, all the civilized peoples have been drawn together by the state of the industrial arts into a single going concern. And for the due working of this inclusive going concern it is essential that that corps of technological specialists who by training, insight, and interest make up the general staff of industry must have a free hand in the disposal of its available resources, in materials, equipment, and man power, regardless of any national pretensions or any vested interests. Any degree of obstruction, diversion, or withholding of any of the available industrial forces, with a view to the special gain of any nation or any investor, unavoidably brings on a dislocation of the system; which involves a disproportionate lowering of its working efficiency and therefore a disproportionate loss to the whole, and therefore a net loss to all its parts.

And all the while the statesmen are at work to divert and obstruct the working forces of this industrial system, here and there, for the special advantage of one nation and another at the cost of the rest; and the captains of finance are working, at cross purposes and in collusion, to divert whatever they can to the special gain of one vested interest and another, at any cost to the rest. So it happens that the industrial system is deliberately handicapped with dissension, misdirection, and unemployment of material resources, equipment, and man power, at every turn where the statesmen or the captains of finance can touch its mechanism; and all the civilized peoples are suffering privation together because their general staff of industrial experts are in this way required to take orders and submit to sabotage at the hands of the statesmen and the vested interests. Politics and investment are still allowed to decide matters of industrial policy which should plainly be left to the discretion of the general staff of production engineers driven by no commercial bias.

No doubt this characterization of the industrial system and its besetting tribulations will seem overdrawn. However, it is not intended to apply to any date earlier than the twentieth century, or to any backward community that still lies outside the sweep of the mechanical industry. Only gradually during the past century, while the mechanical industry has progressively been taking over the production of goods and services, and going over to quantity production, has the industrial system taken on this character of an inclusive organization of interlocking processes and interchange of materials; and it is only in the twentieth century that this cumulative progression has come to a head with such effect that this characterization is now visibly becoming true. . . .

In effect, the progressive advance of this industrial system towards an all-inclusive mechanical balance of interlocking processes appears to be approaching a critical pass, beyond which it will no longer be practicable to leave its control in the hands of business men working at cross purposes for private gain, or to entrust its continued administration to others than suitably trained technological experts, production engineers without a commercial interest. What these men may then do with it all is not so plain; the best they can do may not be good enough; but the negative proposition is becoming sufficiently plain, that this mechanical state of the industrial arts will not long tolerate the continued control of production by the vested interests under the current business-like rule of incapacity by advisement.

In the beginning, that is to say during the early growth of the machine industry, and particularly in that new growth of mechanical industries which arose directly out of the Industrial Revolution, there was no marked division between the industrial experts and the business managers. That was before the new industrial system had gone far on the road of progressive specialization and complexity, and before business had reached an exactingly large scale; so that even the business men of that time, who were without special training in technological matters, would still be able to exercise something or an intelligent oversight of the whole, and to understand something of what was required in the mechanical conduct of the work which they financed and from which they drew their income. Not unusually the designers of industrial processes and equipment would then still take care of the financial end, at the same time that they managed the shop. But from an early point in the development there set in a progressive differentiation, such as to divide those who designed and administered the industrial processes from those others who designed and managed the commercial transactions and took care of the financial end. So there also set in a corresponding division of powers between the business management and the technological experts. It became the work of the technologist to determine, on technological grounds, what could be done in the way of productive industry, and to contrive ways and means of doing it; but the business management always continued to decide, on commercial grounds, how much work should be done and what kind and quality of goods and services should be produced; and the decision of the business management has always continued to be final, and has always set the limit beyond which production must not go. . . .

Through the earlier decades of the machine era these limitations imposed on the work of the experts by the demands of profitable business and by the technical ignorance of the business men, appears not to have been a heavy handicap, whether as a hindrance to the continued development of technological knowledge or as an obstacle to its ordinary use in industry. That was before the mechanical industry had gone far in scope, complexity, and specialization; and it was also before the continued work of the technologists had pushed the industrial system to so high a productive capacity that it is forever in danger of turning out a larger product than is required for a profitable business. But gradually, with the passage of time and the advance of the industrial arts to a wider scope and a larger scale, and to an increasing specialization and standardization of processes, the technological knowledge that makes up the state of the industrial arts has called for a higher degree of that training that makes industrial specialists; and at the same time any passably efficient management of industry has of necessity drawn on them and their special abilities to an ever-increasing extent. At the same time and by the same shift of circumstances, the captains of finance, driven by an increasingly close application to the affairs of business, have been going farther out of touch with the ordinary realities of productive industry; and it is to be admitted, they have also continued increasingly to distrust the technological specialists, whom they do not understand, but whom they can also not get along without. The captains have per force continued to employ the technologists, to make money for them, but they have done so only reluctantly, tardily, sparingly, and with a shrewd circumspection; only because and so far as they have been persuaded that the use of these technologists was indispensable to the making of money.

One outcome of this persistent and pervasive tardiness and

circumspection on the part of the captains has been an incredibly and increasingly uneconomical use of material resources, and an incredibly wasteful organization of equipment and man power in those great industries where the technological advance has been most marked. In good part it was this discreditable pass, to which the leading industries had been brought by these one-eyed captains of industry, that brought the régime of the captains to an inglorious close, by shifting the initiative and discretion in this domain out of their hands into those of the investment bankers. By custom the investment bankers had occupied a position between or overlapping the duties of a broker in corporate securities and those of an underwriter of corporate flotations—such a position, in effect, as is still assigned them in the standard writings on corporation finance. The increasingly large scale of corporate enterprise, as well as the growth of a mutual understanding among these business concerns, also had its share in this new move. But about this time, too, the "consulting engineers" were coming notably into evidence in many of those lines of industry in which corporation finance has habitually been concerned. . . .

The effect of this move has been twofold: experience has brought out the fact that corporation finance, at its best and soundest, has now become a matter of comprehensive and standardized bureaucratic routine, necessarily comprising the mutual relations between various corporate concerns, and best to be taken care of by a clerical staff of trained accountants; and the same experience has put the financial houses in direct touch with the technological general staff of the industrial system, whose surveillance has become increasingly imperative to the conduct of any profitable enterprise in industry. But also, by the same token, it has appeared that the corporation financier of nineteenth-century tradition is no longer of the essence of the case in corporation finance of the larger and more responsible sort. He has, in effect, come to be no better than an idle wheel in the economic mechanism, serving only to take up some of the lubricant.

Since and so far as this shift out of the nineteenth century into the twentieth has been completed, the corporation financier has ceased to be a captain of industry and has become a lieutenant of finance; the captaincy having been taken over by the syndicated investment bankers and administered as a standardized routine of accountancy, having to do with the flotation of corporation securities and with their fluctuating values, and having also something to do with regulating the rate and volume of output in those industrial enterprises which so have passed under the hand of the investment bankers. . . .

Hitherto, then, the growth and conduct of this industrial system presents this singular outcome. The technology—the state of the industrial arts—which takes effect in this mechanical industry is in an eminent sense a joint stock of knowledge and experience held in common by the civilized peoples. It requires the use of trained and instructed workmen—born, bred, trained, and instructed at the cost of the people at large. So also it requires, with a continually more exacting insistence, a corps of highly trained and specially gifted experts, of divers and various kinds. These, too, are born, bred, and trained at the cost of the community at large, and they draw their requisite special knowledge from the community's joint stock of accumulated experience. These expert men, technologists, engineers, or whatever name may best suit them, make up the indispensable General Staff of the industrial system; and without their immediate and unremitting guidance and correction the industrial system will not work. It is a mechanically organized structure of technical processes designed, installed, and conducted by these production engineers. Without them and their constant attention the industrial equipment, the mechanical appliances of industry, will foot up to just so much junk. The material welfare of the community is unreservedly bound up with the due working of this industrial system, and therefore with its unreserved control by the engineers, who alone are competent to manage it. To do their work as it should be done these men of the industrial general staff must have a free hand, unhampered by commercial considerations and reservations; for the production of the goods and services needed by the community they neither need nor are they in any degree benefited by any supervision or interference from the side of the owners. Yet the absentee owners, now represented, in effect, by the syndicated investment bankers, continue to control the industrial experts and limit their discretion, arbitrarily, for their own commercial gain, regardless of the needs of the community.

Hitherto these men who so make up the general staff of the industrial system have not drawn together into anything like a self-directing working force; nor have they been vested with anything more than an occasional, haphazard, and tentative control of some disjointed sector of the industrial equipment, with no direct or decisive relation to that personnel of productive industry that may be called the officers of the line and the rank and file. It is still the unbroken privilege of the financial management and its financial agents to "hire and fire." The final disposition of all the industrial forces still remains in the hands of the business men, who still continue to dispose of these forces for other than industrial ends. And all the while it is an open secret that with a reasonably free hand the production experts would today readily increase the ordinary output of industry by several fold,—variously estimated at some 300 per cent. to 1200 per cent. of the current output. And what stands in the way of so increasing the ordinary output of goods and services is business as usual.

Right lately these technologists have begun to become uneasily "class-conscious" and to reflect that they together constitute the indispensable General Staff of the industrial system. Their class consciousness has taken the immediate form of a growing sense of waste and confusion in the management of industry by the financial agents of the absentee owners. They are beginning to take stock of that all-pervading mismanagement of industry that is inseparable from its control for commercial ends. All of which brings home a realization of their own shame and of damage to the common good. So the engineers are beginning to draw together and ask themselves, "What about it?"

This uneasy movement among the technologists set in, in an undefined and fortuitous way, in the closing years of the nineteenth century; when the consulting engineers, and then presently the "efficiency engineers," began to make scattered corrections in detail, which showed up the industrial incompetence of those elderly laymen who were doing a conservative business at the cost of industry. The consulting engineers of the standard type, both then and since then, are commercialized technologists, whose work it is to appraise the industrial value of any given enterprise with a view to its commercial exploitation. They are a cross between a technological specialist and a commercial agent, beset with the limitations of both and commonly not fully competent in either line. Their normal position is that of an employee of the investment bankers, on a stipend or a retainer, and it has ordinarily been their fortune to shift over in time from a technological footing to a frankly commercial one. The case of the efficiency engineers, or scientific-management experts, is somewhat similar. They too have set out to appraise, exhibit, and correct the commercial short-comings of the ordinary management of those industrial establishments which they investigate, to persuade the business men in charge how they may reasonably come in for larger net earnings by a more closely shorn exploitation of the industrial forces at their disposal. During the opening years of the new century a lively interest centered on the views and expositions of these two groups of industrial experts; and not least was the interest aroused by their exhibits of current facts indicating an all-pervading lag, leak, and friction in the industrial system, due to its disjointed and one-eyed management by commercial adventurers bent on private gain.

During these few years of the opening century the members of this informal guild of engineers at large have been taking an interest in this question of habitual mismanagement by ignorance and commercial sabotage, even apart from the commercial imbecility of it all. But it is the young rather than the old among them who see industry in any other light than its commercial value. Circumstances have decided that the older generation of the craft have become pretty well commercialized. Their habitual outlook has been shaped by a long and unbroken apprenticeship to the corporation financiers and the investment bankers; so that they still habitually see the industrial system as a contrivance for the roundabout process of making money. Accordingly, the established official Associations and Institutes of Engineers, which are officered and engineered by the elder engineers, old and young, also continue to show the commercial bias of their creators, in what they criticize and in what they propose. But the new generation which has been coming on during the present century are not similarly true to that tradition of commercial engineering that makes the technological man an awestruck lieutenant of the captain of finance.

By training, and perhaps also by native bent, the technologists find it easy and convincing to size up men and things in terms of tangible performance, without commercial afterthought, except so far as their apprenticeship to the captains of finance may have made commercial afterthought a second nature to them. Many of the younger generation are beginning to understand that engineering begins and ends in the domain of tangible performance, and that commercial expediency is another matter. Indeed, they are beginning to understand that commercial expediency has nothing better to contribute to the engineer's work than so much lag, leak, and friction. . . .

. . . It would be hazardous to surmise how, how soon, on what provocation, and with what effect the guild of engineers are due to realize that they constitute a guild, and that the material fortunes of the civilized peoples already lie loose in their hands. But it is already sufficiently plain that the industrial conditions and the drift of conviction among the engineers are drawing together to some such end.

Hitherto it has been usual to count on the interested negotiations continually carried on and never concluded between capital and labor, between the agents of the investors and the body of workmen, to bring about whatever readjustments are to be looked for in the control of productive industry and in the distribution and use of its product. These negotiations have necessarily been, and continue to be, in the nature of business transactions, bargaining for a price, since both parties to the negotiation continue to stand on the consecrated ground of ownership, free bargain, and self-help; such as the commercial wisdom of the eighteenth century saw, approved and certified it all, in the time before the coming of this perplexing industrial system. In the course of these endless negotiations betwen the owners and their workmen there has been some loose and provisional syndication of claims and forces on both sides; so that each of these two recognized parties to the industrial controversy has come to make up a loose-knit vested interest, and each speaks for its own special claims as a party in interest. Each is contending for some special gain for itself and trying to drive a profitable bargain for itself, and hitherto no disinterested spokesman for the community at large or for the industrial system as a going concern has seriously cut into this controversy between these contending vested interests. The outcome has been businesslike concession and compromise in the nature of bargain and sale. . . .

These negotiations have necessarily been inconclusive. So long as ownership of resources and industrial plant is allowed, or so long as it is allowed any degree of control or consideration in the conduct of industry, nothing more substantial can come of any readjustment than a concessive mitigation of the owners' interference with production. There is accordingly nothing subversive in these bouts of bargaining between the federated workmen and the syndicated owners. It is a game of chance and skill played between two contending vested interests for private gain, in which the industrial system as a going concern enters only as a victim of interested interference. Yet the material welfare of the community, and not least of the workmen, turns on the due working of this industrial system, without interference. Concessive mitigation of the right to interfere with production, on the part of either one of these vested interests, can evidently come to nothing more substantial than a concessive mitigation.

But owing to the peculiar technological character of this industrial system, with its specialized, standardized, mechanical, and highly technical interlocking processes of production, there has gradually come into being this corps of technological production specialists, into whose keeping the due functioning of the industrial system has now drifted by force of circumstance. They are, by force of circumstance, the keepers of the community's material welfare; although they have hitherto been acting, in effect, as keepers and providers of free income for the kept classes. They are thrown into the position of responsible directors of the industrial system, and by the same move they are in a position to become arbiters of the community's material welfare. They are becoming class-conscious, and they are no longer driven by a commercial interest, in any such degree as will make them a vested interest in that commercial sense in which the syndicated owners and the federated workmen are vested interests. They are, at the same time, numerically and by habitual outlook, no such heterogeneous and unwieldy body as the federated workmen, whose numbers and scattering interest has left all their endeavors substantially nugatory. In short, the engineers are in a position to make the next move.

By comparison with the population at large, including the financial powers and the kept classes, the technological specialists which come in question here are a very inconsiderable number; yet this small number is indispensable to the continued working of the productive industries. So slight are their numbers, and so sharply defined and homogeneous is their class, that a sufficiently compact and inclusive organization of their forces should arrange itself almost as a matter of course, so soon as any appreciable proportion of them shall be moved by any common purpose. And the common purpose is not far to seek, in the all-pervading industrial confusion, obstruction, waste, and retardation which business as usual continually throws in their face. At the same time they are leaders of the industrial personnel, the workmen, of the officers of the line and the rank and file; and these are coming into a frame of mind to follow their leaders in any adventure that holds a promise of advancing the common good.

To these men, soberly trained in a spirit of tangible performance and endowed with something more than an even share of the sense of workmanship, and endowed also with the common heritage of partiality for the rule of Live and Let Live, the disallowance of an outworn and obstructive right of absentee ownership is not likely to seem a shocking infraction of the sacred realities. That customary right of ownership by virtue of which the vested interests continue to control the industrial system for the benefit of the kept classes, belongs to an older order of things than the mechanical industry. It has come out of a past that was made up of small things and traditional make-believe. For all the purposes of that scheme of tangible performance that goes to make up the technologist's world, it is without form and void. So that, given time for due irritation, it should by no means come as a surprise if the guild of engineers are provoked to put their heads together and, quite out of hand, disallow that large absentee ownership that goes to make the vested interests and to unmake the industrial system. And there stand behind them the massed and rough-handed legions of the industrial rank and file, ill at ease and looking for new things. The older commercialized generation among them would, of course, ask themselves: Why should we worry? What do we stand to gain? But the younger generation, not so hard-bitten by commercial experience, will be quite as likely to ask themselves: What do we stand to lose? And there is the patent fact that such a thing as a general strike of the technological specialists in industry need involve no more than a minute fraction of one per cent. of the population; yet it would swiftly bring a collapse of the old order and sweep the timeworn fabric of finance and absentee sabotage into the discard for good and all.

Such a catastrophe would doubtless be deplorable. It would look something like the end of the world to all those persons who take their stand with the kept classes, but it may come to seem no more than an incident of the day's work to the engineers and to the rough-handed legions of the rank and file. It is a situation which may well be deplored. But there is no gain in losing patience with a conjunction of circumstances. And it can do no harm to take stock of the situation and recognize that, by force of circumstance, it is now open to the Council of Technological Workers' and Soldiers' Deputies to make the next move, in their own way and in their own good time. When and what this move will be, if any, or even what it will be like, is not something on which a layman can hold a confident opinion. But so much seems clear, that the industrial dictatorship of the captain of finance is now held on sufferance of the engineers and is liable at any time to be discontinued at their discretion, as a matter of convenience.

What is one to think of this heretical view? It is immediately clear that it is a mixture of realism and unrealism. The vision of a takeover by "engineers" can only be deemed a wishful fantasy: Veblen, who had written in his earlier *Theory of Business Enterprise* that "the machine throws out anthropomorphic habits of thought," is himself the victim of another kind of romantic idealization in the image of the rational engineer, technologist, scientist, turning against the pecuniary-minded business tycoon. Neither in the United States, nor anywhere else, including the former Soviet Union, has control been seized—or even sought—by the designers or custodians of machinery. Books are the sources of revolutionary sentiments, not cogs and gears.

On the other side, there can be no doubt of a real contrast between the outlook of the vice presidents charged with the operation of the production apparatus and that of the executive suite. The objective of the former is hitchless, efficient operation; of the latter, the bottom line, not the production line. The world of corporate affairs depends on efficient operation and can be quite ruthless in seeking to attain it, but it is unavoidably entangled with take-overs, leveraged buyouts, and similar financial transactions that are often of greater immediate importance for its success or failure. The attitude needed to conduct these operations successfully is that of the leader of a raiding party, a view of little use on the production floor.

Thus, from an Olympian height, the interests of "the engineers" may indeed run counter to, or at cross purposes with, those of the directors of "the price system"—a divergence perhaps even more pronounced in our day, when the reach and power of financial maneuvers is much greater than in Veblen's. But I see no signs of any Councils of Technological Workers and Soldiers—neither "just yet," nor in the foreseeable future in any technologically advanced nation. It is an irony of intellectual history that the critic of economics whose scorn was aimed at its conception of the economy as the embodiment of rationality was himself the purveyor of a conception of economic life no less innocent and naive.

JOHN MAYNARD KEYNES

∞

(1883–1946)

Maynard Keynes (he destested his first name and would have been horrified to hear his last pronounced Keenes, not Kaynes) may or may not have been the most brilliant of the great economists, but he was without peer the most worldly. Having distinguished himself at Cambridge, with Marshall as his tutor, thereafter as a member of the hyper-stylish Bloomsbury set, Keynes landed himself a cushy post as the official representative of the British Treasury to the Peace Conference that convened in Paris in June 1919. It was, in retrospect, a turning point in his life. The conference, begun with lofty hopes of repairing the most terrible war in human history, soon settled into a mean-spirited squabble in which the victors sought only to ensure their immediate aims, never mind at whose cost. Keynes resigned in fury and despair, returning to England to make himself famous with a diatribe entitled *The Economic Consequences of the Peace,* in which Keynes laid bare the spirit of the Conference:[57]

Not infrequently, Mr. Lloyd George [The British Prime Minister], after delivering a speech in English, would, during the

[57] *The Economic Consequences of the Peace,* Harcourt Brace and Howe, 1920, pp. 31–32.

period of its interpretation into French, cross the hearthrug to [President Wilson] to reinforce his case by some *ad hominem* argument in private conversation, or to sound the ground for a compromise—and this would sometimes be the signal for a general upheaval and disorder. The President's advisers would press round him, a moment later the British experts would dribble across to learn the result or see that all was well, and next the French would be there, a little suspicious lest the others were arranging something behind them, until all the room were on their feet and conversation was general in both languages. My last and most vivid impression is of such a scene—the President and the Prime Minister as the center of a surging mob and a babel of sound, a welter of eager, impromptu compromises and counter-compromises, all sound and fury signifying nothing, on what was an unreal question anyhow, the great issues of the morning's meeting forgotten and neglected; and Clemenceau silent and aloof on the outskirts—for nothing which touched the security of France was forward—throned, in his gray gloves, on the brocade chair, dry in soul and empty of hope, very old and tired, but surveying the scene with a cynical and almost impish air; and when at least silence was restored and the company had returned to their places, it was to discover that he had disappeared.

He felt about France what Pericles felt of Athens—unique value in her, nothing else mattering; but his theory of politics was Bismarck's. He had one illusion—France; and one dillusion—mankind, including Frenchmen, and his colleagues not least; . . . . The Council of Four paid no attention to [the underlying] issues, being preoccupied with others,—Clemenceau to crush the economic life of his enemy, Lloyd George to do a deal and bring home something that would pass muster for a week, the President to do nothing that was not just and right. . .

But behind these devastating portraits was a socioeconomic landscape sketched out by Keynes with brushstrokes as arresting as, although less flamboyant than, those that caught the public's eye. The landscape provides a remarkable introduction to Keynes's social as well as economic vision:

The Psychology of Society

Europe was so organized socially and economically as to secure the maximum accumulation of capital. While there was some continuous improvement in the daily conditions of life of the mass of the population, Society was so framed as to throw a great part of the increased income into the control of the class least likely to consume it. The new rich of the nineteenth century were not brought up to large expenditures, and preferred the power which investment gave them to the pleasures of immediate consumption. In fact, it was precisely the *inequality* of the distribution of wealth which made possible those vast accumulations of fixed wealth and of capital improvements which distinguished that age from all others. Herein lay, in fact, the main justification of the Capitalist System. If the rich had spent their new wealth on their own enjoyments, the world would long ago have found such a régime intolerable. But like bees they saved and accumulated, not less to the advantage of the whole community because they themselves held narrower ends in prospect.

The immense accumulations of fixed capital which, to the great benefit of mankind, were built up during the half century before the war, could never have come about in a Society where wealth was divided equitably. The railways of the world, which that age built as a monument to posterity, were, not less than the Pyramids of Egypt, the work of labor which was not free to consume in immediate enjoyment the full equivalent of its efforts.

Thus this remarkable system depended for its growth on a double bluff or deception. On the one hand the laboring classes accepted from ignorance or powerlessness, or were compelled, persuaded, or cajoled by custom, convention, authority, and the well-established order of Society into accepting, a situation in

which they could call their own very little of the cake that they
and Nature and the capitalists were co-operating to produce.
And on the other hand the capitalist classes were allowed to call
the best part of the cake theirs and were theoretically free to
consume it, on the tacit underlying condition that they consumed very little of it in practice. The duty of "saving" became
nine-tenths of virtue and the growth of the cake the object of true
religion. There grew round the non-consumption of the cake all
those instincts of puritanism which in other ages has withdrawn
itself from the world and has neglected the arts of production as
well as those of enjoyment. And so the cake increased; but to
what end was not clearly contemplated. Individuals would be
exhorted not so much to abstain as to defer, and to cultivate the
pleasures of security and anticipation. Saving was for old age or
for your children; but this was only in theory,—the virtue of the
cake was that it was never to be consumed, neither by you nor
by your children after you.

In writing thus I do not necessarily disparage the practices of
that generation. In the unconscious recesses of its being Society
knew what it was about. The cake was really very small in proportion to the appetites of consumption, and no one, if it were
shared all round, would be much the better off by the cutting of
it. Society was working not for the small pleasures of today but
for the future security and improvement of the race,—in fact for
"progress." If only the cake were not cut but was allowed to
grow in the geometrical proportion predicted by Malthus of population, but not less true of compound interest, perhaps a day
might come when there would at last be enough to go round,
and when posterity could enter into the enjoyment of *our* labors.
In that day overwork, overcrowding, and underfeeding would
have come to an end, and men, secure of the comforts and necessities of the body, could proceed to the nobler exercises of their
faculties. One geometrical ratio might cancel another, and the
nineteenth century was able to forget the fertility of the species
in a contemplation of the dizzy virtues of compound interest.

There were two pitfalls in this prospect: lest, population still
outstripping accumulation, our self-denials promote not happi-

ness but numbers; and lest the cake be after all consumed, prematurely, in war, the consumer of all such hopes.

But these thoughts lead too far from my present purpose. I seek only to point out that the principle of accumulation based on inequality was a vital part of the pre-war order of Society and of progress as we then understood it, and to emphasize that this principle depended on unstable psychological conditions, which it may be impossible to recreate. It was not natural for a population, of whom so few enjoyed the comforts of life, to accumulate so hugely. The war has disclosed the possibility of consumption to all and the vanity of abstinence to many. Thus the bluff is discovered; the laboring classes may be no longer willing to forego so largely, and the capitalist classes, no longer confident of the future, may seek to enjoy more fully their liberties of consumption so long as they last, and thus precipitate the hour of their confiscation.[58]

There is a radical ring to these words, but it would be a great error to think of Keynes as belonging to the political left. He had almost certainly read Marx, only casually, and it is doubtful if he had yet read (or even heard of) Veblen. The criticism and disdain is that of a disillusioned member of a self-conscious elite—a John Stuart Mill, without Mill's modesty. In an essay entitled "Am I a Liberal?" published in 1925, he declares himself to be anti-conservative—"They offer me neither food nor drink—neither spiritual nor intellectual consolation." "Ought I, then, to join the Labour party?" he asks; and answers: "Superficially that is more attractive, but looked at closer, there are great difficulties. To begin with, it is a class party, and the class is not my class . . . I can be influenced by what seems to me to be Justice and good sense; but the *Class* war will find me on the side of the educated *bourgeoisie*."[59]

Wherever we place Keynes on the ideological spectrum, the sociopolitical setting he describes in *The Economic Consequences of the Peace* would seem to foredoom him to the role of cynical

[58] Ibid, pp. 18f.
[59] Keynes, *Essays in Persuasion*, New York: W. W. Norton, 1963, pp. 323–24.

commentator in the economic world. In fact, he emerged not as cynic, but as reformer—it was not in his nature to sit on the sidelines. Already in 1912, at age twenty-nine, he had been made editor of *The Economic Journal,* England's most prestigious scholarly economic publication. A year later he had written a widely acclaimed small book, *Indian Currency and Finance;* in 1921 published his Cambridge dissertation, the remarkable *Treatise on Probability,* and two years thereafter *A Tract on Monetary Reform,* the last a jeremiad against surrendering deliberate control over the supply of money in favor of an impersonal, and therefore presumably superior, gold standard.

But all this was, in retrospect, a preamble to the writing of his most ambitious book prior to the publication of the *General Theory* in 1936. This was *A Treatise on Money,*[60] over which Keynes labored for seven years, only to tear it up, figuratively speaking, virtually the moment it was born. Clearly the *Treatise* constituted some sort of boundary that had to be crossed before Keynes could venture into the unexplored territory that would take the world by storm in 1936.

Let us therefore glance at it, not to learn its detailed lessons, no longer of much interest, but to familiarize ourselves with the territory that must be left behind. The book, a massive two volumes, opens with a lengthy discussion of the nature of money: a glance at its table of contents will suffice to tell us its general focus:

A TREATISE ON MONEY

Volume I

The Pure Theory of Money

Book I
The Nature of Money

Chapter I
The Classification of Money

[60] John Maynard Keynes, *A Treatise on Money,* (2 vols.) New York: Harcourt, Brace & Co., 1930.

Chapter 2
Bank Money

Chapter 3
The Analysis of Bank Money

Book II
The Value of Money

Chapter 4
The Purchasing Power of Money

Chapter 5
The Plurality of Secondary Price Levels

Chapter 6
Currency Standards

Chapter 7
The Diffusion of Price Levels

Chapter 8
The Theory of Comparisons of Purchasing Power

The chapter titles reveal something about the Treatise that establishes its link with the past. The link is that the analysis of money is essentially focused on *prices,* not on flows of expenditure. The Marshallian vision, which failed to discern anything of special interest in the possibility of dividing social income into consumption and investment expenditures because the *prices* of both types of goods could be explained by a marginalist, supply-and-demand approach, now becomes a stumbling block to Keynes's vision, although not one of which he was yet aware.

We see this difficulty more clearly in Book III, portentously titled *The Fundamental Equations of Money.* Here are the two equations:

(1) $P = \dfrac{E}{O} + \dfrac{I' - S}{R}$, where R is total consumer spending and P is the *price level* of consumers goods

(2) $\Pi = \dfrac{E}{O} + \dfrac{I-S}{O}$, where Π is the *price level* of total output

What do the equations mean? They are vitually impossible to translate into practical terms, and never caught on in the slightest, so I shall relegate their explication to a footnote.* We need only note that they are *price-equations,* with nothing to do with volumes of output: indeed, if these chapters and equations were the sole content of the *Treatise,* the book would not warrant mentioning here. But there is another problem afoot, to which Keynes addresses on some typically colorful (and also elusive) pages. Let me begin with a famous section from Chapter 12 of Book III in this same volume.

The Banana Parable

Let us suppose a community owning banana plantations and labouring to cultivate and collect bananas and nothing else; and consuming bananas and nothing else. Let us suppose, further, that there has been an equilibrium between saving and investment in the sense that the money-income of the community, not spent on the consumption of bananas but saved, is equal to the cost of production of new investment in the further development of plantations; and that the selling price of bananas is equal to their cost of production (including in this the normal remuneration of entrepreneurs). Finally, let us suppose, what is plausible, that ripe bananas will not keep for more than a week or two.

---

*Both equations utilize the term E / O. The term simply divides total income (E) by total output (O), to give us an average cost of production per unit.

Now note the contrast between the two equations. The first reflects any difference between I', which connotes the *cost* (mainly wages) of new investment goods, and S, the value of savings, divided by R, the volume of consumer goods and services. Thus when the cost of investment goods is larger than the savings of the economy, there will be wage and other earnings not offset by savings. This excess will be spent on consumers goods, R, whose average price (P) will therefore rise. If I' is less than S, consumer expenditures and prices will fall.

The crucial term in the second equation compares I—the value, or selling price, of investment goods (not their cost)—and the value of savings. If value is less than savings, there will be losses in the investment sector, whose entrepreneurs cannot lay their hands on the money needed to finance their capital expenditures . These losses will now force a curtailment of expenditures for all kinds of goods (O), and a consequent fall in the price level as a whole. Per contra, if value is greater than savings, there will be profits, and prices will rise.

Into this Eden there enters a Thrift Campaign, urging the members of the public to abate their improvident practices of devoting nearly all their current incomes to buying bananas for daily food. But at the same time there is no corresponding increase in the development of new plantations—for one or other of many reasons: it may be that counsels of prudence are influencing entrepreneurs as well as savers, fears of future over-production of bananas and a falling price-level deterring them from new development; or technical reasons may exist which prevent new development at more than a certain pace; or the labour required for such development may be highly specialised and not capable of being drawn from labour ordinarily occupied in harvesting bananas; or there may be a considerable time-lag between the initial preparations required for development and the date of the bulk of the expenditure eventually required by it. What, in such a case, will happen?

The same quantity of bananas as before will continue to be marketed, whilst the amount of current income devoted to their purchase will, by reason of the thrift campaign, be diminished. Since bananas will not keep, their price must fall; and it will fall proportionately to the amount by which saving exceeds investment. Thus, as before, the public will consume the whole crop of bananas, but at a reduced price-level. This is splendid, or seems so. The Thrift Campaign will not only have increased saving; it will have reduced the cost of living. The public will have saved money, without denying themselves anything. They will be consuming just as much as before, and virtue will be sumptuously rewarded.

But the end is not yet reached. Since wages are still unchanged, only the selling-price of bananas will have fallen and not their cost of production; so that the entrepreneurs will suffer an abnormal loss. Thus the increased saving has not increased in the least the aggregate wealth of the community; it has simply caused a transfer of wealth from the pockets of the entrepreneurs into the pockets of the general public. The savings of the consumers will be required, either directly or through the intermediary of the banking system, to make good the losses of the entrepreneurs. The continuance of this will cause entrepreneurs to seek to protect themselves by throwing their employees out of work or reducing their wages. But even this will not improve their position, since the spending power of the public will be reduced by just as much as the aggregate costs of production. By however much entrepreneurs reduce wages and however many of their employees they throw out of work, they will continue to make losses so long as the community continues to save in excess of new investment. Thus there will be no position of equilibrium until either *(a)* all production ceases and the entire population starves to death; or *(b)* the thrift campaign is called off or peters out as a result of the growing poverty; or *(c)* investment is stimulated by some means or another so that its cost no longer lags behind the rate of saving.

What we see here, only two chapters after the Fundamental Equations have been introduced, is a problem very different from that of price levels. Indeed, it recalls the spectre raised by Malthus of the possibility of a "general glut"—an absence of sufficient demand to absorb the current supply of commodities. (Perhaps we also remember Ricardo's demonstration that this was impossible (see page 120 above). Keynes's parable concerns something like a glut, in which the output of bananas can only be sold at prices that will bankrupt their producers. The element in the situation that plays the crucial role is the act of saving—the deliberate decision not to spend, but to set part of income aside.

In fact, John Stuart Mill had already shown that under certain conditions saving could indeed bring about an inability of total demand to purchase total supply. Mill agreed that it was indeed impossible to have a general glut as long as every seller turned around to become a buyer—but that this equality of supply and demand broke down when money itself became a "commodity." In that case, a seller could accept money *but not spend it again,* perhaps because he was expecting to be able to buy securities or foreign exchange or other commodities more cheaply in the future.[61] Mill's essay appeared after Ricardo's death, so that

[61] J. S. Mill, "Of the Influence of Consumption on Production" (1844), in *Some Unsettled Question of Political Economy,* (1844) New York: Augustus M. Kelley, 1968, pp. 69–72.

we do not know how the latter would have replied. Probably he would have said that selling without buying could not last long, and would therefore present only a passing shock to the system.

In The Banana Parable, Keynes is also interested in the potentially disruptive role that could be played by saving—a far cry from the Fundamental Equations in which saving enters only as it affects price levels. The parable is much less credible than Mill's glut brought on by hoarding, and most readers of the *Treatise* must have dismissed it out of hand—there is no mention, for instance, of the tremendous downward pressure on interest rates that would be expected to follow from a mulish determination to save at any cost. The critics were, of course, right, except for one thing. Keynes seems to have imagined the possibility of problems emerging in a capitalist economy for which no self-correcting remedies would arise—problems rooted in behavior that price changes alone would not correct.

One last reading from the *Treatise*—Volume II, Book IV—points in the same direction.

Chapter 30

Some Historical Illustrations

It has been usual to think of the accumulated wealth of the world as having been painfully built up out of that voluntary abstinence of individuals from the immediate enjoyment of consumption which we call Thrift. But it should be obvious that mere abstinence is not enough by itself to build cities or drain fens. The abstinence of individuals need not increase accumulated wealth;—it may serve instead to increase the current consumption of other individuals. Thus the thrift of a man may lead either to an increase of capital-wealth or to consumers getting better value for their money. There is no telling which, until we have examined another economic factor.

Namely, Enterprise. It is enterprise which builds and improves the world's possessions. Now, just as the fruits of thrift may go to provide either capital accumulation or an enhanced value of money-income for the consumer, so the outgoings of enterprise may be found either out of thrift or at the expense of the consumption of the average consumer. Worse still;—not only may thrift exist without enterprise, but as soon as thrift gets ahead of enterprise, it positively discourages the recovery of enterprise and sets up a vicious circle by its adverse effect on profits. If Enterprise is afoot, wealth accumulates whatever may be happening to Thrift; and if Enterprise is asleep, wealth decays whatever Thrift may be doing.

Thus, Thrift may be the handmaid and nurse of Enterprise. But equally she may not. And, perhaps, even usually she is not. For enterprise is connected with thrift not directly but at one remove; and the link which should join them is frequently missing. For the engine which drives Enterprise is not Thrift, but Profit.

Now, for enterprise to be active, two conditions must be fulfilled. There must be an expectation of profit; and it must be possible for enterprisers to obtain command of sufficient resources to put their projects into execution. Their expectations partly depend on non-monetary influences—on peace and war, inventions, laws, race, education, population and so forth. But the argument of our first volume has gone to show that their power to put their projects into execution on terms which they deem attractive, almost entirely depends on the behaviour of the banking and monetary system.

––––––––

"Were the Seven Wonders of the World built by Thrift?" Keynes asks a paragraph later. "I deem it doubtful," he concludes.

––––––––

THE GENERAL THEORY OF EMPLOYMENT, INTEREST, AND MONEY

––––––––

I first read Keynes's revolutionary book in 1937, understanding very little of it, and I last read it a few weeks ago, preparatory to commencing this daunting resumé of its contents. In the edition I have, now almost sixty years old, there is hardly a page that is not

underlined in part, checked in the margins, decorated with excla-
mation marks, question marks, and obiter dicta: ("very important"
in red; "good idea," in pencil; "Mrs. G not right in QJE"; "U = dis-
inv. of entrep. in own equip., excl. purch. from other entreps.", to
which is added in blue ??; "M $\rightarrow$ D, via 1_2,r,k.") It is a hopeless
book to summarize in a brief paragraph or two, so I shall begin by
reproducing Keynes's own summary, which—as the reader will
soon discover—needs its own summary and explication, to follow.

Chapter 3

The Principle of Effective Demand

II

The outline of our theory can be expressed as follows. When
employment increases, aggregate real income is increased. The
psychology of the community is such that when aggregate real
income is increased aggregate consumption is increased, but not
by so much as income. Hence employers would make a loss if
the whole of the increased employment were to be devoted to
satisfying the increased demand for immediate consumption.
Thus, to justify any given amount of employment there must be
an amount of current investment sufficient to absorb the excess
of total output over what the community chooses to consume
when employment is at the given level. For unless there is this
amount of investment, the receipts of the entrepreneurs will be
less than is required to induce them to offer the given amount of
employment. It follows, therefore, that, given what we shall call
the community's propensity to consume, the equilibrium level
of employment, *i.e.* the level at which there is no inducement to
employers as a whole either to expand or to contract employment, will depend on the amount of current investment. The
amount of current investment will depend, in turn, on what we
shall call the inducement to invest; and the inducement to invest
will be found to depend on the relation between the schedule of
the marginal efficiency of capital and the complex of rates of
interest on loans of various maturities and risks. . . .

This analysis supplies us with an explanation of the paradox of poverty in the midst of plenty. For the mere existence of an insufficiency of effective demand may, and often will, bring the increase of employment to a standstill *before* a level of full employment has been reached. The insufficiency of effective demand will inhibit the process of production in spite of the fact that the marginal product of labour still exceeds in value the marginal disutility of employment.

Moreover the richer the community, the wider will tend to be the gap between its actual and its potential production; and therefore the more obvious and outrageous the defects of the economic system. For a poor community will be prone to consume by far the greater part of its output, so that a very modest measure of investment will be sufficient to provide full employment; whereas a wealthy community will have to discover much ampler opportunities for investment if the saving propensities of its wealthier members are to be compatible with the employment of its poorer members. If in a potentially wealthy community the inducement to invest is weak, then, in spite of its potential wealth, the working of the principle of effective demand will compel it to reduce its actual output, until, in spite of its potential wealth, it has become so poor that its surplus over its consumption is sufficiently diminished to correspond to the weakness of the inducement to invest.

Some words of explanation may help. First, the center of inquiry has changed. It is not the level of prices but the level of employment that has become the focus of analytical attention. This seemingly innocuous change is, in fact, the boundary that had to be crossed before the author of the *Treatise on Money* could become the author of *The General Theory of Employment, Interest, and Money*—note the fifth word of the second title.[62]

In turn, this shift of focus required two wrenching changes in the perception of "the economy" itself. The first was an abandon-

---

[62] John Maynard Keynes, *The General Theory of Employment, Interest, and Money*, New York: Harcourt, Brace and Company, 1964.

ment of the Marshallian conception of it as a congeries of individual markets, each constantly finding a balance between the supply and demand for its product and thereby determining the appropriate level of employment for itself, while simultaneously interacting with other markets to reach a pattern of mutual accommodation. Such a conception, which Keynes said "conquered England as completely as the Holy Inquisition conquered Spain,"[63] presents no reason to believe that all these markets together should fail to generate jobs for anyone willing to work for the wages established by the market system, or in Ricardo's terms, why one should take seriously Malthus's fears of a "general glut."

In contrast, Keynes's view offered a perspective in which the economy was not conceptualized as a structure—inherently a static image—but as a river of output, rising and falling as the proportion of the society's would-be workforce found employment. The river, in turn, is conceived as being made up of two mingled, but independent streams—one made up of expenditures for consumption goods, the other of expenditures for investment goods. Here, of course, are the two categories with respect to which Marshall found no reason to inquire further than their mutual exposure to the forces of supply and demand.

From this new perspective, the level of employment hinges on two factors invisible from the Marshallian view. The first concerns the total volume of consumers' goods in the river of output. Keynes's completely original perception was that society devotes to consumption a portion of its income that rises as its income rises, but not to the full extent of that rise. He called this relationship the Propensity to Consume, and made it an important part of his explanation for the existence of persisting national unemployment. The explanation is that because consumption never keeps pace with income, there is always a growing volume of saving for which investment outlets must be found. In a manner of speaking, this is a translation of the "thrift campaign" of the Banana Parable into the behavioral dynamics of a real life economy.

This obviously gives to the act of investment a strategic impor-

[63] *General Theory*, p. 32.

tance lacking in the Marshallian conception. Keynes has made clear that except for unusual circumstances, such as when an economy makes up for privations suffered during a war, we cannot look to consumer spending alone to bring about high employment. This not only throws a heavy burden on investment, but brings Keynes to identify previously unnoticed obstacles that it must overcome to provide full employment. Here we might once again turn to the text of the *General Theory,* with a fascinating reading from his famous chapter 12 on "The State of Long Term Expectation":

III

The outstanding fact is the extreme precariousness of the basis of knowledge on which our estimates of prospective yield have to be made. Our knowledge of the factors which will govern the yield of an investment some years hence is usually very slight and often negligible. If we speak frankly, we have to admit that our basis of knowledge for estimating the yield ten years hence of a railway, a copper mine, a textile factory, the goodwill of a patent medicine, an Atlantic liner, a building in the City of London amounts to little and sometimes to nothing; or even five years hence. In fact, those who seriously attempt to make any such estimate are often so much in the minority that their behaviour does not govern the market.

In former times, when enterprises were mainly owned by those who undertook them or by their friends and associates, investment depended on a sufficient supply of individuals of sanguine temperament and constructive impulses who embarked on business as a way of life, not really relying on a precise calculation of prospective profit. The affair was partly a lottery, though with the ultimate result largely governed by whether the abilities and character of the managers were above or below the average. Some would fail and some would succeed. But even after the event no one would know whether the average results in terms of the sums invested had exceeded, equalled or fallen short of the prevailing rate of interest; though, if we exclude the exploitation of natural resources and monopolies, it is probable that the actual average results of investments, even during periods of progress and prosperity, have disappointed the hopes which prompted them. Business men play a mixed game of skill and chance, the average results of which to the players are not known by those who take a hand. If human nature felt no temptation to take a chance, no satisfaction (profit apart) in constructing a factory, a railway, a mine or a farm, there might not be much investment merely as a result of cold calculation.

Decisions to invest in private business of the old-fashioned type were, however, decisions largely irrevocable, not only for the community as a whole, but also for the individual. With the separation between ownership and management which prevails to-day and with the development of organised investment markets, a new factor of great importance has entered in, which sometimes facilitates investment but sometimes adds greatly to the instability of the system. In the absence of security markets, there is no object in frequently attempting to revalue an investment to which we are committed. But the Stock Exchange revalues many investments every day and the revaluations give a frequent opportunity to the individual (though not to the community as a whole) to revise his commitments. It is as though a farmer, having tapped his barometer after breakfast, could decide to remove his capital from the farming business between 10 and 11 in the morning and reconsider whether he should return to it later in the week. But the daily revaluations of the Stock Exchange, though they are primarily made to facilitate transfers of old investments between one individual and another, inevitably exert a decisive influence on the rate of current investment. For there is no sense in building up a new enterprise at a cost greater than that at which a similar existing enterprise can be purchased; whilst there is an inducement to spend on a new project what may seem an extravagant sum, if it can be floated off on the Stock Exchange at an immediate profit. Thus certain classes of investment are governed by the average expectation of those who deal on the Stock Exchange as revealed in the price of shares, rather than by the genuine expectations of

the professional entrepreneur. How then are these highly significant daily, even hourly, revaluations of existing investments
carried out in practice?

IV

In practice we have tacitly agreed, as a rule, to fall back on what
is, in truth, *a convention*. The essence of this convention—though
it does not, of course, work out quite so simply—lies in assuming
that the existing state of affairs will continue indefinitely, except
in so far as we have specific reasons to expect a change. This
does not mean that we really believe that the existing state of
affairs will continue indefinitely. We know from extensive experience that this is most unlikely. The actual results of an investment over a long term of years very seldom agree with the initial
expectation. Nor can we rationalise our behaviour by arguing
that to a man in a state of ignorance errors in either direction are
equally probable, so that there remains a mean actuarial expectation based on equi-probabilities. For it can easily be shown that
the assumption of arithmetically equal probabilities based on a
state of ignorance leads to absurdities. We are assuming, in
effect, that the existing market valuation, however arrived at, is
uniquely *correct* in relation to our existing knowledge of the facts
which will influence the yield of the investment, and that it will
only change in proportion to changes in this knowledge; though,
philosophically speaking, it cannot be uniquely correct, since our
existing knowledge does not provide a sufficient basis for a calculated mathematical expectation. In point of fact, all sorts of
considerations enter into the market valuation which are in no
way relevant to the prospective yield.

Nevertheless the above conventional method of calculation
will be compatible with a considerable measure of continuity
and stability in our affairs, *so long as we can rely on the maintenance
of the convention*.

For if there exist organised investment markets and if we can
rely on the maintenance of the convention, an investor can legiti-
mately encourage himself with the idea that the only risk he runs
is that of a genuine change in the news *over the near future*, as to

the likelihood of which he can attempt to form his own judgment, and which is unlikely to be very large. For, assuming that the convention holds good, it is only these changes which can affect the value of his investment, and he need not lose his sleep merely because he has not any notion what his investment will be worth ten years hence. Thus investment becomes reasonably "safe" for the individual investor over short periods, and hence over a succession of short periods however many, if he can fairly rely on there being no breakdown in the convention and on his therefore having an opportunity to revise his judgment and change his investment, before there has been time for much to happen. Investments which are "fixed" for the community are thus made "liquid" for the individual.

It has been, I am sure, on the basis of some such procedure as this that our leading investment markets have been developed. But it is not surprising that a convention, in an absolute view of things so arbitrary, should have its weak points. It is its precariousness which creates no small part of our contemporary problem of securing sufficient investment.

V

Some of the factors which accentuate this precariousness may be briefly mentioned. . . .

There is one feature in particular which deserves our attention. It might have been supposed that competition between expert professionals, possessing judgment and knowledge beyond that of the average private investor, would correct the vagaries of the ignorant individual left to himself. It happens, however, that the energies and skill of the professional investor and speculator are mainly occupied otherwise. For most of these persons are, in fact, largely concerned, not with making superior long-term forecasts of the probable yield of an investment over its whole life, but with foreseeing changes in the conventional basis of valuation a short time ahead of the general public. They are concerned, not with what an investment is really worth to a man who buys it "for keeps", but with what the market will value it at, under the influence of mass psychology, three months or a year hence.

Moreover, this behaviour is not the outcome of a wrong-headed propensity. It is an inevitable result of an investment market organised along the lines described. For it is not sensible to pay 25 for an investment of which you believe the prospective yield to justify a value of 30, if you also believe that the market will value it at 20 three months hence.

Thus the professional investor is forced to concern himself with the anticipation of impending changes, in the news or in the atmosphere, of the kind by which experience shows that the mass psychology of the market is most influenced. This is the inevitable result of investment markets organised with a view to so-called "liquidity". Of the maxims of orthodox finance none, surely, is more anti-social than the fetish of liquidity, the doctrine that it is a positive virtue on the part of investment institutions to concentrate their resources upon the holding of "liquid" securities. It forgets that there is no such thing as liquidity of investment for the community as a whole. The social object of skilled investment should be to defeat the dark forces of time and ignorance which envelop our future. The actual, private object of the most skilled investment to-day is "to beat the gun", as the Americans so well express it, to outwit the crowd, and to pass the bad, or depreciating, half-crown to the other fellow.

This battle of wits to anticipate the basis of conventional valuation a few months hence, rather than the prospective yield of an investment over a long term of years, does not even require gulls amongst the public to feed the maws of the professional;—it can be played by professionals amongst themselves. Nor is it necessary that anyone should keep his simple faith in the conventional basis of valuation having any genuine longterm validity. For it is, so to speak, a game of Snap, of Old Maid, of Musical Chairs— a pastime in which he is victor who says *Snap* neither too soon nor too late, who passes the Old Maid to his neighbour before the game is over, who secures a chair for himself when the music stops. These games can be played with zest and enjoyment, though all the players know that it is the Old Maid which is circulating, or that when the music stops some of the players will find themselves unseated.

Or, to change the metaphor slightly, professional investment may be likened to those newspaper competitions in which the competitors have to pick out the six prettiest faces from a hundred photographs, the prize being awarded to the competitor whose choice most nearly corresponds to the average preferences of the competitors as a whole; so that each competitor has to pick, not those faces which he himself finds prettiest, but those which he thinks likeliest to catch the fancy of the other competitors, all of whom are looking at the problem from the same point of view. It is not a case of choosing those which, to the best of one's judgment, are really the prettiest, nor even those which average opinion genuinely thinks the prettiest. We have reached the third degree where we devote our intelligences to anticipating what average opinion expects the average opinion to be. And there are some, I believe, who practise the fourth, fifth and higher degrees. . . .

VI

These considerations should not lie beyond the purview of the economist. But they must be relegated to their right perspective. If I may be allowed to appropriate the term *speculation* for the activity of forecasting the psychology of the market, and the term *enterprise* for the activity of forecasting the prospective yield of assets over their whole life, it is by no means always the case that speculation predominates over enterprise. As the organisation of investment markets improves, the risk of the predominance of speculation does, however, increase. In one of the greatest investment markets in the world, namely, New York, the influence of speculation (in the above sense) is enormous. Even outside the field of finance, Americans are apt to be unduly interested in discovering what average opinion believes average opinion to be; and this national weakness finds its nemesis in the stock market. It is rare, one is told, for an American to invest, as many Englishmen still do, "for income"; and he will not readily purchase an investment except in the hope of capital appreciation. This is only another way of saying that, when he purchases an investment, the American is attaching his hopes, not so much to its prospective yield, as to a favourable change in the conventional basis of valuation, *i.e.* that he is, in the above sense, a speculator. Speculators may do no harm as bubbles on a steady stream of enterprise. But the position is serious when enterprise becomes the bubble on a whirlpool of speculation. When the capital development of a country becomes a by-product of the activities of a casino, the job is likely to be ill-done. The measure of success attained by Wall Street, regarded as an institution of which the proper social purpose is to direct new investment into the most profitable channels in terms of future yield, cannot be claimed as one of the outstanding triumphs of *laissez-faire* capitalism—which is not surprising, if I am right in thinking that the best brains of Wall Street have been in fact directed towards a different object. . . .

VII

Even apart from the instability due to speculation, there is the instability due to the characteristic of human nature that a large proportion of our positive activities depend on spontaneous optimism rather than on a mathematical expectation, whether moral or hedonistic or economic. Most, probably, of our decisions to do something positive, the full consequences of which will be drawn out over many days to come, can only be taken as a result of animal spirits—of a spontaneous urge to action rather than inaction, and not as the outcome of a weighted average of quantitative benefits multiplied by quantitative probabilities. Enterprise only pretends to itself to be mainly actuated by the statements in its own prospectus, however candid and sincere. Only a little more than an expedition to the South Pole, is it based on an exact calculation of benefits to come. Thus if the animal spirits are dimmed and the spontaneous optimism falters, leaving us to depend on nothing but a mathematical expectation, enterprise will fade and die;—though fears of loss may have a basis no more reasonable than hopes of profit had before.

It is safe to say that enterprise which depends on hopes stretching into the future benefits the community as a whole. But individual initiative will only be adequate when reasonable calculation is supplemented and supported by animal spirits, so that the thought of ultimate loss which often overtakes pioneers, as experience undoubtedly tells us and them, is put aside as a healthy man puts aside the expectation of death.

This means, unfortunately, not only that slumps and depressions are exaggerated in degree, but that economic prosperity is excessively dependent on a political and social atmosphere which is congenial to the average business man. If the fear of a Labour Government or a New Deal depresses enterprise, this need not be the result either of a reasonable calculation or of a plot with political intent;—it is the mere consequence of upsetting the delicate balance of spontaneous optimism. In estimating the prospects of investment, we must have regard, therefore, to the nerves and hysteria and even the digestions and reactions to the weather of those upon whose spontaneous activity it largely depends.

We should not conclude from this that everything depends on waves of irrational psychology. On the contrary, the state of long-term expectation is often steady, and, even when it is not, the other factors exert their compensating effects. We are merely reminding ourselves that human decisions affecting the future, whether personal or political or economic, cannot depend on strict mathematical expectation, since the basis for making such calculations does not exist; and that it is our innate urge to activity which makes the wheels go round, our rational selves choosing between the alternatives as best we are able, calculating where we can, but often falling back for our motive on whim or sentiment or chance.

I have only been able to sketch in the basic outlines of the *General Theory*, leaving aside many important new insights. One such was Keynes's analysis of the rate of interest. Keynes believed that interest was not the reward for *saving*, but for parting with the liquidity of cash. Thus he did not believe that raising interest rates would increase savings, which in any case, he saw as the problem underlying unemployment, not the solution for it. So, too, he was

the first to perceive that increases in spending would have a "mul-
tiplier" effect, so long as we were not fully employed, with the
result that increments of new spending for investment, moving
from recipient to recipient, although diminished each time by saving, would end up creating total incomes that considerably
exceeded the original expenditure. This led, I might add, to a typically Keynesian thrust at the manner in which "sound business
principles" would obscure clear thinking. Speaking of ways to alleviate unemployment he wrote:

If the Treasury were to fill old bottles with banknotes, bury
them at suitable depths in disused coalmines which are then
filled up to the surface with town rubbish, and leave it to private
enterprise on well-tried principles of *laissez-faire* to dig the notes
up again (the right to do so being obtained, of course, by tender-
ing for leases of the note-bearing territory), there need be no
more unemployment and, with the help of the repercussions, the
real income of the community, and its capital wealth also, would
probably become a good deal greater than it actually is. It would,
indeed, be more sensible to build houses and the like; but if there
are political and practical difficulties in the way of this, the above
would be better than nothing. . . .

Ancient Egypt was doubly fortunate, and doubtless owed to
this its fabled wealth, in that it possessed *two* activities, namely,
pyramid-building as well as the search for the precious metals,
the fruits of which, since they could not serve the needs of man
by being consumed, did not stale with abundance. The Middle
Ages built cathedrals and sang dirges. Two pyramids, two
masses for the dead, are twice as good as one; but not so two
railways from London to York. Thus we are so sensible, have
schooled ourselves to so close a semblance of prudent financiers,
taking careful thought before we add to the "financial" burdens
of posterity by building them houses to live in, that we have no
such easy escape from the sufferings of unemployment. We have
to accept them as an inevitable result of applying to the conduct
of the State the maxims which are best calculated to "enrich" an

individual by enabling him to pile up claims to enjoyment which he does not intend to exercise at any definite time.[64]

Many of these innovations in economic thought have by now passed into the conventional wisdom. Other elements have not. In its original presentation, The *General Theory* lacked one powerful validation—a formulation, preferably in diagrammatic form, that carried the psychological persuasiveness of the conventional analysis of supply and demand, with its criss-cross of curves. Attempts to remedy this by a formulation, including a criss-cross, of a goods–market (investment–saving) equilibrium, and a money market (liquidity–money) equilibrium, originally proposed by John Hicks and then endorsed (for a time) by Keynes himself, only generated a dispute as to whether the diagrammatics removed the dynamic, expectations-oriented soul of Keynes's original view in return for the dry husk of a static diagram. The dispute, along with many others, still goes on.

Hence the *General Theory* does not enjoy today the exhalted esteem in which it was held when I first began to make my way through its unfamiliar conceptual terrain and daunting new vocabulary, much of it since discarded. Nonetheless, something of major importance remains. That which we call "the economy" now looks different from the way it appeared to preceding generations of economists. The flow of expenditures and the drain of savings give rise to a level of output and employment that is continually rising and falling like a pingpong ball in a jet of water, as the opposing forces of expansion and contraction find their ever-changing point of balance. Moreover there is no reason to believe that this point must correspond to "capacity" output or "full" employment. On the contrary, if for whatever cause the animal spirits that propel investment are insufficient to bring about high levels of output and employment, the economy will remain in its semi or seriously depressed condition indefinitely.

Thus there is nothing self-curative about a Keynesian decline, unlike the earlier beliefs that as wages fell and interest rates

[64]Op. cit., pp. 129, 131.

declined, sooner or later investment would pick up. In the Keynesian world, as wages fell so did consumption spending, and if the
unease regarding the future continued unappeased, interest rates
would not fall, because holders of cash would not wish to give
up their liquidity for the measly return of a low interest income.
Thus a Keynesian future does not hold put the promise of a Marshallian one. Possibly this is the most profoundly disturbing lesson of the *General Theory.*

It also raises for examination one last aspect of the book—
Keynes's policy prescription to deal with his diagnosis of capitalist malfunction. That malfunction was, of course, the extraordinary, relentless, never-ending depression that hung over the
entire western world during the decade in which *The General
Theory* was written, published, debated, and ulitmately accepted.
Something like a fifth to a quarter of the labor force in the western world was unemployed during that terrible decade. What did
Keynes propose should be done? I think we will be surprised to
find out.

Chapter 24

Concluding Notes on the Social Philosophy towards which the General Theory might lead

I

The outstanding faults of the economic society in which we live
are its failure to provide for full employment and its arbitrary
and inequitable distribution of wealth and incomes. The bearing
of the foregoing theory on the first of these is obvious. But there
are also two important respects in which it is relevant to the
second.

Since the end of the nineteenth century significant progress
towards the removal of very great disparities of wealth and
income has been achieved through the instrument of direct taxation—income tax and surtax and death duties—especially in
Great Britain. Many people would wish to see this process carried much further, but they are deterred by two considerations;

partly by the fear of making skilful evasions too much worth while and also of diminishing unduly the motive towards risk-taking, but mainly, I think, by the belief that the growth of capital depends upon the strength of the motive towards individual saving and that for a large proportion of this growth we are dependent on the savings of the rich out of their superfluity. Our argument does not affect the first of these considerations. But it may considerably modify our attitude towards the second. For we have seen that, up to the point where full employment prevails, the growth of capital depends not at all on a low propensity to consume* but is, on the contrary, held back by it; and only in conditions of full employment is a low propensity to consume conducive to the growth of capital. Moreover, experience suggests that in existing conditions saving by institutions and through sinking funds is more than adequate, and that measures for the redistribution of incomes in a way likely to raise the propensity to consume may prove positively favourable to the growth of capital.

Thus our argument leads towards the conclusion that in contemporary conditions the growth of wealth, so far from being dependent on the abstinence of the rich, as is commonly supposed, is more likely to be impeded by it. One of the chief social justifications of great inequality of wealth is, therefore, removed. I am not saying that there are no other reasons, unaffected by our theory, capable of justifying some measure of inequality in some circumstances. But it does dispose of the most important of the reasons why hitherto we have thought it prudent to move carefully. This particularly affects our attitude towards death duties; for there are certain justifications for inequality of incomes which do not apply equally to inequality of inheritances.

For my own part, I believe that there is social and psychological justification for significant inequalities of incomes and wealth, but not for such large disparities as exist to-day. There are valuable human activities which require the motive of

---

*That is, by a high level of saving.

money-making and the environment of private wealth-ownership for their full fruition. Moreover, dangerous human proclivities can be canalised into comparatively harmless channels by the existence of opportunities for money-making and private wealth, which, if they cannot be satisfied in this way, may find their outlet in cruelty, the reckless pursuit of personal power and authority, and other forms of self-aggrandisement. It is better that a man should tyrannise over his bank balance than over his fellow-citizens; and whilst the former is sometimes denounced as being but a means to the latter, sometimes at least it is an alternative. But it is not necessary for the stimulation of these activities and the satisfaction of these proclivities that the game should be played for such high stakes as at present. Much lower stakes will serve the purpose equally well, as soon as the players are accustomed to them. The task of transmuting human nature must not be confused with the task of managing it. Though in the ideal commonwealth men may have been taught or inspired or bred to take no interest in the stakes, it may still be wise and prudent statesmanship to allow the game to be played, subject to rules and limitations, so long as the average man, or even a significant section of the community, is in fact strongly addicted to the money-making passion.

II

There is, however, a second, much more fundamental inference from our argument which has a bearing on the future of inequalities of wealth; namely, our theory of the rate of interest. The justification for a moderately high rate of interest has been found hitherto in the necessity of providing a sufficient inducement to save. But we have shown that the extent of effective saving is necessarily determined by the scale of investment and that the scale of investment is promoted by a *low* rate of interest, provided that we do not attempt to stimulate it in this way beyond the point which corresponds to full employment. Thus it is to our best advantage to reduce the rate of interest to that point relatively to the schedule of the marginal efficiency of capital at which there is full employment.

There can be no doubt that this criterion will lead to a much lower rate of interest than has ruled hitherto. . . .

I see, therefore, the rentier aspect of capitalism as a transitional phase which will disappear when it has done its work. And with the disappearance of its rentier aspect much else in it besides will suffer a sea-change. It will be, moreover, a great advantage of the order of events which I am advocating, that the euthanasia of the rentier, of the functionless investor, will be nothing sudden, merely a gradual but prolonged continuance of what we have seen recently in Great Britain, and will need no revolution. . . .

III

In some other respects the foregoing theory is moderately conservative in its implications. For whilst it indicates the vital importance of establishing certain central controls in matters which are now left in the main to individual initiative, there are wide fields of activity which are unaffected. The State will have to exercise a guiding influence on the propensity to consume partly through its scheme of taxation, partly by fixing the rate of interest, and partly, perhaps, in other ways. Furthermore, it seems unlikely that the influence of banking policy on the rate of interest will be sufficient by itself to determine an optimum rate of investment. I conceive, therefore, that a somewhat comprehensive socialisation of investment will prove the only means of securing an approximation to full employment; though this need not exclude all manner of compromises and of devices by which public authority will co-operate with private initiative. But beyond this no obvious case is made out for a system of State Socialism which would embrace most of the economic life of the community. It is not the ownership of the instruments of production which it is important for the State to assume. If the State is able to determine the aggregate amount of resources devoted to augmenting the instruments and the basic rate of reward to those who own them, it will have accomplished all that is necessary. Moreover, the necessary measures of socialisation can be introduced gradually and without a break in the general traditions of society. . . .

To put the point concretely, I see no reason to suppose that the existing system seriously misemploys the factors of production which are in use. There are, of course, errors of foresight; but these would not be avoided by centralising decisions. When 9,000,000 men are employed out of 10,000,000 willing and able to work, there is no evidence that the labour of these 9,000,000 men is misdirected. The complaint against the present system is not that these 9,000,000 men ought to be employed on different tasks, but that tasks should be available for the remaining 1,000,000 men. It is in determining the volume, not the direction, of actual employment that the existing system has broken down. . . .

[I]ndividualism, if it can be purged of its defects and its abuses, is the best safeguard of personal liberty in the sense that, compared with any other system, it greatly widens the field for the exercise of personal choice. It is also the best safeguard of the variety of life, which emerges precisely from this extended field of personal choice, and the loss of which is the greatest of all the losses of the homogeneous or totalitarian state. For this variety preserves the traditions which embody the most secure and successful choices of former generations; it colours the present with the diversification of its fancy; and, being the handmaid of experiment as well as of tradition and of fancy, it is the most powerful instrument to better the future.

Whilst, therefore, the enlargement of the functions of government, involved in the task of adjusting to one another the propensity to consume and the inducement to invest, would seem to a nineteenth-century publicist or to a contemporary American financier to be a terrific encroachment on individualism, I defend it, on the contrary, both as the only practicable means of avoiding the destruction of existing economic forms in their entirety and as the condition of the successful functioning of individual initiative.

V

Is the fulfilment of these ideas a visionary hope? Have they insufficient roots in the motives which govern the evolution of political society? Are the interests which they will thwart stronger and more obvious than those which they will serve?

I do not attempt an answer in this place. It would need a volume of a different character from this one to indicate even in outline the practical measures in which they might be gradually clothed. But if the ideas are correct—an hypothesis on which the author himself must necessarily base what he writes—it would be a mistake, I predict, to dispute their potency over a period of time. At the present moment people are unusually expectant of a more fundamental diagnosis; more particularly ready to receive it; eager to try it out, if it should be even plausible. But apart from this contemporary mood, the ideas of economists and political philosophers, both when they are right and when they are wrong, are more powerful than is commonly understood. Indeed the world is ruled by little else. Practical men, who believe themselves to be quite exempt from any intellectual influences, are usually the slaves of some defunct economist. Madmen in authority, who hear voices in the air, are distilling their frenzy from some academic scribbler of a few years back. I am sure that the power of vested interests is vastly exaggerated compared with the gradual encroachment of ideas. Not, indeed, immediately, but after a certain interval; for in the field of economic and political philosophy there are not many who are influenced by new theories after they are twenty-five or thirty years of age, so that the ideas which civil servants and politicians and even agitators apply to current events are not likely to be the newest. But, soon or late, it is ideas, not vested interests, which are dangerous for good or evil.

All in all, it is a surprisingly mild conclusion for so grave an analysis. Keynes's proposed program does not entail any explicit recommendations for government spending to fill the expenditure gap caused by an insufficiency of private spending. He mentions in passing "a somewhat comprehensive socialization of investment," referring in all likelihood to expanded programs of government spending on roads, schools, and other such items of public capital, but there is no blueprint for a permanently enlarged public sector, much less a Welfare State, as we know it. Instead Keynes relies on policies calculated to keep interest rates low and to raise taxes on high incomes and large estates, hoping thereby to reduce the flow of savings. His words—he speaks of the "euthanasia of the rentier"—were hardly calculated to soothe the breast of the agitated conservative, but their bite is much less than their bark, for on the next page he explicitly disavows any system of state socialism, and the chapter ends with something like a celebration of the virtues of a modernized and more reliable capitalism.

In short, what we have read sounds a great deal more like John Stuart Mill than Marx. Those who still equate Keynes's thought with that of Marx evidently do not know his own estimate of the latter's place. In 1934 Keynes writes to Bernard Shaw:

> My feelings about *Das Kapital* are the same as my feelings about the *Koran.* I know it is historically important and I know that many people, not all of whom are idiots, find it a sort of Rock of Ages and continuing inspiration. Yet, when I look into it, it is to me inexplicable that it can have this effect . . . I am sure that its contemporary *economic* value (apart from occasional but inconstructive and discontinuous flashes of insight) is *nil.*[65]

Whatever one may think of this evaluation, it speaks volumes for the man who wrote it. Although he called himself a kind of liberal in his self-placement on the political spectrum, Keynes was better described as an enlightened conservative—enlightened in his awareness of the limitations of business values, conservative in his inability to disavow the larger social arrangements that underpinned those values.

That deeply ingrained point of view was never more unmistakably displayed than at the end of his life when Keynes was a central person—personage would be a more exact description—at the Bretton Woods Conference that sought, with some success, to restore stability and order to a world threatened with international

---

[65] D. E. Moggridge, *Maynard Keynes,* New York: Routledge, 1992, pp. 469–70.

economic disarray. Keynes played a role there that could be described as the exact opposite of those self-centered and myopic figures he had witnessed at the Paris Peace Conference a quarter century earlier. One of the Bretton Woods delegates has given us this portrait:

Today is the 500th anniversary of the Concordat between King's College, Cambridge, and New College, Oxford, and to commemorate the occasion, Keynes gave a small banquet in his room . . . Keynes, who had been looking forward to the event for weeks as excitedly as a schoolboy, was at his most charming. He delivered an exquisite allocution . . . It was an interesting example of the curiously complex nature of this extraordinary man. So radical in outlook in matters purely intellectual, in matters of culture he is a true Burkean conservative. It was all very pianissimo, as befitting the occasion, but his emotion when he spoke of our debt to the past was truly moving.[66]

Whether enlightened conservatism can ultimately muster the strength to reform ill-functioning societies is a faith easier to assert than to demonstrate; but, unhappily, that same criticism can be directed against the ability of radicalism—even moderate radicalism—to perform the same tasks with respect to its own ill-performing systems. That which I find admirable in Keynes is his willingness to wear his political values on his economic sleeve. Whether his theories will continue to shape our general social perceptions we cannot know, but we can hope that his political honesty will continue to inspire them.

[66] Roy Harrod, *The Life of John Maynard Keynes,* New York: Augustus M. Kelley, 1969, p. 577.

JOSEPH ALOIS SCHUMPETER

⌘

(1883–1950)

On the fly leaf of my copy of Joseph Schumpeter's most famous book, *Capitalism, Socialism, and Democracy,* bought in 1947, five years after its publication, I find these words in my handwriting: "Assertive, selective, pompous, and arrogant. The book succeeds by virtue of its omniscient tone, not by its analysis, which is scanty, or its argument, often wrong. Its prophecies have not been borne out." The last refers to what are assuredly the two best-known pronouncements in the book: "Can capitalism survive? No. I do not think it can"; and "Can socialism work? Of course it can."

Why, then, do I now place Schumpeter high among the economists from whom there is something to be learned? The answer is complex, for there is no doubt that Schumpeter is often assertive, pompous, arrogant, and simply wrong. Yet something of great value resides in his work. I see it as a kind of reluctant recognition of the bounded capabilities of economics as a "science"—a recognition all the more remarkable insofar as Schumpeter was a leader in the establishment of econometrics, a new branch of theory-driven statistical inquiry which sought to strengthen the scientific core of economic inquiry. And even here, there are grounds for a

skeptical assessment: elected as the first president of the Econometric Society, Schumpeter was himself an indifferent mathematician,
if indeed one at all.[67]

And what is the saving grace? Let me approach the question by
briefly introducing Schumpeter himself. Joseph Alois was born of
modest parentage in Austria in 1883—the same year as Keynes,
whom he later considered his arch rival (Keynes did not return the
compliment), along with Karl Marx, about whom Schumpeter
wrote with great appreciation, having first identified the real Marx
as a conservative, as we shall see.

His widowed mother remarried well, and young Joseph was
sent to the Theresianum, an exclusive school for sons of the aris-
tocracy. There he adopted the aristocratic style of his school-
mates, although not, I fear, with the inner security that should
accompany them: one suspects that feelings of social inferiority
from those early days underlie much of the later posturing.* There
was never any doubt, however, that he was a brilliant student;
and at age 27, while serving as financial advisor to an Egyptian
princess, he published his second book, *The Theory of Economic
Development*.[68] The book did not make an immediate impression,
but slowly made him known, especially after an English translation in 1934. It is here that our own inquiry begins.

The *Theory* interests us for a special reason—its striking and
wholly original picture of a key figure within the system, the entrepreneur. Curiously, for all his importance, the entrepreneur-capi-
talist exists as little more than a shadow in previous economic
scenarios. We never actually meet any of Smith's masters, such as
the owner of the famous pin factory, and have no idea of what he
and his brethren actually do, aside from scheming to cheat the

[67] See Richard Swedberg, *Schumpeter: A Biography*, Princeton, N.J.: Princeton University Press, 1991, I, pp. 117–18.
*I cannot resist a reference to *The Worldly Philosophers* (6th ed., p. 298), which tells
how Schumpeter married the charming daughter of an apartment superintendent
"whom he had sent to schools in Paris and Switzerland to equip her to be his wife."
That was indeed the story he circulated. In point of fact, she had worked as a maid
in France. (Robert Loring Allen, *Opening Doors: The Life and Work of Josef Schumpeter*,
New Brunswick, N.J.: Transaction Publishers, 1991, Vol. I, p. 197.) He did, however,
love her dearly and never fully recovered from her early death.
[68] New York: Harper & Bros., 1942; 2d ed., 1947.

public (see page 95 above). We do not catch so much as a glimpse of Ricardo's capitalists at work, and have no inkling as to their activities as businessmen or their reactions to their impending loss of income to the landlords. In Marx's great drama, the capitalist appears as Mr. Moneybags, collecting surplus value, or playing the role of predator or prey in the battle of capitals, but his actual economic duties or decisions are left undescribed. Even with Marshall, where we watch the rise and decline of business fortunes, there is no attention to what men in business actually do.

With Schumpeter this changes. We now have a sharp, if somewhat romantic, description of the character and the duties of a key person in the capitalist world, and as a very important consequence, a new perspective within which to regard capitalism itself. Here we must start with the tableau within which the entrepreneur comes to life, a tableau that Schumpeter calls a "circular flow" economy. Perhaps borrowing from Quesnay and Cantillon and Walras, Schumpeter believed that one could only understand how a commercial society worked if one pictured what such a society would look like if it merely reproduced itself, year in and year out. This is certainly not because Schumpeter believed that a circular flow was an accurate representation of a capitalist system. On the contrary, he strongly felt that capitalism was unique in history because of its ceaseless and self-generated changefulness. The purpose of starting from a circular flow, where, in his words, "the same products are produced every year in the same way,"[69] was that only in such an imaginary system, from which all dynamism had been removed, could one put one's finger on the agency of endemic change. It would be, of course, the entrepreneur.

We should take a moment to realize what the circular flow entails. As a consequence of its frozen condition, something like the Ricardian and Millian stationary state prevails. Competition now forces employers to pay workers the full value of their efforts, with the result that there are no profits over and above the wages of management. It is a world in which Say's Law is the law of the

---

[69] Schumpeter, supra cit., p. 108.

land: "For every supply," writes Schumpeter, "there awaits some-where in the economic system a corresponding demand, for every demand a corresponding supply."*

I will not go further into the description of a circular flow econ-omy with its Walrasian-like general equilibrium, nor raise the obvi-ous objection that no capitalism could maintain itself in such a condition of inanimation. Schumpeter would admit all that with an impatient wave of his hand. The point, he would insist, is that only from such a *reductio ad absurdum* can one locate the crucial means by which real capitalism gains its life force. The answer, as we can anticipate, lies in the activity of a class of individuals who take it upon themselves to upset the circular flow by inventing and redesigning the products, and rearranging the processes of business life in the hope of making a profit from the disequilibria that their activities will bring about.

In *Capitalism, Socialism, and Democracy* we will explore at some length the long-term consequences of this dynamization ("Can capitalism survive? No. I do not think it can."). At this junc-ture, however, the entrepreneurial capitalist deserves our attention because he embodies another Schumpeterian concept—namely, the natural elite whence the body of entrepeneurs emerge. Below he addresses the question of how it comes about that some capital-ists become entrepreneurs, whereas others remain mere passive administrators of unchanging businesses. The answer lies in the uneven distribution of talents or "aptitudes":

... [T]hese aptitudes are presumably distributed in an ethni-cally homogeneous population just like others, that is, the curve of their distribution has a maximum ordinate, deviations on either side of which become rarer the greater they are. Similarly we can assume that every healthy man can sing if he will. Per-haps half the individuals in an ethnically homogeneous group have the capacity for it to an average degree, a quarter in pro-

----

*Say's Law, promulgated in his *Treatise on Political Economy* in 1803, maintained that every act of production always generates enough income to buy back its output, whence the saying "Supply creates its own Demand." For Schumpeter's version, op. cit., p. 108.

gressively diminishing measure, and, let us say, a quarter in a measure above the average; and within this quarter, through a series of continually increasing singing ability and continually diminishing number of people who possess it, we come finally to the Carusos. Only in this quarter are we struck in general by singing ability, and only in the supreme instances can it become the characterising mark of the person. . . .

Let us apply this: Again, a quarter of the population may be so poor in those qualities, let us say here provisionally, of economic initiative that the deficiency makes itself felt by poverty of their moral personality, and they play a wretched part in the smallest affairs of private and professional life on which this element is called for. We recognize this type and know that many of the best clerks, distinguished by devotion to duty, expert knowledge, and exactitude, belong to it. Then comes the "half," the "normal." These prove themselves to be better in the things which even within the established channels cannot be "dispatched" but must also be "decided" and "carried out." Practically all business persons belong here, otherwise they would never have attained their positions; most represent a selection—individually or hereditarily tested. . . . From there, rising in the scale we come finally into the highest quarter, to people who are a type characterised by super-normal qualities of intellect and will. Within this type are not only many varieties (merchants, manufacturers, financiers, etc.,) but also a continuous variety of degrees of intensity in "initiative" . . . Many a one can steer a safe course, where no one has yet been; others follow where first another went before; still others only in the crowd, but in this among the first. . . .*

Last, what drives the entrepreneur to exercise his leadership talents? Schumpeter writes:

First of all, there is the dream and the will to found a private kingdom, usually, though not necessarily, also a dynasty. The

*Op. cit., pp. 81–82, n. 2. Oddly, this crucial passage was only added in the second edition of the book, and then as a footnote.

modern world really does not know any such positions, but what may be attained by industrial or commercial success is still the nearest approach to medieval lordship possible to modern man. Its fascination is especially strong for people who have no other chance of achieving social distinction. The sensation of power and independence loses nothing by the fact that both are largely illusions. Closer analysis would lead to discovering an endless variety within this group of motives, from spiritual ambition down to mere snobbery. . . .

Then there is the will to conquer; the impulse to fight, to prove oneself superior to others, to succeed for the sake, not of the fruits of success, but of success itself. From this aspect, economic action becomes akin to sport—there are financial races, or rather boxing-matches. The financial result is a secondary consider-ation, or at all events, mainly valued as an index of success, and as a symptom of victory. Again we should find countless nuances, some of which, like social ambition, fade into the first group of motives. And again we are faced with a motivation characteristically different from that of "satisfaction of wants". . . .

Finally there is the joy of creating, of getting things done, or simply of exercising one's energy and ingenuity. This is akin to a ubiquitous motive, but nowhere else does it stand out as an independent factor of behavior with anything like the clearness with which it obtrudes itself in our case. Our type seeks out dif-ficulties, changes in order to change, delights in ventures.

Only with the first groups of motives is private property as the result of entreprenurial activity an essential factor in making it operative. With the other two it is not. Pecuniary gain is indeed a very accurate expression of success, especially of *relative* suc-cess, and from the standpoint of the man who strives for it, it has the additional advantage of being an objective fact and largely independent of the opinion of others. These and other peculiari-ties incident to the mechanism of "acquisitive" society make it very difficult to replace it as a motor of industrial development . . . What other stimuli could be provided, and how they could be made to work as well as the "capitalistic" ones do, are questions which are beyond our theme. They are taken too lightly by social reformers. . . . But they are not insoluble, and may be answered by detailed observation of the psychology of entrepreneurial activity, at least for given times and places.[70]

It is hard to know what to make of this mixture of sophistication, élitism, and naiveté. I do not think anyone would take Schumpeter's analysis of the role or motives of entrepreneurial behavior as the basis for an investigation to be put to econometric testing. But neither do I think this was his purpose. Schumpeter is trying to put his finger on an aspect of economics that had been almost totally neglected since Adam Smith's observations in his *Theory of Moral Sentiments.* This is to locate the roots of the activity vital for capitalism. Schumpeter finds it in the realm of social or political motivation rather than that of economics, with its near-exclusive emphasis on rational calculation.

We will be tracing the consequences of this view of entrepreneurial behavior when we turn shortly to a consideration of the book from which we began our study of Schumpeter—*Capitalism, Socialism, and Democracy.* But first, one additional application deserves our brief attention. It is the role of "irrational" behavior in explaining a phenomenon in which Schumpeter had always been interested—business cycles. Cycles are the focus of the last chapter of *The Theory of Economic Development,* and will be examined again during the 1930s in a two volume study. The later book, *Business Cycles,* was much more ambitious—its subtitle reads *Theoretical, Historical, and Statistical Analysis of the Capitalist Process*—but it is generally agreed that most of the two volumes consist of rather tedious business history, and that the remaining portion, devoted to explaining why booms and busts seemed to come in a *cyclical* pattern, offered little that was not already in the final chapter of *The Theory of Economic Development.**

---

[70] Op. cit., pp. 93–94.
*There was one notable change in the later book. Business cycles now meet with respect. In *The Theory of Economic Development,* they did not: "How exaggerated the popular conceptions of the ravages caused by a depression are, is shown by any official investigation of crises." (p. 246) But this was written 20 years before the 1930s.

Why do cycles attract Schumpeter's attention? The answer, although not the historical detail that will be presented in *Business Cycles,* again lies in the earlier *Theory of Economic Development.* It is Schumpeter's attribution of economic growth to entrepreneurial energy. For the question then arises, as Schumpeter puts it, why is not growth a smooth and continuous process, "similar to the organic growth of a tree?" Schumpeter looks to various causes for business turndowns, ranging from accidents," such as crop failures, various malfunctions of supply or demand, to credit breakdowns, "panics," and the like. None seemed to contain a self-repeating element. This now leads Schumpeter to the conclusion that cycles arise not because disturbances appear in the system, but because these disturbances appear "in groups or swarms." This is particularly the case with respect to those growth-producing "disturbances" that arise because of the introduction of new and untried processes or products. Schumpeter has already explained the problem as follows:

Why do entrepreneurs appear, not continuously, that is, singly in every appropriately chosen interval, but in clusters? *Exclusively because the appearance of one or a few entrepreneurs facilitates the appearance of others, and those the appearance of more, in ever-increasing numbers* [his italics].

This means, first, that for the reasons explained [previously] the carrying out of new combinations is difficult and only accessible to people with certain qualities, as is best seen by visualizing an example from earlier times or the economic situation in the stage that most resembles an economy without development. ... Only a few people have these qualities of leadership and only a few in such a situation, that is a situation which is not itself already a boom, can succeed in this direction. However, if one or a few have advanced with success many of the difficulties disappear. Others can then follow these pioneers, as they will clearly do under this stimulus of the success now attainable. Their success again makes it easier, through the increasingly complete removal of the obstacles analyzed [earlier], for more people to follow suit, until finally the innovation becomes familiar and the acceptance of it a matter of free choice.

Secondly, since as we have seen the entrepreneurial qualification is something which, like many other qualities, is distributed in an ethnically homogenous group according to the law of error, the number of individuals who satisfy progressively diminishing standards in this respect continually increases. . . .

Thirdly, this explains the appearance of entrepreneurs in clusters and indeed up to the point of eliminating entrepreneurial profit, first of all in the branch of industry in which the pioneers appear. Reality also discloses that every normal boom starts in one or a few branches of industry (railway building, electrical, and chemical industries, and so forth), and that it derives its character from the innovations in the industry where it begins. But the pioneers remove the obstacles for the others not only in the branch of production in which they first appear, but, owing to the nature of these obstacles, *ipso facto,* in other branches as well. . . . Hence the first leaders are effective beyond their immediate sphere of action and so the group of entrepreneurs increases still further and the economic system is drawn more rapidly and more completely than would otherwise be the case into the process of technological and commercial reorganization which constitutes the meaning of periods of boom.

Fourth, the more the process of development becomes familiar and a mere matter of calculation to all concerned, and the weaker the obstacles become in the course of time, the less the "leadership" that will be needed to call forth innovations. Hence the less pronounced will become the swarm-like appearance of entrepreneurs and the milder the cyclical movement. . . . The progressive trustification of economic life acts in the same direction. . . .

Fifthly, the swarm-like appearance of new combinations easily and necessarily explains the fundamental features of periods of boom. It explains why increasing capital investment is the very first symptom of the coming boom, why industries producing the means of production are the first to show supernormal stimulation, above all why the consumption of iron increases. It explains the appearance of new purchasing power in bulk, thereby the characteristic rise of prices during booms, which obviously no reference to increased need or increased costs can explain. Further, it explains the decline of unemployment and the rise of wages, the rise in the interest rate, the increase in freight, the increasing strain on bank balances and bank reserves, and so forth, and, as we have said, the release of secondary waves—the spread of prosperity over the whole economic system.

It is a bravura, although by no means a wholly convincing exposition, which had considerable impact in its time, not least in introducing the term "pioneer" into much business cycle literature. The key matter of cyclicality, however, remains elusive—granting that "swarming" may intensify the boom, why does not the expansion, once made a matter of routine, go on indefinitely? Schumpeter is silent about this. But I have nonetheless chosen to reproduce the passages from his business cycle chapter for two reasons. One, as I have already said, is that Schumpeter's elitist view of the distribution of talents is again put to use, with at least some clarificatory gain as a result.

. . . No therapy can permanently obstruct the great economic and social process by which businesses, individual positions, forms of life, cultural values and ideals, sink in the social scale and finally disappear. In a society of private property and competition, this process is the necessary complement of the continual emergence of new economic and social forms and of continually rising real incomes of all social strata. The process would be milder if there were no cyclical fluctuations, but it is not wholly due to the latter and it is completed independently of them. These changes are, theoretically and practically, economically and culturally, much more important than the economic stability upon which all analytical attention has been concentrated for so long. And in their special way both the rise and fall of families and firms are much more characteristic of the capitalist economic system, of its culture and its results, than any of the things that can be observed in a society which is stationary in the sense that its processes reproduce themselves at a constant rate.[71]

The second reason will be found in the remarkable paragraph above—the conclusion to the chapter and the book. The paragraph sounds a note of pessimism that takes us by surprise because we have not been prepared for it in this celebration of entrepreneurialism. As such, the mixture of celebration and resignation serves as a bridge to our next reading—the remarkable *Capitalism, Socialism, and Democracy*—which would not appear until thirty years later. I have no idea whether Schumpeter had already worked out in his mind the scenario of that powerful book, but the paragraph above reveals that if it was not in his conscious mind, it was assuredly somewhere in what he would later call the "preanalytic" level of socioeconomic vision.

CAPITALISM, SOCIALISM, AND DEMOCRACY

The great book starts with Marx: Marx the Prophet, Marx the Sociologist, Marx the Economist, Marx the Teacher. It is a Marx whom Schumpeter approaches as admirer, and student—never as devotee or sycophant. Furthermore, that which Schumpeter takes from Marx is not his dialectical method, materialist view of history, or even specific model of capitalism. That would seem to leave little behind. But Schumpeter's appreciation is based on something else—an approach to economic inquiry that never loses sight of its sociological and political roots, its value-laden core. This approach gives to Schumpeter's scenario, even when it is manifestly in error, an importance that cannot be dismissed.

We will see that quality as we proceed, but I must make one last observation about the chapter behind us. Schumpeter ultimately finds his affinity with Marx because in *Capital* he perceives "beneath the fantastic glitter of dubious gems a distinct conservative implication. And after all," he muses, "Why not? No serious argument ever supports any "ism" unconditionally. To say that

---

[71] Op. cit., p. 255.

Marx, stripped of phrases, admits of interpretation in a conservative sense is only saying that he can be taken seriously."[72] I am
not sure what light these reflections throw on Marx, but they
surely illumine their author.

One finishes Part I on Marx, and turns the page to Part II, *Can
Capitalism Survive?* We know the answer, but not the argument
until we reach the third paragraph:

The thesis I shall endeavor to establish is that the actual and
prospective performance of the capitalist system is such as to
negative the idea of its breaking down under the weight of economic failure, but that its very success undermines the social
institutions which protect it, and "inevitably" creates conditions
in which it will not be able to live and which strongly point to
socialism as the heir apparent. My final conclusion therefore
does not differ, however much my argument may, from that of
most socialist writers and in particular from that of all Marxists.
But in order to accept it one does not need to be a socialist. Prognosis does not imply anything about the desirability of the
course of events that one predicts. If a doctor predicts that his
patient will die presently, this does not mean that he desires it.
One may hate socialism or at least look upon it with cool criticism, and yet foresee its advent. Many conservatives did and do.

The next chapter is, in effect, an update of the conclusion of
Smith's Chapter I in *The Wealth*, which concludes, we will recall,
by reminding us that the "accommodation . . . of an industrious
and frugal peasant . . . exceeds that of many an African king, the
master of ten thousand naked savages" (see page 82 above). In
more sophisticated terms, Schumpeter reminds us of a similar
change that has characterized the world since Smith's day.

One way of expressing our result is that, if capitalism repeated
its past performance for another half century starting with 1928,
this would do away with anything that according to present

---

[72] *Capitalism, Socialism, Democracy,* 2d ed., New York: Harper & Bros., 1947.

standards could be called poverty, even in the lowest strata of the population, pathological cases alone excepted. . . .

Verification is easy. There are no doubt some things available to the modern workman that Louis XIV himself would have been delighted to have yet was unable to have—modern dentistry for instance. On the whole, however, a budget on that level had little that really mattered to gain from capitalist achievement. Even speed of traveling may be assumed to have been a minor consideration for so very dignified a gentleman. Electric lighting is no great boon to anyone who has money enough to buy a sufficient number of candles and to pay servants to attend to them. It is the cheap cloth, the cheap cotton and rayon fabric, boots, motorcars and so on that are the typical achievements of capitalist production, and not as a rule improvements that would mean much to the rich man. Queen Elizabeth owned silk stockings. The capitalist achievement does not typically consist in providing more silk stockings for queens but in bringing them within the reach of factory girls in return for steadily decreasing amounts of effort.

From this first hopeful overview, the argument moves to one of causality: what has brought about this long upward movement? The answer will not surprise us.

The essential point to grasp is that in dealing with capitalism we are dealing with an evolutionary process. It may seem strange that anyone can fail to see so obvious a fact which moreover was long ago emphasized by Karl Marx. Yet that fragmentary analysis which yields the bulk of our propositions about the functioning of modern capitalism persistently neglects it. Let us restate the point and see how it bears upon our problem.

Capitalism, then, is by nature a form or method of economic change and not only never is but never can be stationary. And this evolutionary character of the capitalist process is not merely due to the fact that economic life goes on in a social and natural environment which changes and by its change alters the data of economic action; this fact is important and these changes (wars, revolutions and so on) often condition industrial change, but they are not its prime movers. Nor is this evolutionary character due to a quasi-automatic increase in population and capital or to the vagaries of monetary systems of which exactly the same thing holds true. The fundamental impulse that sets and keeps the capitalist engine in motion comes from the new consumers' goods, the new methods of production or transportation, the new markets, the new forms of industrial organization that capitalist enterprise creates.

As we have seen in the preceding chapter, the contents of the laborer's budget, say from 1760 to 1940, did not simply grow on unchanging lines but they underwent a process of qualitative change. Similarly, the history of the productive apparatus of a typical farm, from the beginnings of the rationalization of crop rotation, plowing and fattening to the mechanized thing of today—linking up with elevators and railroads—is a history of revolutions. So is the history of the productive apparatus of the iron and steel industry from the charcoal furnace to our own type of furnace, or the history of the apparatus of power production from the overshot water wheel to the modern power plant, or the history of transportation from the mailcoach to the airplane. The opening up of new markets, foreign or domestic, and the organizational development from the craft shop and factory to such concerns as U.S. Steel illustrate the same process of industrial mutation—if I may use that biological term—that incessantly revolutionizes the economic structure *from within*, incessantly destroying the old one, incessantly creating a new one. This process of Creative Destruction is the essential fact about capitalism. It is what capitalism consists in and what every capitalist concern has got to live in. This fact bears upon our problem in two ways.

First, since we are dealing with a process whose every element takes considerable time in revealing its true features and ultimate effects, there is no point in appraising the performance of that process *ex visu* of a given point of time; we must judge its performance over time, as it unfolds through decades or centuries. A system—any system, economic or other—that at *every* given point of time fully utilizes its possibilities to the best advantage may yet in the long run be inferior to a system that does so at *no* given point of time, because the latter's failure to do so may be a condition for the level or speed of long-run performance.

Second, since we are dealing with an organic process, analysis of what happens in any particular part of it—say, in an individual concern or industry—may indeed clarify details of mechanism but is inconclusive beyond that. Every piece of business strategy acquires its true significance only against the background of that process and within the situation created by it. It must be seen in its role in the perennial gale of creative destruction; it cannot be understood irrespective of it or, in fact, on the hypothesis that there is a perennial lull.

Thus we begin to unravel the argument that capitalism *cannot* survive, by recounting the reasons for its success—"the perennial gale of creative destruction"—by which its energies are mobilized and stimulated. Schumpeter takes a chapter to develop the thesis that the outcome of this gale is the evolution of atomistic competition—one small firm against another, as in Adam Smith's world of pin factories—to a new world of competitive "monopolies." "What we have got to accept," he concludes at the end of Chapter VIII, "is that [large-scale industry] has come to be the most powerful engine of . . . progress and in particular of the long-run expansion of total output. . . . In this respect, perfect competition is not only impossible but inferior, and has no title of being set up as a model of ideal efficiency."

That question now leads to a more difficult one. If we agree with Schumpeter that irregular, but persistent growth has been the pattern of the past, can we with any confidence extend that trajectory into the future? Could a "vanishing of investment opportunity"—Schumpeter uses a much-repeated phrase of the late 1930s and prewar 1940s—draw a line between past achievement and future prospects?

Schumpeter dismisses such gloomy views. The fears that we face a declining rate of population growth, with a corresponding decline in purchasing, are likened to the outmoded fears of the past that population would outrun resources; do not forget that we are dealing with the prospects of more than fifty years ago. The same confidence enables him to shrug at the danger that we will use up our resources—Schumpeter relies on technological progress to produce an "embarras de richesse" of both foodstuffs and resources. Might there not, then, be a "closing of the frontier" for new investment? It is dismissed with a trenchant observation: "The conquest of the air may well be more important than the conquest of India was—we must not confuse geographical frontiers with economic ones." But could we not exhaust these technological frontiers? We are assured that "Technological possibilities are an uncharted sea"; that "there is no reason to expect slackening of the rate of output through exhaustion of technological possibilities."

It must be clear that Schumpeter does not expect to have laid to rest all the fears that capitalism's historical record of expansion will come to a halt. The purpose of the chapter is, rather, a typically Schumpeterian ploy in giving his opponents all the cards, and nonetheless beating them at their own game. In the chapters we have just summarized in passing he has "demonstrated" that the conventional fears for its demise are much exaggerated, to say the least. The next four chapter titles now tell us what lies ahead: let us follow them to discover why the answer to the question "Can Capitalism Survive?" is negative.

Chapter XI

The Civilization of Capitalism

... Capitalist civilization is rationalistic "and anti-heroic." The two go together of course. Success in industry and commerce requires a lot of stamina, yet industrial and commercial activity is essentially unheroic in the knight's sense—no flourishing of swords about it, not much physical prowess, no chance to gallop the armored horse into the enemy, preferably a heretic or heathen—and the ideology that glorifies the idea of fighting for fighting's sake and of victory for victory's sake understandably withers in the office among all the columns of figures. Therefore, owning assets that are apt to attract the robber or the tax gatherer and not sharing or even disliking warrior ideology that conflicts with its "rational" utilitarianism, the industrial and commercial bourgeoisie is fundamentally pacifist and inclined to insist on the application of the moral precepts of private life to international relations. It is true that, unlike most but like some other features of capitalist civilization, pacifism and international morality have also been espoused in non-capitalist environments and by precapitalist agencies, in the Middle Ages by the Roman Church for instance. Modern pacifism and modern international morality are nonetheless products of capitalism.

In view of the fact that Marxian doctrine—especially Neo-Marxian doctrine and even a considerable body of non-socialist opinion—is, as we have seen in the first part of this book, strongly opposed to this proposition it is necessary to point out that the latter is not meant to deny that many a bourgeoisie has put up a splendid fight for hearth and home, or that almost purely bourgeois commonwealths were often aggressive when it seemed to pay—like the Athenian or the Venetian common-wealths—or that no bourgeoisie ever disliked war profits and advantages to trade accruing from conquest or refused to be trained in warlike nationalism by its feudal masters or leaders or by the propaganda of some specially interested group. All I hold is, first, that such instances of capitalist combativeness are not, as Marxism has it, to be explained—exclusively or primarily— in terms of class interests or class situations that systematically engender capitalist wars of conquest; second, that there is a difference between doing that which you consider your normal business in life, for which you prepare yourself in season and out of season and in terms of which you define your success or failure, and doing what is not in your line, for which your normal work and your mentality do not fit you and success in which will increase the prestige of the most unbourgeois of professions; and third, that this difference steadily tells—in international as well as in domestic affairs—against the use of military force and for peaceful arrangements, even where the balance of pecuniary advantage is clearly on the side of war which, under modern circumstances, is not in general very likely. As a matter of fact, the more completely capitalist the structure and attitude of a nation, the more pacifist—and the more prone to count the costs of war—we observe it to be. . . .

But I am not going to sum up as the reader presumably expects me to. That is to say, I am not going to invite him, before he decides to put his trust in an untried alternative advocated by untried men, to look once more at the impressive economic and the still more impressive cultural achievement of the capitalist order and at the immense promise held out by both. I am not going to argue that that achievement and that promise are in themselves sufficient to support an argument for allowing the capitalist process to work on and, as it might easily be put, to lift poverty from the shoulders of mankind. . . .

However, whether favorable or unfavorable, value judgments about capitalist performance are of little interest. For mankind is not free to choose. This is not only because the mass of people are not in a position to compare alternatives rationally and always accept what they are being told. There is a much deeper reason for it. Things economic and social move by their own momentum and the ensuing situations compel individuals and groups to behave in certain ways whatever they may wish to do—not indeed by destroying their freedom of choice but by shaping the choosing mentalities and by narrowing the list of possibilities from which to choose. If this is the quintessence of Marxism then we all of us have got to be Marxists. In consequence, capitalist performance is not even relevant for prognosis. Most civilizations have disappeared before they had time to fill to the full the measure of their promise. Hence I am not going to argue, on the strength of that performance, that the capitalist intermezzo is likely to be prolonged. In fact, I am now going to draw the exactly opposite inference.

Chapter XII

Crumbling Walls

I. THE OBSOLESCENCE OF THE ENTREPRENEURIAL FUNCTION

In our discussion of the theory of vanishing investment opportunity, a reservation was made in favor of the possibility that the economic wants of humanity might some day be so completely satisfied that little motive would be left to push productive effort still further ahead. Such a state of satiety is no doubt very far off even if we keep within the present scheme of wants; and if we take account of the fact that, as higher standards of life are attained, these wants automatically expand and new wants emerge or are created, satiety becomes a flying goal, particularly if we include leisure among consumers' goods. However, let us glance at that possibility, assuming, still more unrealistically, that methods of production have reached a state of perfection which does not admit of further improvement.

A more or less stationary state would ensue. Capitalism, being essentially an evolutionary process, would become atrophic. There would be nothing left for entrepreneurs to do. They would find themselves in much the same situation as generals would in a society perfectly sure of permanent peace. Profits and along with profits the rate of interest would converge toward zero. The bourgeois strata that live on profits and interest would tend to disappear. The management of industry and trade would become a matter of current administration, and the personnel would unavoidably acquire the characteristics of a bureaucracy. Socialism of a very sober type would almost automatically come into being. Human energy would turn away from business. Other than economic pursuits would attract the brains and provide the adventure.

For the calculable future this vision is of no importance. But all the greater importance attaches to the fact that many of the effects on the structure of society and on the organization of the productive process that we might expect from an approximately complete satisfaction of wants or from absolute technological perfection can also be expected from a development that is clearly observable already. Progress itself may be mechanized as well as the management of a stationary economy, and this mechanization of progress may affect entrepreneurship and capitalist society nearly as much as the cessation of economic progress would. In order to see this it is only necessary to restate, first, what the entrepreneurial function consists in and, secondly, what it means for bourgeois society and the survival of the capitalist order.

We have seen that the function of entrepreneurs is to reform or revolutionize the pattern of production by exploiting an invention or, more generally, an untried technological possibility for producing a new commodity or producing an old one in a new way, by opening up a new source of supply of materials or a new outlet for products, by reorganizing an industry and so on. Railroad construction in its earlier stages, electrical power production before the First World War, steam and steel, the motorcar, colonial ventures afford spectacular instances of a large genus which comprises innumerable humbler ones—down to such things as making a success of a particular kind of sausage or toothbrush. This kind of activity is primarily responsible for the recurrent "prosperities" that revolutionize the economic organism and the recurrent "recessions" that are due to the disequilibrating impact of the new products or methods. To undertake such new things is difficult and constitutes a distinct economic function, first, because they lie outside of the routine tasks which everybody understands and, secondly, because the environment resists in many ways that vary, according to social conditions, from simple refusal either to finance or to buy a new thing, to physical attack on the man who tries to produce it. To act with confidence beyond the range of familiar beacons and to overcome that resistance requires aptitudes that are present in only a small fraction of the population and that define the entrepreneurial type as well as the entrepreneurial function. This function does not essentially consist in either inventing anything or otherwise creating the conditions which the enterprise exploits. It consists in getting things done.

This social function is already losing importance and is bound to lose it at an accelerating rate in the future even if the economic process itself of which entrepreneurship was the prime mover went on unabated. For, on the one hand, it is much easier now than it has been in the past to do things that lie outside familiar routine—innovation itself is being reduced to routine. Technological progress is increasingly becoming the business of teams of trained specialists who turn out what is required and make it work in predictable ways. The romance of earlier commercial adventure is rapidly wearing away, because so many more things can be strictly calculated that had of old to be visualized in a flash of genius. . . .

But this affects the position of the entire bourgeois stratum. Although entrepreneurs are not necessarily or even typically elements of that stratum from the outset, they nevertheless enter it in case of success. Thus, though entrepreneurs do not *per se* form a social class, the bourgeois class absorbs them and their families and connections, thereby recruiting and revitalizing itself currently while at the same time the families that sever their active relation to "business" drop out of it after a generation or two. Between, there is the bulk of what we refer to as industrialists, merchants, financiers and bankers; they are in the intermediate stage between entrepreneurial venture and mere current administration of an inherited domain. The returns on which the class lives are produced by, and the social position of the class rests on, the success of this more or less active sector—which of course may, as it does in this country, form over 90 per cent of the bourgeois stratum—and of the individuals who are in the act of rising into that class. Economically and sociologically, directly and indirectly, the bourgeoisie therefore depends on the entrepreneur and, as a class, lives and will die with him, though a more or less prolonged transitional stage—eventually a stage in which it may feel equally unable to die and to live—is quite likely to occur, as in fact it did occur in the case of the feudal civilization.

To sum up this part of our argument: if capitalist evolution—"progress"—either ceases or becomes completely automatic, the economic basis of the industrial bourgeoisie will be reduced eventually to wages such as are paid for current administrative work excepting remnants of quasi-rents and monopoloid gains that may be expected to linger on for some time. Since capitalist enterprise, by its very achievements, tends to automatize progress, we conclude that it tends to make itself superfluous—to break to pieces under the pressure of its own success. The perfectly bureaucratized giant industrial unit not only ousts the small or medium-sized firm and "expropriates" its owners, but in the end it also ousts the entrepreneur and expropriates the bourgeoisie as a class which in the process stands to lose not only its income but also what is infinitely more important, its function. The true pacemakers of socialism were not the intellectuals or agitators who preached it but the Vanderbilts, Carnegies and Rockefellers. This result may not in every respect be to the taste of Marxian socialists, still less to the taste of socialists of a more popular (Marx would have said, vulgar) description. But so far as prognosis goes, it does not differ from theirs.

Chapter XIII

Growing Hostility

From the analysis of the two preceding chapters, it should not be difficult to understand how the capitalist process produced that atmosphere of almost universal hostility to its own social order to which I have referred at the threshold of this part. The phenomenon is so striking and both the Marxian and the popular explanations are so inadequate that it is desirable to develop the theory of it a little further.

The capitalist process, so we have seen, eventually decreases the importance of the function by which the capitalist class lives. We have also seen that it tends to wear away protective strata, to break down its own defenses, to disperse the garrisons of its entrenchments. And we have finally seen that capitalism creates a critical frame of mind which, after having destroyed the moral authority of so many other institutions, in the end turns against its own; the bourgeois finds to his amazement that the rationalist attitude does not stop at the credentials of kings and popes but goes on to attack private property and the whole scheme of bourgeois values. . . .

Of course, the hostility of the intellectual group—amounting to moral disapproval of the capitalist order—is one thing, and the general hostile atmosphere which surrounds the capitalist engine is another thing. The latter is the really significant phe-nomenon; and it is not simply the product of the former but flows partly from independent sources, some of which have been mentioned before; so far as it does, it is raw material for the intellectual group to work on. There are give-and-take relations between the two which it would require more space to unravel than I can spare. The general contours of such an analysis are however sufficiently obvious and I think it safe to repeat that the role of the intellectual group consists primarily in stimulating, energizing, verbalizing and organizing this material and only secondarily in adding to it.

Chapter XIV

Decomposition

Faced by the increasing hostility of the environment and by the legislative, administrative and judicial practice born of that hos-tility, entrepreneurs and capitalists—in fact the whole stratum that accepts the bourgeois scheme of life—will eventually cease to function. Their standard aims are rapidly becoming unattain-able, their efforts futile. The most glamorous of these bourgeois aims, the foundation of an industrial dynasty, has in most coun-tries become unattainable already, and even more modest ones are so difficult to attain that they may cease to be thought worth the struggle as the permanence of these conditions is being increasingly realized.

Considering the role of bourgeois motivation in the explana-tion of the economic history of the last two or three centuries, its smothering by the unfavorable reactions of society or its weaken-ing by disuse no doubt constitutes a factor adequate to explain a flop in the capitalist process—should we ever observe it as a permanent phenomenon—and one that is much more important than any of those that are presented by the Theory of Vanishing Investment Opportunity. It is hence interesting to observe that that motivation not only is threatened by forces external to the bourgeois mind but that it also tends to die out from internal causes. There is of course close interdependence between the two. But we cannot get at the true diagnosis unless we try to disentangle them.

One of those "internal causes" we have already met with. I have dubbed it Evaporation of the Substance of Property. We have seen that, normally, the modern businessman, whether entrepreneur or mere managing administrator, is of the executive type. From the logic of his position he acquires something of the psychology of the salaried employee working in a bureaucratic organization. Whether a stockholder or not, his will to fight and to hold on is not and cannot be what it was with the man who knew ownership and its responsibilities in the full-blooded sense of those words. His system of values and his conception of duty undergo a profound change. Mere stockholders of course have ceased to count at all—quite independently of the clipping of their share by a regulating and taxing state. Thus the modern corporation, although the product of the capitalist process, socializes the bourgeois mind; it relentlessly narrows the scope of capitalist motivation; not only that, it will eventually kill its roots.

Still more important however is another "internal cause," viz., the disintegration of the bourgeois family. The facts to which I am referring are too well known to need explicit statement. To men and women in modern capitalist societies, family life and parenthood mean less than they meant before and hence are less powerful molders of behavior; the rebellious son or daughter who professes contempt for "Victorian" standards is, however incorrectly, expressing an undeniable truth. . . . The phenomenon by now extends, more or less, to all classes. But it first appeared in the bourgeois (and intellectual) stratum and its symptomatic as well as causal value for our purposes lies entirely there. It is wholly attributable to the rationalization of everything in life, which we have seen is one of the effects of capitalist evolution. In fact, it is but one of the results of the spread of that rationalization to the sphere of private life. All the other factors which are usually adduced in explanation can be readily reduced to that one.

As soon as men and women learn the utilitarian lesson and

refuse to take for granted the traditional arrangements that their social environment makes for them, as soon as they acquire the habit of weighing the individual advantages and disadvantages of any prospective course of action—or, as we might also put it, as soon as they introduce into their private life a sort of inarticulate system of cost accounting—they cannot fail to become aware of the heavy personal sacrifices that family ties and especially parenthood entail under modern conditions and of the fact that at the same time, excepting the cases of farmers and peasants, children cease to be economic assets. These sacrifices do not consist only of the items that come within the reach of the measuring rod of money but comprise in addition an indefinite amount of loss of comfort, of freedom from care, and opportunity to enjoy alternatives of increasing attractiveness and variety—alternatives to be compared with joys of parenthood that are being subjected to a critical analysis of increasing severity. The implication of this is not weakened but strengthened by the fact that the balance sheet is likely to be incomplete, perhaps even fundamentally wrong. For the greatest of the assets, the contribution made by parenthood to physical and moral health—to "normality" as we might express it—particularly in the case of women, almost invariably escapes the rational searchlight of modern individuals who, in private as in public life, tend to focus attention on ascertainable details of immediate utilitarian relevance and to sneer at the idea of hidden necessities of human nature or of the social organism. The point I wish to convey is, I think, clear without further elaboration. It may be summed up in the question that is so clearly in many potential parents' minds: "Why should we stunt our ambitions and impoverish our lives in order to be insulted and looked down upon in our old age?"

We have rediscovered what from different standpoints and, so I believe, on inadequate grounds has often been discovered before: there is inherent in the capitalist system a tendency toward self-destruction which, in its earlier stages, may well assert itself in the form of a tendency toward retardation of progress.

I shall not stay to repeat how objective and subjective, economic and extra-economic factors, reinforcing each other in
imposing accord, contribute to that result. Nor shall I stay to
show what should be obvious and in subsequent chapters will
become more obvious still, viz., that those factors make not only
for the destruction of the capitalist but for the emergence of a
socialist civilization. They all point in that direction. The capitalist process not only destroys its own institutional framework but
it also creates the conditions for another. Destruction may not be
the right word after all. Perhaps I should have spoken of transformation. The outcome of the process is not simply a void that
could be filled by whatever might happen to turn up; things and
souls are transformed in such a way as to become increasingly
amenable to the socialist form of life. With every peg from under
the capitalist structure vanishes an impossibility of the socialist
plan. In both these respects Marx's *vision* was right. We can also
agree with him in linking the particular social transformation
that goes on under our eyes with an economic process as its
prime mover. What our analysis, if correct, disproves is after all
of secondary importance, however essential the role may be
which it plays in the socialist credo. In the end there is not so
much difference as one might think between saying that the
decay of capitalism is due to its success and saying that it is due
to its failure.

But our answer to the question that heads this part posits far
more problems than it solves. In view of what is to follow in this
book, the reader should bear in mind:

First, that so far we have not learned anything about the kind
of socialism that may be looming in the future. For Marx and for
most of his followers—and this was and is one of the most serious shortcomings of their doctrine—socialism meant just one
definite thing. But the definiteness really goes no further than
nationalization of industry would carry us and with this an
indefinite variety of economic and cultural possibilities will be
seen to be compatible.

Second, that similarly we know nothing as yet about the precise way by which socialism may be expected to come except

that there must be a great many possibilities ranging from a gradual bureaucratization to the most picturesque revolution. Strictly speaking we do not even know whether socialism will actually come to stay. For to repeat: perceiving a tendency and visualizing the goal of it is one thing and predicting that this goal will actually be reached and that the resulting state of things will be workable, let alone permanent, is quite another thing. Before humanity chokes (or basks) in the dungeon (or paradise) of socialism it may well burn up in the horrors (or glories) of imperialist wars.*

Third, that the various components of the tendency we have been trying to describe, while everywhere discernible, have as yet nowhere fully revealed themselves. Things have gone to different lengths in different countries but in no country far enough to allow us to say with any confidence precisely how far they will go, or to assert that their "underlying trend" has grown too strong to be subject to anything more serious than temporary reverses. Industrial integration is far from being complete. Competition, actual and potential, is still a major factor in any business situation. Enterprise is still active, the leadership of the bourgeois group still the prime mover of the economic process. The middle class is still a political power. Bourgeois standards and bourgeois motivations though being increasingly impaired are still alive. Survival of traditions—and family ownership of controlling parcels of stock—still make many an executive behave as the owner-manager did of old. The bourgeois family has not yet died; in fact, it clings to life so tenaciously that no responsible politician has as yet dared to touch it by any method other than taxation. From the standpoint of immediate practice as well as for the purposes of short-run forecasting—and in these things, a century is a "short run"**—all this surface may be more

---

*Written in the summer of 1935. [This and the following footnote are Schumpeter's, added for the second edition].

**This is why the facts and arguments presented in this and the two preceding chapters do not invalidate my reasoning about the possible economic results of another fifty years of capitalist evolution. The thirties may well turn out to have been the last gasp of capitalism—the likelihood of this is of course greatly increased by the current war. But again they may not. In any case there are no *purely economic* reasons why capitalism should not have another successful run which is all I wished to establish.

important than the tendency toward another civilization that slowly works deep down below.

We turn the page to read Part III: "Can Socialism Work?" with its famous first sentence.

Part III is a great deal less interesting than its predecessor, not only because of its obvious invalidation by history, but because the internal argument is less intriguing than when Schumpeter is arguing for the inevitability of capitalism's demise—an inevitability, please note, that is given a half-century deferment in the first sentence of the last footnote on page 323, and perhaps an indefinitely longer one in the last sentence.

There is, in fact, only one aspect of Schumpeter's discussion of socialism that I find intriguing, because it mirrors once again the fundamental pre-cognitive vision from which he begins. We find it in Chapter XVIII, "The Human Element." I shall first reproduce the telltale passages, in which he discusses whether profound changes in attitudes will be needed to create socialism—examining the question in terms of three sectors: agriculture, industrial and service employees, and management—and then pose my question.

. . . We can first exclude the agrarian sector which could be expected to offer the most serious difficulties. Our socialism would still be socialism if the socialist management confined itself to a kind of agrarian planning that would only in degree differ from the practice that is already developing. Settling a plan of production; rationalizing location (land use); supplying farmers with machinery, seeds, stock for breeding purposes, fertilizers and so on; fixing prices of products and buying them from farmers at these prices—this is all that would be necessary and yet it would leave the agrarian world and its attitudes substantially intact. There are other possible courses. But what matters to us is that there is one which could be followed with very little friction and could be followed indefinitely without impairing the claim of the society to being called socialist.

Second, there is the world of the laborer and of the clerk. No reform of souls, no painful adaptation would be required of them. Their work would remain substantially what it is—and it would, with an important qualification to be added later, turn out similar attitudes and habits. From his work the laborer or clerk would return to a home and to pursuits which socialist fancy may denote as it pleases—he may, for instance, play proletarian football whereas now he is playing bourgeois football—but which would still be the same kind of home and the same kind of pursuits. No great difficulties need arise in that quarter.

Third, there is the problem of the groups that not unnaturally expect to be the victims of the socialist arrangement—the problem, roughly speaking, of the upper or leading stratum. It cannot be settled according to that hallowed doctrine which has become an article of faith much beyond the socialist camp, viz., the doctrine that this stratum consists of nothing but overfed beasts of prey whose presence in their economic and social positions is explicable only by luck and ruthlessness and who fill no other "function" than to withhold from the working masses—or the consumers, as the case may be—the fruits of their toil; that these beasts of prey, moreover, bungle their own game by incompetence and (to add a more modern touch) produce depressions by their habit of hoarding the greater part of their loot; and that the socialist community need not bother about them beyond seeing to it that they are promptly ousted from those positions and prevented from committing acts of sabotage. Whatever the political and, in the case of the subnormal, the psychotherapeutic virtues of this doctrine, it is not even good socialism. For any civilized socialist will, when on his good behavior and intending to be taken seriously by serious people, admit many facts about the quality and the achievements of the bourgeois stratum which are incompatible with such a doctrine, and go on to argue that its upper ranks are not going to be victimized at all but that, on the contrary, they too are to be freed from the shackles of the system which oppresses them morally no less than it oppresses the masses economically. From this standpoint which agrees with the teaching of Karl Marx, the way is not so very far to the conclusion that a cooperation of the bourgeois elements may make all the difference between success and failure for the socialist order.

The problem, then, posits itself like this. Here is a class which, by virtue of the selective process of which it is the result, harbors human material of supernormal quality and hence is a national asset which it is rational for any social organization to use. This alone implies more than refraining from exterminating it. Moreover, this class is fulfilling vital functions that will have to be fulfilled also in socialist society. We have seen that it has been and is causally associated with practically all the cultural achievements of the capitalistic epoch and with as much of its economic achievements as is not accounted for by the growth of the laboring population—with all the increase, that is, in what is usually called the productivity of labor (product per man-hour). And this achievement has been in turn causally associated with a system of prizes and penalties of unique efficiency that socialism is bound to abolish. Therefore the question is, on the one hand, whether the bourgeois stock can be harnessed into the service of socialist society and, on the other hand, whether those of the functions discharged by the bourgeoisie which socialism must take away from it can be discharged by other agents or by other than bourgeois methods, or by both.

I do not think we need pursue the matter much further. Schumpeter will answer the question above in the affirmative: yes, the bourgeois manager, possessed of his supernormal talents, will of course adjust to bureaucratic organization, not so very different from the organization of advanced capitalism. Indeed, in the Part on Democracy (which I cannot cover in this book), bureaucracy will also be found compatible with—even indispensable for—democratic government in a technologically advanced society.

So we see now why Schumpeter answers the original question "Can Socialism Work?" with such an assured "Of course it can." The reason is that he sees socialism as very similar to a highly advanced capitalism. To be sure, work tasks will be somewhat ameliorated and income differentials will be somewhat more egalitarian, but these are developments that one might argue would arrive from the dynamic of capitalism itself. Put that way, the only question would be, why should socialism not work; and for this Schumpeter has no answer.

Is there a final word to be said about this remarkable work, at once so bold and so smug, so radical and so truly conservative? I see little purpose in trying to come up with a single valued appraisal of a work whose charm and value lie in its ability to combine diametrical opposites and to persuade irreconcilable ideas to lie down together peacefully. Perhaps I could suggest that the book deserves to be first in line in a category called Economic Science Fiction, but Schumpeter might not like being put together with Utopian socialists. I think I could then assuage his feelings by calling the category Scientific Imagination, in which his would be the only book on the shelf.

There remains one last Schumpeterian opus to be looked at, the magisterial *History of Economic Analysis,* published in 1954, after his death.[73] Over a thousand pages long, combining the most extraordinary scholarship without a trace of pedantry, deeply learned but of course opinionated, it is a masterwork without equal. It cannot be read cover to cover, but must be kept on a shelf and pulled out when one wants to know something about this or that turning in the course of economic thought, about this or that character, small or large, this or that ramification of its central ideas. There is nothing remotely like it.

Here I want to feature it for another reason. Early on, I said that I thought Schumpeter's single most notable contribution was his reluctant recognition of the bounded extent of economics as a science—a recognition all the more remarkable insofar as Schumpeter himself was so keen on advancing its scientific status. We have already seen one extremely important aspect of that recognition in the unabashed emphasis accorded to matters that are ordinarily allowed to lie quiescent—worse, unknown—below the

---

[73] *History of Economic Analysis,* edited from manuscript by Elizabeth Boody Schumpeter, New York: Oxford University Press, 1954.

analytic surface: sociological patterns, cultural aspirations, class characteristics that play decisive roles in his depiction of what capitalism (and to a lesser extent socialism) is and how it works.

In the *History* another, even more iconoclastic, nonscientific element is openly introduced. It is the direct consideration of that most dangerous of all adulerants to scientific thought: ideology. Let me quote Schumpeter's remarkable words: "In every scientific venture," he writes, "the thing that comes first is Vision. That is to say, before embarking upon analytic work of any kind we must first single out the set of phenomena we wish to investigate, and acquire 'intuitively' a preliminary notion of how they hang together or, in other words, of what appear from our standpoint to be their fundamental properties."

This is a bold statement. For the acknowledged prior necessity for Vision raises a fundamental challenge to analysis as the sovereign task of economic inquiry. Unavoidably, the explicit recognition accorded to Vision brings in its train an acknowledgement of the role played by subjective elements—differing preferences, values, or simply cognitive abilities that may profoundly affect the "facts" to which we apply our analytical skills. To the extent that these subjective matters then enter the foundation on which analysis stands, we introduce elements whose influence must of necessity interfere with the "scientificity" of our analytic ambitions, and whose buried presence can never be lost to sight with regard to any conclusions to which our analytic work may lead.

Analytical effort [he continues] starts when we have conceived our vision of the set of phenomena that caught our interest, no matter whether this set lies in virgin soil or in land that had been cultivated before. . . . Now it should be perfectly clear that there is a wide gate for ideology to enter into this process. In fact, it enters on the very ground floor, into the preanalytic cognitive act of which we have been speaking. Analytic work begins with material provided by our vision of things, and this vision is ideological almost by definition. It embodies the picture of things as we see them, and wherever there is any possible motive for wishing to see them in a given rather than another light, the way in which we see things can hardly be distinguished from the way in which we wish to see them.[74]

Having admitted the power of ideology, Schumpeter now tries to contain it. He suggests that there are protective counter-forces that will limit, if not entirely eliminate, its dangers. The principal protective element is the methodological procedures that guide our analytical work. The suggested remedy, I fear, is not as effective as Schumpeter hopes. For what are the "rules" that will play this all-important role? Schumpeter does not spell them out. The text ends shortly after this passage—or rather, as we know from remarks of the editor, it continues in untyped pages found among his papers intended for this part of the *History,* and now appended to the chapter. Three lengthy pages in fine type deserve to be read carefully (pp. 44–47), but I think the excerpt below, from the first paragraph of these pages, sums up what will follow:

While it is hoped that the foregoing treatment of the ideology problem will help the reader understand the situation within which we have to work, and put him on guard without imbuing him with a sterile pessimism concerning the 'objective validity' of our methods and results, it must be admitted that our answer to the problem, consisting as it does of a set of rules by which to locate, diagnose, and eliminate ideological delusion, cannot be made as simple and definite as can the usual glib assertion that the history of scientific economics is or is not a history of ideologies. We have had to make large concessions to the former view, concessions that challenge the scientific character of all those comprehensive philosophies of economic life . . . which are, to many of us, the most interesting and most glamorous of the creations of economic thought. Worse than this, we have had to recognize, on the one hand, that although there exists a mechanism that tends to crush out ideologies automatically, this may be a time-consuming process that meets with many resistances and, on the other hand, that we are never safe from the current

---

[74] History, op. cit., p. 42.

intrusion of new ideologies to take the place of vanishing older ones.

This disarming admission is now followed by a promise to discuss four examples of such anti-ideological safeguards. Unfortunately Schumpeter does not proceed beyond the first. . . . Thereafter the unfinished chapter returns (via a parenthesized insert added by the editor) to the commencement of the section on ideology, bringing us full circle to material we have already covered. Thus, if Schumpeter confronts the problem of vision more directly than any previous economist, including Marx, it cannot be said that he effectively removes its threat with respect to the objectivity of analysis.*

I am not so sure, myself, that ideology is an impurity to be eliminated, so much as an ingredient to be recognized; but that is a matter for another time. Here, the reluctant bravery shown by Schumpeter in recognizing the admixture of vision and analysis, of values and facts, seems an excellent way to sum up the contribution of this most quixotic of the worldly philosophers. It is very easy to recognize Schumpeter's weaknesses, to call him "assertive, pompous, and arrogant" as I did so audaciously when I was in my twenties; but for all that, there is something in his introspective awareness that will continue to educate us, whatever happens to the scientific effort to clarify the world around us.

---

*Adapted from R. Heilbroner, "Was Schumpeter Right After All?" *J. Econ. Perspectives*, Vol. 7, No. 3 (Summer 1993), pp. 88–90. This long footnote seems an appropriate place to suggest an answer to a question that has long puzzled me. It is why Schumpeter has chosen such an unlikely hero for his vast sweep of economic writers. The hero of the *History of Economic Analysis* is not Smith, Ricardo, Mill, Marx, Marshall, Keynes—certainly not Keynes, his arch rival. It is Léon Walras. But I now see that in Schumpeter's recognition of the contest between analysis and ideology—a contest in which ideology always seems to infiltrate analysis—one can find an answer. It is that Walras, with his insistence on separating pure from applied economics comes closer than anyone to fulfilling Schumpeter's hopes for a nonideologically contaminated economics. Whether one can call a system of general equilibrium a value-free depiction of capitalism I leave to the reader to decide. But there is certainly a claim to such a status in Walras's effort to create a "pure" economics; and one can see the appeal that such an idea would have to an economist who himself declared that capitalism could not survive and that socialism would assuredly work. Say what one will, Schumpeter is an interesting man, not less so when, as I think to be the case here, he is a victim of wishful thinking. Would that more practitioners of the worldly philosophy had his imagination and boldness.

VII

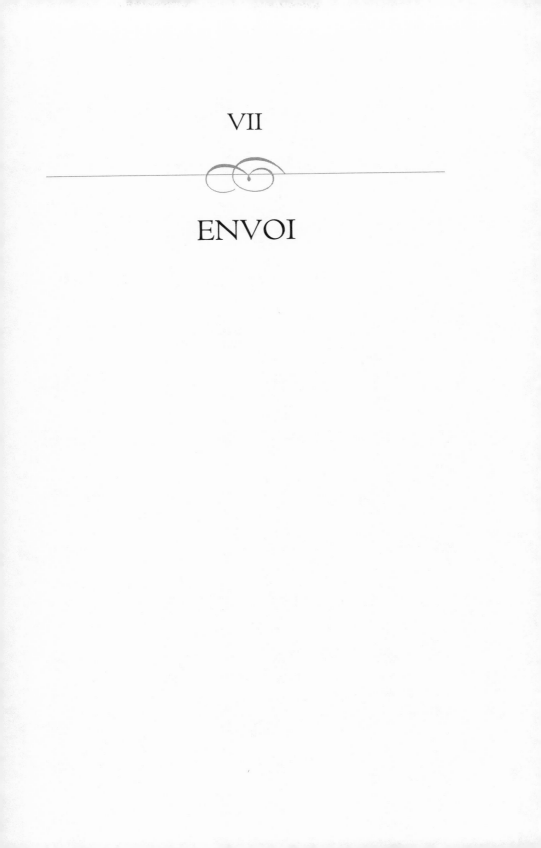

ENVOI

ENVOI

Is there a meta-history of economic thought—an overarching narrative that gives shape to the work of its great figures? The question is not an easy one to answer, but I know no better way to conclude our inquiry. Moreover the question fits the judgments often expressed in these pages as comments on the works of the great economists. Some of those comments have been aimed at analytical confusions, such as the Physiocratic treatment of rent as a "gift of nature."* But by far the greater part of my criticisms have been directed at the visions that preceded the analytical expositions themselves. To take a second example from Physiocracy, we recall Turgot's words that "another part of society . . . had come to *prefer* the occupation of preparing . . . the products of the soil to growing them,"** a curious way to describe the historical process by which poor farmers were forced from the land to become proletarian workers.

Now I must confront my own criticisms by asking if they are not themselves value laden. My answer is that indeed they are,

*See page 40, above.
**See page 43, Section IV, my comment.

although I hope in a fashion that has been explicit from the start—namely, that economics is inextricably sociopolitical in nature. But even that does not yet fully express my own value orientation. For I further believe that the sociopolitical aspect of economics applies in particular—perhaps even exclusively—to social orders whose economies manifest three properties: they are driven by a restless desire to accumulate capital, knit together by largely unregulated markets, and divided into two realms, one private, one public. In a word, they are modern capitalist societies.

Such societies do indeed require the special analytics of economics if we are to understand how they hang together and why they display the dynamics that are their most egregious feature. That is the vaunted achievement of economics featured in these pages as the "scenarios" that display these analytical elucidations at their most interesting. But I have also focused on the great scenarios for another reason. It is that they all express, more clearly than in any other application of economics, the manner in which pre-cognitive visions (as Schumpeter called them) imbue economic analytics with valuational—Schumpeter called it "ideological"—content.

We are already familiar with that general conclusion. What is important at this juncture, however, is to recognize that these value-laden scenarios can provide us with the meta-history of our subject for which we have been looking. Moreover, that overarching narrative now seems rather easy to describe. It takes the form of a steady movement of inquiry from political economy to economics—that is, from investigations that unashamedly recognize the value-laden elements in their analytical concepts, to expositions that ignore, or worse, are unaware of their presence. What clearer evidence could there be than to compare the principal actors in the scenarios of Smith, Ricardo, Mill, and of course Marx, with those of Jevons, Walras, Marshall, and even Keynes. In the first group the drama concerns the fate of sociopolitical strata in society; in the second, the fortunes of a shapeless group of individuals. It follows that the first scenarios describe the changing outlook for the social order itself, whereas the second group describes shifts in income distributions, but not in relative class positions.

To what can we attribute this change in perspectives? One reason is itself political—the evolution of social outlooks from the mid-eighteenth century in which political economy was born and flourished, to the mid-to-late-nineteenth century in which it began to decline. The first period was essentially aristocratic in its beliefs, taking for granted the inevitability and rightness of class stratification, the second tending to deny the importance or even presence of classes under the growing predominance of democratic political, and capitalist economic viewpoints. It is worth noting, in this regard that Marshall preferred the broad term "Economics" to the narrower "Political Economy" because he explicitly construes the key word "political" as referring to the "exigencies of party organization," not to the class nature of a capitalist order.[75]

Thus cleansed, economics beats a steady retreat from a self-conception as a social inquiry toward that of "science"—biology being Marshall's interesting choice. We see this in the growing lack of interest in sociological and political considerations in the "models" that increasingly represent the preferred mode of analytical exposition. Only well-behaved behavioral forces—mainly maximizing and optimizing—can be considered in these expositions, not forces that do not lend themselves to mathematical representation, such as irrational decision-making, servile obedience, or boundless ambition. It follows that considerations of "relevance" are low on the list of analytic prerequisites—relevance to what? In the same fashion, economic policy takes a back seat to the pursuit of expositional "rigor": As I have written elsewhere, a visitor from Mars picking up a mainstream economics journal might be forgiven for mistaking it for a journal of physics.

Does this meta-narrative have a foreseeable ending? It is all too easy to imagine one in which the practitioners of "scientific" economics pursue their present course with the tenacity of the medi-

[75] Marshall, op. cit., p. 43; xiv.

eval schooolmasters. But I can also imagine, if not easily foresee, another path of development. The system of capitalism is today under many new pressures emanating from powerful technologies, unprecedented exposure to international financial and investment flows, emerging ecological threats, and intensified political instabilities. These challenges may be what is finally needed to reinvigorate the tradition of political economy that has been celebrated in this book.

Thus I can hope for the emergence of a new interest in political economy, perhaps resurrected by a corps of dissenting economists—the counterpart of Veblen's technicians. Such a corps would seek a mode of economic inquiry whose analytic conclusions started from an effort to take full cognizance of the sociopolitical realities of our time, whatever the difficulties they may pose for the construction of elegant models. This hope may prove as unrealistic as Veblen's expectations for a reconstitution of the price system under the guidance of its disillusioned engineers. But I would not have written this book if I did not believe that a rekindling of the tradition of political economy was within the realm of possibility. That would indeed be a happy ending to the teachings of the worldly philosophy.

INDEX